Praise for *The Business of Changing the World*

"Salesforce.com serves as a great model for Google and any other company that wants to try to do what we know in our hearts is the right thing: stewardship of our troubled times. *The Business of Changing the World* reveals exactly how salesforce.com—and many other inspiring companies—are doing well by doing good."

—Larry Brilliant, MD, Executive Director,
Google Foundation and Google.org

"Marc Benioff has brought much needed innovation to corporate philanthropy. He's a leader who has always been able to see a greater good and a better way that is now well documented in *The Business of Changing the World*."

—Charles Phillips, President and member of
the Board of Directors, Oracle Corporation

"Do corporate and shareholder interests diverge greatly from the social imperatives around us? *The Business of Changing the World* importantly responds with a resounding NO by highlighting brilliant examples of the power that businesses can deliver by espousing a culture of caring. It's not about the money. The winning formula incorporates innovation, volunteerism, and leadership—or what Marc Benioff calls *Integrated Philanthropy*."

—Harry McMahon, Vice Chairman, Merrill Lynch & Co., Inc.

"Becoming a valued partner in our local communities and a global society has become a key imperative in building a company that will thrive in the twenty-first century. The collective passion and energy of the private sector can make a profound impact in the quality of life and the opportunities afforded the less fortunate around the world. *The Business of Changing the World* is a wonderful roadmap into how global business leaders are making it happen."

—Stratton Sclavos, Chairman and CEO, Verisign

"I was personally inspired by the stories in this book. It is great to see so many companies doing great things for the communities they serve. I am convinced that this not only helps those in need, it makes our companies far better."

—Maynard Webb, Chief Operating Officer, (retired), eBay

The Business of
Changing the
World

The Business of Changing the
World

TWENTY GREAT
LEADERS ON
STRATEGIC CORPORATE
PHILANTHROPY

Marc Benioff
and
Carlye Adler

McGRAW-HILL

New York / Chicago / San Francisco / Lisbon / London / Madrid / Mexico City
Milan / New Delhi / San Juan / Seoul / Singapore / Sydney / Toronto

The McGraw·Hill Companies

3 4 5 6 7 8 9 0   DOC/DOC   0 9 8 7

ISBN-13: 978-0-07-148151-9
ISBN-10: 0-07-148151-6

McGraw-Hill books are available at special quantity discounts to use as premiums and sales promotions, or for use in corporate training programs. For more information, please write to the Director of Special Sales, McGraw-Hill Professional, Two Penn Plaza, New York, NY 10121-2298. Or contact your local bookstore.

This book is printed on acid-free paper.

Library of Congress Cataloging-in-Publication Data

Benioff, Marc.
   The business of changing the world : twenty great leaders on strategic corporate philanthropy / by Marc Benioff and Carlye Adler.
        p.   cm.
   ISBN 0-07-148151-6 (hardcover : alk. paper)
   1. Corporations—Charitable contributions.   I. Adler, Carlye.   II. Title.

HG4028.C6B455   2006
361.7'65—dc22   2006015477

*This book is dedicated to Karen Southwick,
the coauthor of* Compassionate Capitalism, *an award-winning
journalist, and a thoughtful woman who made the world a better place.
Karen passed away in 2004 after a courageous battle with cancer;
we miss her greatly.*

CONTENTS

FOREWORD

The responsibility to lead the world's largest corporations falls to several hundred chief executive officers who, by the very nature of their job descriptions, are no strangers to the ever-shifting character of stakeholder expectations. From quarter to quarter and year to year, a successful CEO must act in the best interest of the company that he or she manages, remaining sharply attuned to the sometimes conflicting demands of an enormous cast of customers, employees, analysts, suppliers, vendors, investors or owners, and many others.

As the essays in this book attest, it is clear to a leading set of CEOs that a new stakeholder demand has surfaced and is here to stay: companies must generously and consistently support the communities in which they operate.

Many business leaders would argue that this expectation is utopian. To summarize their viewpoint, businesses provide sufficient value to society if they operate efficiently, use resources judiciously, provide employment, and deliver goods and services that support a healthy economy.

As an advocacy body that works with a diverse range of top corporate leaders, nonprofit partners, the media, the independent sector, and government institutions, the Committee to Encourage Corporate Philanthropy (CECP) can aver that indeed the rules are no longer that simple. CECP board member Rochelle Lazarus, chairman and CEO of Ogilvy & Mather Worldwide, summarizes the new paradigm best: "The debate about whether corporate philanthropy is right for the bottom line is over. The market has spoken and said it cares whether companies are good citizens; these issues do in fact matter to society. Engaging your company in corporate philanthropy is now part of being a good CEO."

The good news for corporations is that giving back, when conceived and executed thoughtfully, creates a win-win scenario for businesses and the public. From eradicating disease and improving childhood literacy rates, to boosting employee job skills, opening new markets, and heightening brand recognition, business and society stand to benefit greatly if companies can demonstrate programmatic effectiveness, fiscal accountability, and good stewardship in their philanthropic contributions.

It's Not About Logos Anymore

Although several longstanding, innovative corporate giving programs present commendable exceptions to the rule, for many companies philanthropy has traditionally been a reactionary gesture of goodwill. As a result, in the mind of the public, corporate donations are commonly assumed to be just another form of advertising; after all, aren't corporate logos printed in scale with the size of the donation made?

In reality, the shape, scope, and motivation behind corporate giving has changed dramatically in recent years. Large-scale volunteerism projects, product donations, disaster relief strategies, issue awareness campaigns, research and development, and public policy work are all standard undertakings for today's top corporate giving professionals.

CECP research on corporate givers shows that the median company in our 2004 survey of large multinationals grants \$32 million annually. Given the huge sums of money involved, it is no wonder that a more rigorous economic and scientific approach is now being applied to the field of corporate philanthropy. With more and more resources flowing from the private sector into the nonprofit sector each year, companies have become exponentially more sophisticated about why, where, and how they give.

If Philanthropy Reduces Profits, Why Do Corporations Give?

While the reasons for giving are as diverse as the companies that practice philanthropy, most companies cite both societal and business reasons for giving. The two most often-mentioned benefits to society are: improved quality of life and capacity-building for the nonprofits themselves.

What do these benefits mean? To support the capacity of nonprofits, a corporation must focus on fortifying the inner workings of the nonprofit partners with which it works. This requires that companies, in addition to assisting with specific community projects that a nonprofit undertakes, must provide management and strategy consulting to the nonprofit organization to ensure its longevity and effectiveness. Assisting with scalability and sustainability issues ensures that nonprofits make ongoing commitments to serve their constituencies.

Improved quality of life captures a spectrum of positive outcomes. For example, some companies invest in broadening awareness of social issues, such as domestic violence or breast cancer. This may involve public education as much as it does assisting victims. Other companies set up programs to facilitate access to services for those in need, such as free eye exams in remote areas or wholesome food for malnourished children. Other companies put their energy into job-training and skill-building programs. The environment, arts and culture, health and human services, and education are all examples of focus areas that feed into the idea that it is crucial to help build thriving communities. Thriving communities, in turn, are obviously good for business.

In the words of Robert Forrester, CECP board member and chairman and CEO of Payne, Forrester & Associates, LLC: "The highest aspirations for corporate philanthropy should be to encourage and nurture the nonprofit and philanthropy communities. These sectors are key to producing the healthy, civil societies required for business competition to flourish."

In addition to adding societal value and fostering the healthy societies upon which all businesses depend, corporate philanthropy can provide direct benefits on the corporate side as well. A strong corporate philanthropy program directly supports employee recruitment, retention, skill-building, teamwork, and morale. Similarly, it can foster improved relationships with customers, vendors, and suppliers. In some cases, philanthropy initiatives can facilitate the creation of new products and the penetration of new markets regionally and internationally.

These are just a few examples of what motivates companies to give. CECP recommends that corporations develop programs tailored to their own corporate strengths. Often, a mixed portfolio of cash, in-kind contributions, volunteerism, and pro bono services is the most sustainable solution. It is the work of each company to define the business and societal outcomes that it is looking to achieve and what resources it is best suited to provide. Often, this entails leveraging the company's competitive business advantages.

The Role of the CEO in Corporate Philanthropy

Just as with all important, companywide initiatives, a focused and engaged CEO sets the tone for a company's philanthropy program. CECP encourages its CEO members to seek and create opportunities to serve as corporate giving advocates, practitioners, educators, and spokespersons to advance the case for philanthropy and to inspire other business leaders to make a lasting commitment to community giving.

Whatever the tactic, when a CEO participates in corporate philanthropy activities, he or she sends a clear message internally and externally that the company is serious about corporate philanthropy. CECP is extremely encouraged by the results of a recent survey we conducted of more than 30 companies, in which 74 percent of giving officers reported strong senior executive engagement (via their CEO or other senior management) with their philanthropic programs.

Where Do We Go from Here?

While the new expectations for corporate philanthropy are challenging, it must be acknowledged that the means to solving some of the world's most pressing problems rest in the private sector. In the service of society, corporations are able to leverage incredible assets, including product donations, volunteers, professional services, technology, and unsurpassed distribution channels. Tapping the extensive resources of the corporate world to strategically match social, community, and public needs can create immense benefits for all parties.

CECP believes that we are about to enter a new phase of philanthropy in which large corporations, rather than working independently on philanthropic initiatives, will begin to come together with greater frequency to take on the big, complex issues facing the world community. Pharmaceutical companies have already begun to make such strides by working together to help eradicate curable diseases affecting millions of people in Africa, Asia, and the Americas. In the United States, we have seen examples of companies pooling employee volunteers in large-scale "days of service." Creative collaborative ideas are in the drafting stages at several companies, and CECP fully expects the trend of cooperation to continue.

The Business of Changing the World: A Call to Action

Underlying each of the case studies presented in the following pages is the acknowledgment that there is a profound interdependency between businesses and the communities in which they operate. As I reflect on the themes of this book, one very concrete *call to action* rises to the surface: now is time for all players in the private sector to identify the ways in which they can join in this movement. A growing network of distinguished corporate leaders is actively working to effect positive change through corporate philanthropy, and there is room and reason enough for us all to help advance the cause.

Charles H. Moore
Executive Director
Committee to Encourage Corporate Philanthropy

The Committee to Encourage Corporate Philanthropy is the only international forum of business CEOs and chairpersons pursuing a mission exclusively focused on corporate philanthropy. Membership includes more than 125 CEOs and chairpersons who represent companies that account for nearly 50 percent of reported corporate giving in the United States. Visit www.CorporatePhilanthropy.org for more information.

ACKNOWLEDGMENTS

This book would not have been possible without the assistance, energy, and passion of Suzanne DiBianca, executive director of the salesforce.com/foundation. Suzanne's tireless work and determination have made my dream of integrating philanthropy into our business model an everyday reality, and it is my hope that the tremendous knowledge, support, and fine editing skills she's contributed to this book will help other companies incorporate giving back into their business models.

A sincere thank-you to Charlie Moore, Cari Parsons, Margaret Coady, and Sarah Munro at the Committee to Encourage Corporate Philanthropy (CECP) for your generous introductions, wise insights, and most of all, inspiration.

Special thanks to Alan Hassenfeld, a brave and compassionate soul, who offered his support, advice, and personal story when this book was still in the conceptual stages and who remained steadfastly committed throughout the process.

A heartfelt thank-you to Michael Dell and Kevin Rollins for committing to participate in this project from the very beginning. Your involvement inspired many others to contribute.

We are deeply grateful to all of the business leaders who graciously agreed to participate in this book: Michael Milken, Jeffrey Swartz, Peter Gabriel, Phil Marineau, Craig Barrett, Larry Fish,

Marilyn Carlson Nelson, JP Garnier, Mike Eskew, Laura Scher, Klaus Schwab, Steve Case, Jim Donald, Akinobu Kanasugi, Steve Burd, and John Morgridge. Each of you has made the world a better place, and we are confident that your accomplishments will continue to inspire others to do so.

There were many people at each company profiled who were generous and patient enough to help coordinate interviews, provide background information, check facts, and carry each chapter to completion. Thank you to Sandy Marks, Lori Pollock, Jane Englebardt, Karen Davis, Stephanie Duarante, Pat Nathan, Deborah McNair, John McGrath, Michelle Hanson, Karen Vantrease, Geoffrey Moore, Robin Sherman, Robin Giampa, Kate King, Annie Parsons, Leanne Penfold, Gillian Caldwell, E.J. Bernacki, Dan McMackin, Dave Stangis, Tracy Koon, Bill Wray, Geralyn Tatangelo, Heather Campion, Blake Jordan, Debra Norberg, Doug Cody, Nancy Pekarek, Sandy Maddonni, Anne Luesing, Pamela Hartigan, Ben Binswanger, Caroline Wong, Katherine Cheng, Soon Beng Yeap, Audrey Lincoff, Hitoshi Suzuki, Keisuke Ohta, Larree Renda, Brian Dowling, Karen Darnell, Abby Smith, and Tae Yoo.

In the publishing world, we are forever indebted to Jeffrey Krames, at McGraw-Hill, who personally committed to this project and ushered it to completion in record speed. We are grateful to Daina Penikas, Laura Libretti, and Alex Schwartz for their hard work and careful attention.

We were lucky enough to work with Jim Levine, agent extraordinaire, who appreciated our vision and made it a reality.

Finally, to the members of the salesforce.com family who have provided smart ideas, enthusiastic effort, and unwavering support: Laura Pavlolich, Makiko Akabane, Isabel Kelly, Bruce Francis, Jennifer Keavney, Sue McGilpin, Caryn Marooney, Lynne Benioff, and Ruthie Johnson. We are grateful to all of our employees— who have made salesforce.com a leading global public company while contributing more than 30,000 hours volunteering in the community; assisting over 1,000 nonprofit organizations using the donated salesforce.com technology effectively; and empowering youth throughout the world. They have proven that integrating philanthropy into business isn't a lofty idea, but the secret weapon for twenty-first century companies to achieve success.

FORCE OF CHANGE

Marc Benioff

I'm amazed by the potential of more companies employing integrated philanthropic initiatives at earlier stages in their life cycle. What if this were done on an even more massive scale?

I t's somewhat ironic that I decided that America's companies don't do enough for their communities at the exact time I was spending $100 million on corporate philanthropic programs.

It was 1997 and I was an executive at Oracle Corporation when CEO Larry Ellison tapped me to help start the company's first major philanthropic initiative. Larry was motivated to launch a corporate philanthropy program after Colin Powell stood up with the five living presidents and launched America's Promise— a program that challenged the nation to make a greater commitment to its youth. Oracle's effort, called Oracle's Promise, was designed to get computers into underserved schools. All of a sudden, I was living in two worlds. I spent half of my time in management meetings and the other half at schools in south-central Los Angeles, Washington, DC, Northern Ireland, and Israel.

Although the program allowed us to place thousands of computers in hundreds of schools worldwide (and earned Larry recognition on the *Oprah Winfrey Show*), our small team felt as if the effort fell short of leveraging Oracle's full philanthropic potential.

Initially, I had been pumped up, but ultimately, I was let down. I often thought back to Colin Powell's call to America's companies to "take the lead" in getting involved in youth service projects and his suggestion to give employees paid time off to participate in these programs. I realized that philanthropy was about more than writing a check and knew that if we had been able to draw on Oracle's full assets—its employees, its customers, its products, and its partners—we could have made a much bigger contribution.

That was a defining moment that helped inspire my belief in "integrated philanthropy." There are many extremely generous business leaders who are some of the world's biggest and most noted philanthropists. Private philanthropy is different from corporate philanthropy, though. Many executives (I'm not going to mention any names) must take the next step to strategically use their company as a vehicle to give back to the community. It's not always easy. I learned the hard way that, to be truly successful, corporate philanthropic programs must be woven into the fabric of the organization. It must become an inherent part of the culture of the company. I've since found that the easiest way to do that is simply to start from the very beginning.

At salesforce.com, we have integrated philanthropy into our corporate culture from the inception of our company, and we have seen the difference that can be made with that model. Shortly after we started salesforce.com (in a rented apartment next to my own) in late-1999, we launched the salesforce.com/foundation, a 501(c)3 public charity, with a mission to provide access to technology to youth in underserved communities and funding for youth entrepreneurship and education programs globally. Alongside private funding sources, we placed 1 percent of the corporation's shares of stock upon founding into the foundation. We also committed to donating 1 percent of company profits to the community (realized through product donations) and 1 percent of employee working hours to community service. The 1-1-1 model—equity, profits, and employee time—was designed to ensure that as our business grew so would our contribution to the communities in which we operate.

We built the foundation in tandem with the company and designed systems to ensure that the importance of social service was ingrained in the culture. The team sits alongside our salesforce.com employees. The two-day orientation for all new hires includes a half day of volunteerism to demonstrate to newcomers that this as a true priority of the company. Most of our company meetings include reports on our community service projects. By committing to the community from the beginning, giving back has become part of the salesforce.com DNA. By leveraging the energy of our entire ecosystem—employees, partners, and customers—we have been able to make contributions that have even exceeded my expectations.

In July 2000 the salesforce.com/foundation opened its first after-school technology center at a neighboring YMCA, providing free access to underserved youth. (It was personally rewarding for me to have Colin Powell—the original inspiration for this effort—in attendance). Since then, we have created more than 60 technology centers and media programs with schools and nongovernment organizations in 12 countries including Kenya, Israel, Japan, Ireland, and Singapore. Our over 2,000 employees have embraced the effort with fervor and donated over 30,000 hours to the communities that we serve. Corporations including Time Warner, Dell, and Cisco have joined our effort, donating services, time, and people. Together we've been able to reach more than 100,000 people worldwide with access to the Internet and state of the art technology programs.

As salesforce.com has grown from a start-up business into a successful global company, our foundation has developed a broader footprint for expansion. In the past few years we have opened foundation offices in New York, Dublin, London, and Tokyo. Each staff member in those regions is responsible for facilitating grants administration, supporting employee volunteerism, and helping to empower nonprofits that are using the salesforce.com software for free. In the summer of 2004, we witnessed the true financial power of our integrated model. The salesforce.com initial public offering raised more than $12 million for the foundation—and proved the capability of pre-IPO companies to make a positive difference, if only they make an early financial commitment of equity. In addition to funds raised from salesforce.com equity, about half of our employees make annual stock or cash contributions through the matching gifts program; we also receive donations from outside individuals. Today the foundation is worth more than $18 million. It's my personal goal to raise $100 to $200 million for the foundation over the next ten years in cash and equity contributions.

The foundation's impact is measured in many ways: employee and nonprofit satisfaction levels reported after the completion of a volunteer project; student performance and youth engagement as a result of our technology or education investments; nonprofit usability rates and improvement in organizational efficacy. For me, though, the most powerful impact is measured in the stories of the people and organizations we've reached and worked with over time. Something of particular importance to us and that we believe distinguishes our foundation is our ability to "stay the course" with these young people over many years.

Take Theo, for example. We met Theo at one of our original technology centers in San Francisco six years ago. Theo has grown up with us—not only because he was 5 feet 2 inches when we met him and stands at 6-foot-7 today—but because we've seen him transform from a rudderless 12-year-old into a confident, driven, and passionate college-bound young man.

Shortly after we met Theo, he began to express interest and demonstrate talent in many of the multimedia opportunities we offered. We worked with him in *Bus 24*, a youth-produced film that documents a bus line that travels from one of the poorest to one of the richest neighborhoods in San Francisco and depicts the diversity of people met along the way. The film, which gave all the young people involved opportunities to gain skills in video production, editing, and interviewing, was shown at the San Francisco International Film Festival and proved to be a great hit. The experience also proved to be the impetus for Theo to get more involved with our foundation. He began to come to our offices every day after school. We hired him to do administrative work for the foundation and paid him $8 an hour. (Now we pay him $11.) He also received free tutoring in math from Dominic Paschel, a salesforce.com employee in investor relations. Theo's math grade soared from an F to a B, and he became more and more interested in school.

This fall, Theo will be the first in his family to attend college. We'll be paying for it—a promise we made to Theo long ago. It's not just the money that's given Theo the motivation to plan for his future, though. We believe it was the individual attention and access to opportunities previously beyond Theo's imagination that has made the biggest difference.

Many times, it is the work of a salesforce.com employee that introduces the foundation to the most interesting opportunities to effect change. In 2002 Eugene Hillery, a finance employee in Dublin, applied for a foundation grant to travel to the St. Martin's Girls' School in Kibagare, a slum outside of Nairobi in Kenya. The school is focused exclusively on the education of poor, orphaned girls. The grant was used to supply the school with eight comput-ers and an Internet connection. It was incredible when the girls in the school, very excited about the new technology available to them, began to e-mail us. We then sent them a video camera to help increase their resources and opportunities. They sent a movie back to us immediately. Their film, *What If*, depicted what life was like in the slums of Africa. "What if we had the opportunity to do more," they wondered. "What if we had the opportunity to be something else?"

We wanted to give these girls—all of whom had never left Nairobi—some of those opportunities. We invited the three girls who made the film, Mary, Kule, and Rosemary, to come to our annual users' conference "Dreamforce"—in San Francisco. The girls stayed at the executive director of the foundation's house for 10 days, learned about business and life here, and honed their technology skills by making a film about the conference.

Last year the girls graduated high school. All three went on to higher education—the first generation to do so for each of their families. Mary decided to study nursing, Kule began to pursue law, and Rosemary chose a career in Web development. Unbeknownst to us, Eugene, the employee who first introduced us to these girls, and his family generously began paying for their college tuition. The foundation has since committed to funding a portion of their college education and has extended the program to include more students at St. Martin's. Eugene is deeply committed to further building a relationship with the St. Martin's school via media programs and scholarships and continues to be very involved in these girls' lives.

We've found that a great deal can be achieved through product donations as well. There are more than 1,000 nonprofits that are using the salesforce.com product for free. United Way, Red Cross, Stanford University, the Elizabeth Glazier Pediatrics AIDS Foundation, and the Special Olympics are just some examples of nonprofits that are using the salesforce.com tool for donor management, volunteer management, and other key data tracking to better manage their organizations. The Bronx Lab School in New York uses the tool to help track attendance, test scores, and disciplinary actions. On the heels of that success, a pilot implementation is currently being replicated in 30 additional New York City schools. It's exciting to see that as our product has become more sophisticated and customizable, our ability to benefit our nonprofit partners has immensely increased.

The salesforce.com/foundation has enriched our communities— as well as our company and our lives. Eighty-five percent of our global workforce is active in philanthropy. (The national average is 18 percent.) Our employees contribute in many different ways— from painting an orphanage in the mountains of Poland, to playing Santa Claus at a local housing project, to serving as a mentor for a child who needs a little extra math help, to wiring a school in Kenya—these are the real stars who make our programs shine. Our success would not be possible without their desire to contribute and their generous spirit. They tell us, though, that the foundation is the secret weapon that keeps them grounded. People are here to do more than just make money—they want to help make the world a better place during their time here. This is another thing that distinguishes our company and helps us to attract and retain phenomenal employees.

I'm in awe of the individual efforts of all of our employees. One IT staffer has spent every Monday for the past three years at a salesforce.com/foundation technology lab, sharing his professional skills and mentoring the students. One of our high-performing sales employees just took his six paid community service days to teach lessons and participate in the rebuilding of a school in a very poor part of Brazil. Our president of EMEA (Europe, the Middle East, and Asia) has pledged to give £350,000 over the next 10 years to "Teach First," an organization that empowers and supports teachers. Our employees know how to make community service a part of their lives and they know the rewards of giving back. I know that some of these people will go off and start their own companies, just like I did, and I believe these future leaders will employ models of integrated philanthropy in their own companies and lives.

Every year, corporate philanthropic foundations pour $30 billion into their endeavors in the United States alone.

This is really what gets me so excited. I'm amazed by the potential of more companies employing integrated philanthropic initiatives at earlier stages in their life cycle. What if this were done on an even more massive scale? Consider what would happen if a top-tier venture-capital firm required the companies in which it invested to place 1 percent of their equity into a foundation serving the communities in which they do business. If embraced, this new model could dramatically increase the percentage of overall corporate donations and even lead to what *Fortune* magazine writer David Kirkpatrick has called "the end of philanthropy" and prove the true power of the integrated community service model.

Every year, corporate philanthropic foundations pour *$30 billion* into their endeavors in the United States alone. While that's a big number, many of these efforts occur in isolation with little or no relationship to the communities in which they operate, the people they employ, or their corporate missions. We are excited, though, that it appears the philanthropic landscape is changing. Companies are beginning to see the potential of this integrated approach. For example, executives at Google followed the salesforce.com/foundation's lead and agreed to put 1 percent of its equity aside in its early stages. Post-IPO, their philanthropic dollars are hovering around $1 billion.

Now, more than ever, companies are trying to create programs that are more strategic—and ultimately more successful. We've found, though, that the written testimonies and best practices on this subject are lacking. We are often asked *how* we implemented our integrated approach, what others are doing, and the specific information on what works and what doesn't in terms of setting up these kinds of programs. We've seen it as part of our mandate to respond and promote our philosophy with businesses and community members around the world. We work with many companies to share our model and help them integrate their own programs. It's been energizing to see companies such as Google and our business partners, including GOT technology, make public commitments to follow our lead. We're excited to watch other companies like iRobot, PalmOne, Antenna and many others further develop the model. In 2004, we published *Compassionate Capitalism*, the first-ever best practices guide for corporate philanthropy. This book, *The Business of Changing the World*, tells the story of leaders who have achieved success in this area—many of whom have inspired us—and all of whom we believe will encourage future leaders to realize that companies of all sizes can and *should* help to make the world a better place through the use of their own resources.

Building salesforce.com from a start-up company with a big dream to a public company with a big impact has been one of the most exciting experiences of my life. Building the foundation from an intellectual idea to a practical reality that has served 100,000 people in need has been one of the most rewarding. By creating these symbiotic organizations, I have received the most remarkable opportunity to lead an organization that makes "doing good" an integral part of doing well. The result is a professional achievement that can't be beat: I feel better every day doing this work.

The Business of Changing the World

A FAMILY TRADITION: HASBRO

Hasbro's isn't just a story about the actualization of the American Dream. . . . Hasbro is also a pioneer of the integrated corporation; early on, it expanded its reach beyond the playroom and into the community.

Alan Hassenfeld sometimes refers to himself as "Kid No. 1," and as the chairman of the $3 billion toy company Hasbro, it's an appropriate nickname that belies his modus operandi. In his mid-50s, the always upbeat Hassenfeld—who looks like a cross between Gene Wilder and Alfred E. Newman—still wears rubber bands on his wrists (he says it's good luck), and gets down-right giddy when he talks about "guys" like Mr. Potato Head and G.I. Joe. And frankly, there's no reason not to. Mr. Potato Head, the first toy to be advertised on TV, and G.I. Joe, the first doll for boys (they coined the term "action figure" to make it more palatable), were revolutionary concepts and the building blocks of a company that has made Alan and his family a fortune.

Alan, who grew up amid these toy icons (he says G.I. Joe put him through college), is the third-generation of his family to run Hasbro. The company was founded in Providence, Rhode Island, in 1923 by his grandfather, Henry, and grand-uncle, Helal. As immigrants from Poland, the Hassenfeld brothers started their business selling fabric-covered pencil-boxes and other school supplies. Henry's son, Merrill (Alan's father), became president in the 1940s, about the same time the company sold its first toy—doctors' and nurses' kits. Mr. Potato Head, which debuted in the 1950s, was the company's first big success. (At that time, it only came with parts; kids used a real potato!) The company introduced G.I. Joe a decade later, and went public on the American Stock Exchange in 1968.

About 10 years later, the company suffered a devastating loss when Merrill Hassenfeld had a heart attack at work and died. He was 61. Alan's older brother, Stephen, then the company president, became chairman and CEO. With Stephen at the helm, Hasbro went gangbusters. It acquired one of the world's most famous game companies Milton Bradley, the maker of Chutes & Ladders, Candy Land, and the Game of Life, which gave Hasbro a rich stable of enduring favorites—a godsend in the fickle toy business. (The game division now makes up 40 percent of the company's revenue.) Employing savvy marketing, smarter toy selection, and better financial control, Stephen turned Hasbro into a Fortune 500 company.

In 1989, when the company had annual sales of $1.4 billion, tragedy struck Hasbro once again. Forty-seven-year-old Stephen died of pneumonia, a complication of AIDS. Alan, who himself was president of the company at the time, stepped up to become CEO. Alan had been a creative writing major at the University of Pennsylvania and considered himself more a "free spirit" than a titan of industry (the calculator at his desk is made by Playskool), but his drive to keep the company independent—buyout offers were made at this vulnerable time—and his passion for Hasbro's 8,200 employees helped take the company to another level. Under Alan's leadership, the company beat rival Mattel to acquire Tonka—bringing Play-Doh, Nerf, and Monopoly into the Hasbro family. Alan's eye for the wacky and wonderful has also helped Hasbro continue its tradition of innovation. In 1998, it created an electronic pet called Furby. (If you don't know it, ask your kids; 40 million were sold in three years.) He took a bet on licensing Pokémon, the Japanese cartoon that would later become a worldwide phenomenon.

In 2003, with a desire to establish a solid succession plan, and after a year of serious consideration, Alan Hassenfeld stepped down as CEO and promoted longtime Hasbro executive Al Verrecchia to the post. Alan remains chairman, but the change marks the first time in the company's history that a Hassenfeld is not in the CEO spot. And, for Alan, that's an important point: "I wanted to show the world that the road to the top is open," he says.

For the past number of years many traditional toy companies, Hasbro included, have struggled with waning sales due to increased competition from electronic gadgets and video games. Hasbro is currently bolstering its electronics offerings, something that seems to be paying off as its new portable personal video player for kids, Videonow Color, was named "Best Toy of 2004" at the first annual Ultimate Toy Awards. At the same time, many of Hasbro's classic icons are just as relevant as when they first debuted. G.I. Joe, who just celebrated his fortieth birthday, still continues his heroics. Mr. Potato Head, who in his 50-plus years has quit smoking, gotten married, and had children (the so-called spuds are named Julienne and Chip), entertains each new generation of kids—now as a video game character.

◄o►

Hasbro's isn't just a story about the actualization of the American Dream, or a tale about the triumphs and tragedies of a business. Hasbro is also a pioneer of the integrated corporation; early on, it expanded its reach beyond the playroom and into the community.

While the first two generations of management had a personal interest in giving back to the community, it was the founders' grandchildren, Stephen and Alan, who made it a formal pursuit. In 1983 the company established the Hasbro Charitable Trust, which is funded on an annual basis by the company. Each year the trust donates more than $1.5 million in grant money and more than a million toys to the communities in which it operates and to children worldwide. A separate giving arm, the Hasbro Children's Foundation, which the company also contributes to on a yearly basis, has awarded more than $42 million in grants to hundreds of national organizations since Stephen founded it in 1984. On Valentine's Day, 1994, a personal dream of Alan's was realized when Hasbro Children's Hospital opened in Providence, Rhode Island. (To help fund it, the Hasbro Charitable Trust contributed $2.5 million and Alan raised another $2.5 million from donors all over the world.)

But it's not just about giving money away. As part of a truly integrated corporation, in 1999 the company launched a program that dedicates 1 percent of corporate time to local community service projects. Employees are encouraged to spend four hours a month, paid by Hasbro, volunteering in the community.

Hasbro, known as the crown jewel when it comes to ethics in the toy industry, has been widely recognized as a model of social responsibility. In 2003, *BusinessWeek* listed the company as one of the top 15 corporate donors in the United States, based on contributions and in-kind donations. In 2004, the New York–based Committee to Encourage Corporate Philanthropy honored Hasbro with its Excellence in Corporate Philanthropy award for demonstrating outstanding executive commitment and innovation in corporate giving.

Alan says that as chairman of Hasbro most of his daily focus is on corporate governance and philanthropy. He paraphrases the philosophy of Winston Churchill: "You make a living by what you do," he says. "You make a life by what you give." Currently, he sits on the board of 10 charitable organizations, including Operation Smile, the World Scholar Athlete Games, and the Rhode Island Community Food Bank, which he hopes will achieve his goal of making the state hunger free in the next two years.

We make a living by what we get. We make a life by what we give.

WINSTON CHURCHILL

On a trip to New York to raise money for one of his current projects—an effort to establish a global standard for the ethical manufacturing of toys—Alan Hassenfeld took a break to meet with us to discuss the "debt" he believes he owes to the children of the world, and why—more than ever—it's important to pay that debt back.

WHY GIVE?

Alan G. Hassenfeld, Chairman, Hasbro

I see my job to be a catalyst to lead others to make a difference.

My passion for philanthropy definitely stems from my family. My grandfather and his two brothers came here from Poland and started a company in 1923. Later, during the Second World War, the village they came from, Ulanov, was completely destroyed. Even though they were safely in America, they never forgot where they came from, and they sponsored other villagers to come to America. We grew up with that.

Dad was passionate about philanthropy—especially Jewish philanthropy; he was responsible for the first factory in Jerusalem, Jerusalem Pencil Limited. He was also the head of United Way in Rhode Island. When it came to giving, dad crossed all boundaries. He was one of those people (and I don't think I totally inherited these genes), who couldn't say "No."

When dad died in 1979, it was a difficult time. Hasbro had a much smaller base then—we were doing about $70 million—and the year that dad passed away we lost about $7 million. Of course, it was difficult for us personally as well. We were a close family—we ate dinner together almost every night growing up—and my dad, brother, and I worked together at Hasbro. Surprisingly, Dad didn't leave anything to his philanthropic pursuits when he died. In a letter he left to us, he explained, "I'm not leaving my shares to charity because I believe in living charity." He went on to say that there were things that he might have chosen to give to that maybe if he had more time, or maybe in our lifetimes, he wouldn't feel as strongly about. He wanted us to continue in his tradition, but he wanted us give to organizations that were important to us, that gave us pleasure.

We've tried to follow through with that and give to organizations that matter to us. At Hasbro, the organizations that matter most are the ones that directly benefit children. While our company's success has come from hard work, entrepreneurial spirit, and the great people working with us, our success is mostly thanks to our market—children and the family. If there is a debt that I owe, or my family owes, it is to the children of the world for letting us become what we've become. (Some people might refer to this as Jewish guilt!)

What we've learned over many years is that there are different ways a corporation can give. At Hasbro, we have established five different arms of giving.

The first is the Hasbro Charitable Trust, which works with the communities in which Hasbro and its subsidiaries operate. The trust gets more than 15,000 requests a year. Recently, the trust led the campaign for Rhode Island to become the first hunger-free state. There are 12 million children in the United States who go hungry every day—that's a pretty tough number. We gave an initial gift and helped to raise more than $8 million from individuals and community organizations to build a new facility for the Rhode Island Community Food Bank. (Mr. Potato Head helped out too. We put him on license plates holding a sign that said "Rhode Island Community Food Bank Help End Hunger." The plates carried an additional charge, which went to the Food Bank.) What's most important is that the new facility opened in

January 2004, and we're feeding kids that otherwise may have gone hungry.

In addition to monetary giving, the trust gets thousands of toy donation requests annually. To that end, we set up something called the Children's Giving Tree, which gives a toy to every child in need. When we first started it in Rhode Island, we gave away 40,000 toys. In 2004 we gave away 65,000 toys in Rhode Island and 35,000 in Springfield, Massachusetts, where our Milton Bradley and Parker Brothers offices are located. Worldwide, we estimate that we impact more than 1.3 million children through this program. We couldn't do this alone; we've partnered with World Vision, a wonderful organization that is one of the largest international relief agencies. They help us bring toys to orphanages and children in distressed situations. For example, we sent 25,000 toys, including Nerf footballs, Play-Doh, and Koosh balls (we can't send toys that would require batteries, since many people can't afford them) to Honduras after the awful devastation of Hurricane Mitch. Over the years, we've sent toys to refugee children in Nicaragua, Grenada, and Kosovo and to orphanages in Mongolia, Peru, and Romania.

Our second major arm of giving is the Children's Foundation, which my brother Steve set up 20 years ago. It has a separate outside board that helps advise on issues such as pediatrics, homelessness, abuse, and literacy. The foundation is inundated with upwards of 5,000 grant requests a year. When we look at grants, we are interested in supporting start-up programs that can become self-funding. We are especially passionate about finding programs that we can use as a model and replicate in other parts of the United States or elsewhere in the world. A perfect example of something we've had this type of success with is Boundless Playgrounds, which designs and builds playgrounds where kids with disabilities and regular kids can play together. We gave the seed money to fund that program in 1996; now there are more than 70 of them in the United States and one in Canada benefiting more than 5 million children with special needs.

The foundation looks for opportunities to make a long-term impact. Over the past 20 years we've learned that meeting the immediate needs of children is not enough. That's why, for example, we set up the September 11th Children's Fund (this is different than the September 11th Fund), which we established to help children and families who were deeply impacted by the tragedy. There had been a lot of money pouring in, but we were concerned that the money would not be used properly. (And, unfortunately, as we later learned, that did happen.) We wanted to set up something that helped children two to three years down the road—when the nightmares are still vivid and fewer resources are allocated to help. With the support of other sponsors around the world, we were able to parlay our initial grant into $5 million to fund the program. The fund helps to provide mental health care, mentorship, story-telling programs, and other social services to more than 3,000 children who lost a parent or witnessed the terrorist attack.

Recently, the trust and the foundation joined forces to create a similar long-term focused initiative for tsunami relief. Immediately after the disaster we saw an outpouring of money like never before. People saw the pictures—the horror of it came into their living rooms. We know, though, months later people begin to forget. I was in Thailand during the tsunami; I witnessed the devastation firsthand. I don't like to talk about what I saw, but I know that there are children without parents and children with serious trauma issues who will need to be provided for years from now. We decided instead of focusing on the right-now by providing food and water, our organization would help plan for what these children need next, when many people have forgotten them. Similar to the September 11th Children's Fund, we are focusing on physical and mental health issues, as well as building two schools, two child care facilities (each have the capacity to service 1,000 kids), and a children's medical clinic.

Our programs are successful because we've hired people who are exclusively dedicated to the foundation and the trust. They evaluate grants and do site visitations. They are amazing. Additionally, we have a board at the foundation that has someone of every child discipline on it, and we network. Nothing gets approved without scrutiny. It's been this way since the 1980s. If you don't foster the programs with the right people, it's not going to work.

The third giving arm is my family's foundation. This gives us an opportunity to do things that we are passionate about, but that may not be appropriate for the Hasbro Charitable Trust or Children's Foundation to sponsor. For example, I love supporting the Afghan women's resource centers. I believe in order to change this world (that has gone a little bit crazy!), women hold the clue. They are really the nucleus of the family, and we desperately must empower women in the developing world to break the cycle of violence. Believing that, I jumped on the opportunity to do something in Afghanistan. Remember, education was gone from there for 25 years. We needed to set up centers to teach literacy and skills. I'm proud to say that we have three centers up and running.

The family giving arm serves another purpose, too. At Hasbro we have limited resources, and there have been times when we have had to be careful and cut back what we could give away. When that happens, the family foundation will try to make up the difference. That way, we never have to cut back when it comes to trying to positively impact children's lives.

There are other areas of giving that don't have direct monetary value in the way writing a check or donating a toy does, but they are just as important. One of them is volunteerism. Hasbro's CEO, Al Verracchia, and I, and before that, my brother and dad and grandfather, believe in being part of the community. At Hasbro we like to say that we are about "caring and sharing," and as part of that mission we give our people four hours a month paid to do volunteer work. Their efforts make a difference in our communities, but it also boosts employee morale. My peers at the company are able to hold their head up very high.

The fifth arm of giving is advocacy. I see it as my job to be a catalyst to lead others to make a difference. There's this old awful saying, "a fish rots from the head." Basically, to me that means it's the job of the chairman or CEO to set the ethics of the company. And if the leadership truly believes in what it is saying and acts accordingly, that emanates through the entire corporation.

We've seen that domino effect happen at Hasbro. Our office in Hong Kong just participated in the Dragon Boat Races to raise money to support an Operation Smile mission in China. That particular mission operated on 175 kids with cleft palates. What's amazing is that with their fund-raising effort and a 45-minute operation, they were able to positively change the lives of 175 children forever. Similarly, our London office is initiating wonderful things. That office is committed to helping raise funds for DEBRA, an organization that helps children suffering from a rare skin disorder, epidermolysis bullosa. It also supports Theodora Clown Doctors, an organization that trains "clown doctors," who visit seriously ill children trying to make them laugh and enjoy normal kid things. Our employees in Ireland sponsored a national game-playing week to help raise money for Our Lady's Hospital for Sick Children in Crumlin. They gave six or seven games to each participating school (20 percent of the schools in Ireland participated) and each student brought in 2 euros (€2) to participate in the program. The goal was to raise about €25,000, but the program ended up generating more than €70,000. It was a simple program with a big impact. In fact, the Prime Minister of Ireland met with me to discuss it.

Last Christmas, we did something really different as part of our efforts to energize our employees and partners on our philanthropic efforts. We had a get-together with all our people and brought in some of the people involved in the programs that we have granted money to, such as Sister Emerita McGann, a wonderful nun in Appalachia who every Christmas helps us distribute toys to kids in need, and Matthew Cavedon, a 14-year-old who uses a wheelchair and who has become an important advocate for Boundless Playgrounds. The program was remarkable at showing the impact our company has made, and it made our employees feel like an integral part of it—there wasn't a dry eye in the house (mine included) by the time we finished. We beamed the program to our offices around the world, and we videotaped it as well. After, we gave each of our employees the one-hour video to take home to share with their families. That's how we try to get families involved. That's how we try to pass on this tradition.

While it is our goal to convert those who don't yet have "religion," we know that there are staunch naysayers. The economist Milton Friedman believes in giving every bit back to the shareholders and that none of the profits should be spent on other efforts. I debunk that theory; I don't think Milton was right about our time. Today there are pressures on good governance and doing the right thing.

On the consumer side, we are hearing more and more that people care where a product is made, and they care about the people who are making the product. With technology the way it is today, we are living in a world of great transparency. We not only have cell phones, but we have cell phones with cameras. If something is wrong in a factory, an image can instantly be sent to a computer, and before long, the world will know about it. Nobody wants to buy a product that has blood on it, so I think that cleaning up our industries isn't only the right thing to do, it's necessary for survival.

Although we would all like to say that we are, no company is 100 percent "clean." Right now, in the toy industry, we are working on something to help change that. The goal is to set up a global standard for the ethical manufacturing of toys. Currently, there's no one standard for any industry that every country must adhere to. I'm trying to raise $5 million in three years from as many people as possible to help fund this effort. I've been to London, Tokyo, Hong Kong, and San Francisco raising money, and I can't believe how receptive people have been. We raised $500,000 in one night in Hong Kong alone. People see the writing on the wall: if you want to be part of the twenty-first century, you must be socially responsible.

At Hasbro we don't give to get recognition; we give because it's the right thing to do. We've learned, though, that it's also the profitable thing to do. If a corporation has a clean, good reputation when times are difficult, people tend to support that more than they would necessarily support anybody else.

In all industries, we talk about investment spending: investment spending in new technology; in new computer systems; in new products; in the marketplace. We see our marketplace as children all the world over. We have to invest in bettering that market; otherwise we cannot be successful. Similarly, we can't have a strong bottom line without having strong communities around us. It is from our communities that we draw our employees, our customers, our supporters, and our critics. Without vibrant, active communities we lose our own vitality.

Twenty-five years ago, my dad left us with a letter that stressed how important it is to make a difference in our lifetimes. Trying to make a difference in our communities has made all the difference to us as a company, and to my family personally. As my generation gets ready to pass the baton in the near future, we hope to pass on the idea of living charity, so that we can all enjoy the rich rewards of affecting positive change.

WHAT I HATE ABOUT PHILANTHROPY

- I hate the big dinners! There are times when the honoree is not deserving. (I will not give examples because I'll be damned.) We would rather support a cause by giving a grant than paying for a table and sending people to a dinner.
- Wasted money! Too often people give big sums of money, and a lot of that money is wasted. Make sure you push people to make every penny of the dollar you give away work.
- Some people think they should wait to give their money away until after they die. They think the amount will be greater if they wait. How do you tell a starving child, "I'm sorry there's nothing for you, just wait a couple of years"?

CHAPTER 2

DELIVERING ON
ITS LEGACY: UPS

Remember that the story is to be about us—not about me. No single individual should be given a disproportionate share of credit. . . .

JIM CASEY

The people at UPS are probably too practical to believe in ghosts, but it's obvious that the spirit of Jim Casey—the entrepreneur who founded UPS in 1907 and who was involved until he passed away in 1983 at 95 years of age—is still alive at the company. Management discusses leadership philosophies at an event called a Jim Casey Evening; each year a UPSer who has made the greatest contribution to his or her community is honored with the Jim Casey Community Service Award; and UPSers share a penchant for reciting Jim Casey quotes. (Among them: "While building up others you will build up yourself"; "Good management is an attitude inspired by the will to do right"; and "Determined people, working together, can do anything.")

In the almost 100 years since Jim Casey founded UPS, the company has emerged as a $42 billion global corporation, the third largest employer in the United States, and one of the most recognized brands in the world. As it has grown, UPS has remained steadfast in actively maintaining the values with which it was created. Among other things, there are books about Jim; an official archivist who records quotes, speeches, and stories; and a 407,000-member workforce that is aware—and in awe of—the principles of the founder. Jim seems to permeate everything at UPS. When making a big decision, chairman and CEO Mike Eskew admits to asking himself, "What would Jim do?" In fact, Jim seems to come up dozens of times in any conversation. "I probably shouldn't do this interview," Mike told us when we met to discuss UPS's inclusion in this book. "Jim taught us not to crow."

The story of UPS begins with a 19-year-old Jim Casey who borrowed $100 from a friend and launched the American Messenger Company. Headquartered in Seattle in a small office below a saloon, Jim's brother George and a handful of their teenage friends delivered packages, carried notes, and took trays of food from restaurants. Deliveries were made by foot or bicycle, and eventually motorcycles (there were only a few cars in existence; department stores used horses and wagons to deliver merchandise). Jim slept in the office so that he could offer 24-hour service—including weekends and holidays. The company did well against its competition, mostly because of Jim's mantra: "Best Service and Lowest Rates."

The company used a "consolidated delivery" system, which made business more efficient by combining packages going to the same neighborhoods. It used zone rates based on the travel distance for delivery. Jim gave drivers the same routes so that they had the opportunity to get to know their customers. (The personalized attention that ensued earned the company a reputation for good service.) In 1913 the company acquired its first delivery car—a Model-T Ford—and it changed its name to Merchants Parcel Delivery. A few years later it expanded beyond Seattle and changed its name—this time to United Parcel Service (UPS).

The following years were revolutionary for UPS. It launched new services such as automatic daily pickup calls, additional delivery attempts, and the return of undeliverable items, which propelled it ahead of the competition. In 1924 it debuted a technological innovation that would shape its future: the first conveyor belt system for handling packages. In 1930 UPS extended its reach to deliver for large department stores on the East Coast. Shortly after World War II, UPS made the bold decision to compete head-to-head with the U.S. Postal Service and offer delivery service between any two addresses, rather than just from retail stores. To do so, UPS would have to receive authority from each state to move packages within its borders. In 1953, Chicago and New York became the first cities outside of California where UPS was able to send to and from any address, and over the next two decades it worked to obtain authorization to ship freely in all states. By 1975 UPS became the first package delivery company to deliver to every address in the continental United States.

While working to secure delivery on the ground, UPS also ramped up its service by air. It was the first delivery company to provide air service via privately operated airlines in 1929, but the service was soon stopped due to a lack of volume during the Great Depression. It resumed air operations in 1953, and UPS Blue Label Air became available in every state by 1978. As the demand for air parcel delivery increased, UPS extended Next Day Air service to 48 states and Puerto Rico by 1985. That same year, it began deliveries to six European countries. In 1988, UPS became authorized by the Federal Aviation Administration (FAA) to operate its own aircraft. Formed in little more than one year, UPS Airlines was the fastest-growing airline in FAA history. Today, UPS Airlines—with a fleet of 268 jets, which they call "brown tails," is the ninth largest airline in the world.

As UPS grew—it reached more than one million regular customers by 1993—it spent billions to develop new technologies to stay efficient. It created an electronic clipboard to help drivers track packages with a digital picture of a recipient's signature (no pens needed) and allow drivers to stay in constant contact with headquarters for changing schedules and traffic patterns.

UPS also expanded beyond package delivery by launching new services and businesses. In 1995 it formed the UPS Logistics Group, now called UPS Supply Chain Solutions, to provide global supply chain management solutions, freight transportation, and consulting services. In 1998 UPS Capital was founded to provide financial products and services. UPS Supply Chain Solutions manages goods for UPS customers. (If someone orders a digital camera from Nikon.com, for example, the request is filled and sent by UPS. If someone needs an engine part for his or her Bentley, it doesn't come from the headquarters in the United Kingdom, but from a UPS warehouse in the United States. And, if someone sends back a faulty Toshiba laptop, it isn't returned to the company, but fixed by a dedicated staff member at UPS.) Jim Casey was famous for saying, "Anybody can deliver a package." With UPS's entry into new lines of business it's clear that the company does a whole lot more.

In addition to an emphasis on personal service and a drive to innovate, Jim instilled a commitment to his employees and the community. Jim and his siblings founded the Annie E. Casey Foundation—named after their mother—and the first grants went to support a camp for children in Seattle. The Casey Foundation, which now has $3 billion in assets, is the largest foundation dedicated to improving the lives of disadvantaged children and families in the United States. Jim also launched the UPS Foundation, in 1951, as a way for the company to give back. Giving to the community is a tradition that has remained strong. In 2004, the UPS Foundation donated nearly $40 million to charitable organizations worldwide, and for many years UPS and its employees have led the United States in supporting the annual United Way campaign. (The company and its employees donated $54.2 million to United Way in 2004—an all-time record.)

It's not just money, though. UPS is dedicated to investing time too. More than 30,000 employees are involved in its "Neighbor-to-Neighbor" volunteer program, which has a full-time employee assigned to matching employees with volunteer opportunities based on skills, interests, and time availability. UPS also organizes a "Global Volunteer Week," and 2004 saw the number of volunteers and volunteer hours triple as employees in 35 countries dedicated more than 13,000 hours to building homes in the Philippines, reading to hospitalized children in Nigeria, and working in a soup kitchen in Belgium.

While UPS feels it owes something to its community ("If they do well, we do well," says Mike), it also feels that it owes something to its employees. Jim said that employees should be not just workers, but owners of stock. The company was 100 percent owned by its employees and retirees until 1999, when it offered shares of its stock to the public for the first time. Today employees own almost 50 percent of the stock. Being publicly traded hasn't changed UPS that much, though. "We manage this place for the long term. We think about not the next quarter, but the next quarter of a century," Mike says. And ownership has amounted to a more committed workforce, as Jim predicted.

The company promotes from within, which has further encouraged an invested employee population. (Mike, who became chairman and CEO in 2002, has spent his whole career at UPS, first designing a parking lot and later, briefly working as a driver.) While drivers must adhere to strict guidelines—among them to hold the truck keys on their pinkie to avoid fumbling—they also have rich rewards. Drivers earn top union wages (up to $70,000 or more a year), senior drivers get up to nine weeks paid annual leave, and medical insurance premium costs are paid for by the company. In 2002 the Teamsters president said, "UPS is not our enemy. . . . If there were more companies like UPS, America would be a better place." UPS is also a better place for it: drivers average 16.2 years on the job—four times longer than the typical American worker. And with no mandatory retirement age, drivers such as Marty Peters, 82 years old, just celebrated his fifty-ninth year with the company.

For 21 consecutive years, UPS was rated "America's Most Admired" company in its industry by *Fortune* and it's been honored among the top in the world on social responsibility. When it comes to embracing diversity, UPS is among the top corporations as well. *Fortune* consistently names it to the "50 Best Companies for Minorities," *DiversityInc* magazine includes it on its "Top 50 Companies for Diversity," and it has been honored as Corporate Citizen of the Year by the NAACP and by the Urban League. It's also been recognized among "America's Top Corporations for Women Business Enterprises" by the Women's Business Enterprise National Council (WBENC). UPS's environmentally sustainable practices, which include having one of the quietest, most fuel-efficient aircraft in the industry and making a commitment to reduce nonhazardous waste, have made it the only delivery company listed on the inaugural list of 2005 Global 100 Most Sustainable Corporations in the World, which was announced at the World Economic Forum in Davos, Switzerland.

While UPS—with one high-tech facility that can sort 304,000 packages an hour (40 percent of them without any human intervention)—looks different than the company Jim Casey created, much of it still feels the same. Mike continues in Jim's footsteps, not just by serving as a trustee of the UPS Foundation and The Annie E. Casey Foundation, but by keeping a modest attitude that means sharing an administrative assistant and eating lunch in the company cafeteria. He agreed to participate in this book if we focused our chapter on Jim Casey and UPS—not on him. (It eerily echoes what Jim told a journalist writing a piece for *The New Yorker*, in 1947: "Remember that the story is to be about us—not about me. No single individual should be given a disproportionate share of credit for the development of the United

Parcel Service you are writing about today.") Mike met with us a week before he and his wife, as well as some other UPSers, traveled to a remote part of Poland to build a school. It's something they've done before in China, Mexico, and the United States—and it's something that demonstrates the spirit of Jim Casey is alive and channeled through the folks who run UPS today.

Remembering Jim Casey

Mike Eskew, Chairman and CEO, UPS

In God we trust, everything else we measure.

At UPS we live by a set of core values, and those values are the things that Jim Casey put in place. Over our 100-year history, things have changed. Our purpose has changed, our mission has changed, and our strategy has changed. We've changed our products, we've changed the way we go to customers, and we've even changed our logo. While we've changed a lot of things, the things that have never changed are the values that Jim gave us. He told us:

- Take your jobs and families and communities seriously, but never yourself.
- When you say you are going to do something, do it; and do the right thing, not just the easy or quick or convenient thing.

We think about Jim when we make big decisions. It may seem that walking around with an anchor of values that never changes must be inhibiting, but it's not. It's almost liberating. We have a compass that we believe points us in the right direction. It gives us the guidelines in which to move—as opposed to restrictions so that we don't move.

From the beginning, Jim had the philosophy that to endure, a business depended on its reputation. That meant earning the trust of its customers, its employees, and the communities it serves. We keep that alive by passing on stories about Jim. We talk about how he invited the Teamsters to come in in the 1930s. We know about how during the Great Depression he gathered plant managers for a meeting and asked them to come back with a name of a family that was struggling—half of them came back with names, and Jim helped those families. The employees who didn't come back with names—the ones who demonstrated that they didn't think enough about others—never went very far at UPS.

Jim was very bright and very inquisitive. He loved to learn, loved to read, loved to see new things, but unfortunately he was only able to complete school to the sixth grade. His father passed away when he was 14 and he had been working since he was 11 to help support his family. That's when Jim first started his career in deliveries. It was fascinating to talk with him about what some of his jobs entailed working as a messenger: he carried pitchers of beer—known as "rushing a growler"—from saloons to residences; he went after bail money at the request of prisoners in jail; he was hired to "shadow" someone and report back on his whereabouts. Jim later said, "The messenger boy of that day was not engaged in a particularly edifying occupation." Although Jim wasn't the type to lament his own circumstances, he understood that there were going to be an awfully lot of needy kids in the future. He wanted them to have the chance that he didn't have.

Jim started the Annie E. Casey Foundation and the UPS Foundation to try to give people opportunities. Some UPSers, including myself, are involved in the Casey Foundation, and we believe we are spending his money the way he would want us to. But the way we give back as a company is through the UPS Foundation, which is funded by a percentage of our profits. The UPS Foundation has three major initiatives, which include programs to support family and workplace literacy, hunger relief and improved nutrition, and national volunteerism.

We started the effort to improve adult literacy in 1989 as a way to offer adults and families tools that will make a brighter future available. We've since given more than $11.9 million, and we've worked with more than 300 nonprofits. We've seen the results: more than 42,000 adults and their families have achieved a marked increase their literacy skills. Our program to end hunger also began in 1989 through our Prepared and Perishable Food Rescue Initiative. We've invested nearly $15 million in hundreds of local organizations throughout the country, which have helped provide people with more than 240 million pounds of food. One of the organizations we've seen a lot of success with is the Campus Kitchens Project, a national leadership development program, which brings college students, dining service professionals, and community organizations together to combat hunger through teaching food preparation and culinary skills to unemployed and underemployed men and women. The UPS Foundation recently gave a $250,000 grant, which will allow Campus Kitchens to add another eight locations, launch 20 new community service learning partnerships, recruit dozens of new volunteers, and increase the volume of meals and services provided. Last year we made reducing obesity and improving nutrition a core part of our efforts because we believe that poor nutrition is one of the reasons that kids and adults aren't performing as well as they could.

The third effort of the UPS Foundation is our newest initiative and perhaps the one that I am most excited about. It's a program that's designed to increase and improve volunteerism. We know that volunteers are the lifeblood of nonprofit organizations, but at the same time these people who have generously given their time find that they aren't being used well. They often report back with disappointment that they just stood around and weren't used effectively and didn't make a difference.

At UPS we love to measure everything—in fact we have a saying, "In God we trust, everything else we measure"—so we decided to use this skill set to create a program that helps national and local organizations better recruit, train, and manage volunteers. By measuring effectiveness, we believe that we can discover the best ways to use volunteers, increase the number of volunteers on the roster, and eventually, improve the impact on the community.

I'm excited about these new efforts because we see it starting to take hold with the pilot programs we've launched with United Way, Big Brothers Big Sisters, and 100 Black Men. We are seeing that these programs help us find and keep great volunteers. As we meet and review the programs, we are learning that pieces can be replicated—not only at the big foundations already described, but at smaller places as well.

This effort is important to us because volunteerism is something at the very heart of UPS. We believe that just a little dirt under the fingernails is more powerful than ink on a check. We have something very unique called the Community Internship Program. UPS started it in 1968; it was a time in the United States when we were just coming to grips with the difficulties in the inner cities and Jim felt it was time to get our people to understand what life was like for people who had it differently than we did.

The Community Internship Program gives UPS that opportunity. Each year we select top performers in mid-level management positions, who have high advancement potential, and we ask them to leave their jobs for an entire month. They travel to one of four rural and urban communities unfortunately afflicted with poverty, homelessness, drugs, crime, and gang warfare. The interns live and eat on-site. They immerse themselves in community projects—day and night—for the whole month. The projects involve everything from tutoring preschool children, orphans, or kids who have AIDS to teaching résumé and interviewing skills to prisoners or at-risk teens, to visiting nursing homes and mental health facilities. Our interns have answered calls with police officers, clothed people who didn't have enough to wear, and bathed sick people—they do whatever is necessary at any given moment.

We invest $10,000 per intern in this program. It pays off many times over, though. There are thousands of things that the interns tell us, and there are many things—the look in someone's eyes, or the feeling of witnessing something they've never seen before—that they can't tell us about fully. What we do see in the managers, though, is that walking in the other guy's shoes changes perspectives. We've seen that after completing the program, managers tend to look at employee matters in a less rigid way. They tend to listen with more empathy. The internship changes individual managers—they change the rest of us.

This program is so essential because at UPS we see the community like no one else. Our drivers knock on doors in every city, in every village, in every street. We see everyone—the hungry, the homeless, the undereducated, the abused. These people are our next generation of employees and our next generation of customers. Through the internships, our current UPSers gain an understanding of what their lives are like. It's made our people stronger. It's made them more capable to deal with what is thrown at them. (A lot is: among other things they have pulled people out of burning cars, put out house fires with garden hoses, and saved dogs that were hit by cars.) The internship has also made all of our employees more compassionate.

I got this terrific letter from a customer not too long ago, it goes back in time, it says:

Early in November of 1982 my wife and I were blessed with our second child, a son Nicholas, and after being awake the better part of two days I decided to go home to feed the dog and to catch up on a little sleep. About 20 minutes into my nap the phone rang it was my wife. She was distraught with news from the doctors that something was wrong with our son. They told her that they were fairly certain that he was born with Down Syndrome. They told her that he would more than likely require constant professional care based on their early observations. When I heard this news I literally felt as though I'd been punched in the stomach.

At that moment the doorbell rang. It was a UPS driver I'd never seen before. She took one look at me and asked, "What's wrong, what's happened to you?" I told her what I just heard and she asked me to come out on the porch. She had something to say to me. We talked for about 30 minutes. She told me she had worked with kids like Nicholas back in New York. She gave me assurances that everything would work out and that everything would be fine. She made sure to tell me how to handle the news with his sister, Maria, and other members of the family. After feeling much better about things, I remarked how great it must be to have a job where you can spend time talking to someone when you felt like it, when she responded, "I just took my lunch with you."

The funny thing about this UPS driver is that I had never seen her before that day and I have never seen her since. I call her my UPS angel and I am grateful to her to this very day. Nick is now 21 years old and the joy of our family. He's handsome and healthy and strong. People are attracted by his magnetic personality. The doctors were wrong; the UPS angel was right.

What's incredible is that we get letters like that all the time. It sounds funny, but there's something honest and noble about what our people do. They understand that they have an obligation to their customers and their communities. They become a part of people's lives.

After 33 years with UPS, it's hard to know when I do something if it stems from something in me, or, if it's UPS. I don't mean to shortchange my parents or my friends, but those thousands of experiences that we hear about Jim Casey, the beliefs that come back about our next generation from our interns, and the stories that our drivers tell us, have made us all better. It's given us a heart and a soul and a conscience.

At some point you say, "I owe Jim." For me, that meant getting involved in the Casey Foundation. More than 14 million, or 21 percent of all kids under 18 years old, live in poverty. It's a higher proportion than what existed 30 years ago. You see these kids come in—they are foster kids and call themselves Casey kids—and they talk about the conditions that they've lived in and the vastly bettered conditions since they have become Casey kids. It makes it so clear that investing in this program, keeping at it, really makes a difference. It's been incredible to see how some of the programs that Casey does have been replicated with juvenile care and health care. What started with my doing what I thought Jim would want me to do has become what I want to do.

If Jim Casey were watching down, he would tell us that we are not moving fast enough, and we are not aggressive enough, and we have to serve our customers better. He'd tell us—as he has told us before—that we have to be "constructively dissatisfied." It's not to complain. It's not to, as Jim would say, "gripe" about it; he would simply tell us that if we are constructively dissatisfied, we can do better. It's part of this continuous improvement.

Every once in a while Jim would say, "Not too bad over there; you've done a good job." I think Jim would also tell us he was proud of us. He would like what we are doing globally. He told us that in some of his last years: "Bear in mind you are only serving a fraction of the world's population—there's a lot of places and lands for you to touch and places to do the things that we know we can do." As we trade and create partnerships with other countries, it does more than enable commerce, it connects people and cultures. The quality of life goes up around the world—especially in the neediest parts of the world. Jim would tell us to keep reaching out—except to do more of it. He would say, "Don't rest on your laurels. Keep thinking about the next generation. I did for you."

MIKE ESKEW EXPLAINS HOW COMMUNITIES AND COMPANIES CAN BE "IN LOCKSTEP"

There are things that we have done to support the community that have proven to be very good for us as well. When companies move in lockstep with their communities incredible things can happen. Take for example, the 60,000 folks whom we've hired through the Welfare-to-Work program. When we first started the program, there was concern from some that perhaps these people didn't have the work ethic that UPSers have developed over the years. We soon learned that wasn't the case, though. These people liked coming to work, and most came to work every day. It was a great opportunity for us: it gave us a terrific workforce and it gave us a different perspective. Diversity—whether it's diversity of work experience, age, gender, or thought—makes companies richer. We achieved a different kind of diversity and we became a better company.

We started another program, which has also helped us enhance our workforce while providing something that the community needed. We were growing at our hub in Louisville and we realized that we were about to run out of qualified employees. At the same time we learned that there was an enormous unemployment rate and undereducated population in parts of Kentucky and Indiana—geographically close to where we needed to hire people. We came up with a program called School-to-Work. It was originally designed to give high school seniors an opportunity to gain work experience as well as earn college credits by taking preliminary college courses. Students in the program could attend classes at their high school in the morning, work at UPS as package handlers from 11 a.m. to 3 p.m. and take a Jefferson Community College course twice a week in the UPS classroom (the classroom is at our Worldport headquarters, where UPS package sorters work).

The School-to-Work program also serves as a feeder program for Metropolitan College, which is a university facilitated by UPS, the University of Louisville, Jefferson Community College and Technical College that offers students a free college education and part-time paid jobs at UPS. As students graduate from School-to-Work they can seamlessly transition to a paid college career at Metro College.

It made it easier for an entire population to work and go to school because the class times and work times were designed to work together. And, as a UPS employee, the students receive health coverage, a 401(k) plan, vacation pay, and a starting salary of $8.50 an hour. Through something we call Earn and Learn we also pay for full-time or part-time employees' school tuition, books, room and board, and we give bonuses for passed classes. We've spent more than $60 million on the program and have had more than 40,000 employees participate. It's paid for itself many times over: we've been rewarded with a stable workforce that is awfully mature and committed.

CHAPTER 3

HOW TO MAKE BOOTS AND SAVE THE WORLD: TIMBERLAND

The company took the idea of service a step further by offering a "Service Sabbatical," where employees can take a three- to six-month paid leave to lend their professional skills to a nonprofit organization.

Although Jeff Swartz swept floors and painted walls at the Timberland factory when he was a kid, he was discouraged from ever being seriously employed by the company started by his grandfather, Nathan Swartz, (a.k.a. "Papa Nathan") and run by his father, Sidney Swartz. Working in the New England shoe manufacturing business was a roller coaster of a way to make a living. (It was dangerous too; Papa Nathan sliced off part of his finger on one of the machines.) Papa Nathan dreamed a different future for Jeff and encouraged him to "get a profession" and become a doctor, lawyer, or accountant. "My grandson is not going to be a *schlepper*," he said.

Jeff usually listened to Papa Nathan—he had studied Russian to speak with him in his native tongue and still shares stories his grandfather had imparted to him—but he blatantly chose not to follow his career counsel. And, today, as the CEO of Timberland—now a global brand—Papa Nathan can rest assured that Jeff is not a *schlepper*. Under Jeff's leadership, revenues have charged from around $860 million in 1998 (the year Jeff became

CEO) to $1.5 billion in 2005. In addition to his business acumen, Jeff took Papa Nathan's moral beliefs (his mantra was "You got to do for others") and applied them to building creative partnerships and sponsoring innovative programming. As a result, he has established Timberland as an icon for socially responsible businesses worldwide.

The seeds for Timberland were planted in 1918 when Nathan Swartz, a Russian immigrant, began work as an apprentice at a small Boston outfit called the Abington Shoe Company. He learned to cut leather, stitch seams, attach soles, and craft fine leather boots. In a classic "coming to America" success story, he worked hard and rose in the ranks, and in 1952 he bought a 50 percent stake in the company. A few years later, he purchased the remaining interest and brought his sons, Sidney and Herman, to work with him. In 1965 Abington introduced a new technology—injection molding, at the time used to make items such the View-Master stereoscopes and furniture parts—to the footwear industry. With the newfound ability to fuse the soles to leather uppers without any stitching, Abington produced its first guaranteed waterproof leather boots.

For a decade Abington had been making private-label boots for various companies, but in 1973 it decided its new rugged waterproof boot was so innovative that it should be kept as its own. It was called Timberland, and by 1978, when the boot comprised more than 80 percent of the company's production, the company officially changed its focus—and its name.

From then on, known as the Timberland Company, business expanded to include casual and boat shoes. Sidney, who had begun as a trainee on the production line at Abington and later became the company treasurer, took the reigns in 1986. He opened the company's first international subsidiary in Italy and helped to launch the company's first dress shoe line. From there, the company branched out into men's and women's apparel, accessories, and leather goods.

In the summer of 1978, right after Jeff graduated high school and was preparing to start at Brown University in the fall, Nathan died—killed by a drunk driver. Jeff decided that after college he would return to Timberland and continue the family legacy. (Out of respect for his father, Sidney had never asked Jeff to join, but had always hoped it would remain a family business.) After graduating from Brown and earning an MBA from Dartmouth, Jeff joined Timberland in 1986.

The company went public a year later, but structured a deal with two types of stock shares so that the Swartz family would always maintain control. (The family held stock with 10 votes per share, while the public was sold stock with a single vote per share.) In 1991, the company switched from being listed on the American Stock Exchange to the New York Stock Exchange, and began trading under the symbol TBL. (Currently, the family owns 20 percent of all shares and has 68 percent of voting control.)

Jeff, who had been COO since 1991, continued to expand the scope of the business—he helped introduce boots, shoes, and apparel for kids and grew licensing agreements to include watches, wallets, and travel gear—and was elevated to president and CEO in 1998. He was 38 years old. Sidney remained chairman and maintained an active role. It was a plan they were able to pull off in part because the family controlled the voting shares, but more importantly, it proved to be the right decision for the family and outside shareholders alike.

Over the past five years, Timberland's earnings averaged 20 percent growth, sales averaged 10 percent growth, and the company has no debt, which is especially impressive in tough economic times. While the company has emerged as a global values brand (it has 200 stores around the world), the original yellow boot continues to be one of Timberland's most popular styles. Now customizable in endless color combinations (Burgundy! Cornflower! Pink!), the product has not only maintained a strong following with its traditional audience, but captured an urban consumer as well. Several rap artists have adopted the rugged boot they call "Tims" and made it the favorite footwear of hip-hop culture.

—◄◦►—

The unlikely ability for the original product to simultaneously serve as a utilitarian boot and a status symbol for urban youth echoes the unlikely way Timberland serves simultaneously as a for-profit business and a vehicle for social justice. In 1988 Timberland became a founding sponsor of the not-for-profit organization City Year, making it the first youth service corps launched entirely through private sector support. City Year, a Boston-based "urban Peace Corps," offers 17 to 24 year olds from diverse backgrounds the opportunity to do community service full-time for one year. The programming is mostly focused on educational initiatives; City Year participants serve as mentors in public schools and run after-school programs that focus on social issues such as domestic violence prevention and AIDS awareness.

To date, Timberland, has invested about $20 million in funds and in-kind donations (it provides every City Year corps member with a uniform), but it's not about handouts. City Year New Hampshire shares Timberland's headquarters in Stratham, New Hampshire, and both organizations have grown together. Since partnering with Timberland, corporations such as Cisco, Comcast, and Bank of America have also invested in City Year. Today, the growing partnerships mean that the nonprofit has 750 young people dedicating themselves to making a difference in 15 cities in the United States and in South Africa.

From the groundbreaking City Year partnership, Timberland wholeheartedly embraced the idea of integrating social justice into its business model. Timberland has had a long-running program to direct a percentage of sales from its infant booties to Share Our Strength, an organization that raises consumer awareness about children's hunger. It also partners with the Student Conservation Association, the nation's leading provider of conservation service opportunities, and the Harlem Children's Zone, a nonprofit organization that enhances the quality of life for children and families in New York City.

Partnership at Timberland does not mean writing a check—employees are encouraged to actively participate. It launched the "Path of Service" program, where employees receive paid leave to do community volunteer work. (It began with 16 hours a year, and was upped to 40.) The initiative has enabled Timberland employees to restore an abandoned African-American cemetery in Danville, Kentucky; create a garden at the Girls' After School Academy in San Francisco; and organize a bike ride in New Hampshire that raises money to fight cancer.

The company took the idea of service a step further by offering a "Service Sabbatical," where employees can take a three- to six-month paid leave to lend their professional skills to a nonprofit organization. Volunteerism spans far beyond the folks who work at Timberland headquarters: the company created an annual day of service called Serv-a-palooza in an effort to unite employees, vendors, and community partners in more than 20 countries. In a recent Serv-a-palooza, volunteers in Japan cleaned a beach; teams in Italy, England, and Germany built trails and planted gardens; and 1,000 people in New Hampshire dedicated their time to the Humane Society, Meals on Wheels, and neighborhood schools. To date, Timberland employees have dedicated 330,000 working hours to make their communities better.

Doing well by doing good is a holistic effort at Timberland that also incorporates environmental responsibility (including finding renewable and sustainable sources of energy, using organic cotton in some of its products, and purchasing 100 percent postconsumer recycled content cardboard to make its shoe boxes). It also applies its ethics in every corner of the world in which it operates.

Timberland has products made in more than 35 countries and has a "Global Business Alliance" department which offers creative programming including worker training programs, microlending for factory workers and, among other things, ensures that workplace conditions are fair, safe, and nondiscriminatory.

Everyone Timberland does business with—vendors, tanneries, suppliers, licensees, and distributors—are bound by a Code of Conduct, which the company created in 1994 and has since translated into 20 languages. Third parties perform assessments to ensure that Timberland and its business partners are following the guidelines. The assessments have uncovered some problematic issues, and while Timberland will leave the factories if the conditions don't improve, it prefers to first try to effect change by working with local organizations to train managers and better conditions so that factories won't close and workers won't lose their jobs. (Examples of working to create change in the factories include helping its apparel and accessory vendors in China meet expectations for compensation systems; conducting training for 1,500 workers that focused on human rights, local labor law, and the Code of Conduct in the Dominican Republic; and sponsoring an HIV/AIDS awareness event in Vietnam).

Everyone Timberland does business with is bound by a Code of Conduct, which the company created in 1994 and has since translated into 20 languages.

Timberland represents the apex in innovation in corporate social responsibility and has been widely recognized as such. In 2002, it was a recipient of the Ron Brown Award for Corporate Leadership, an annual Presidential award presented to companies that have shown commitment empowering employees and communities. (The award, which is presented at a White House cer-emony, is a tribute to Ron Brown, a former U.S. Secretary of Commerce.) The company has been honored with the Corporate Excellence Award by the New York–based Committee to Encour-age Corporate Philanthropy and has topped many magazines' "Best Companies to Work For" lists.

In his essay, Jeff talks about the origins of the partnership with City Year. It's a genuine and often funny personal account about how he tied his corporation to the community—and how it changed his company, and his life, for the better.

A SHARING OF STRENGTH

Jeffrey Swartz, President and CEO, Timberland

The notion of interdependence—that you are your brother's or sister's keeper—was always part of our business model.

I grew up in a family business, which for us meant working in a factory. That was where my dad was, and that's where our livelihood was—or wasn't. I have very powerful visual and sensory memories of it. One time, when I was about 13 years old, as the factory was churning at its usual breakneck pace, I noticed my dad standing in the shadows with another man. It caught my attention because Dad was (and still is) a get-things-done kind of guy—not someone to be off on the sidelines. I saw that their heads were bent together and then Dad reached into his pocket and gave this guy a wad of cash.

Now, I knew that Dad always had cash on him, in fact, we used to call him "The Bank of Sidney," but I wasn't sure what that exchange was all about. Later that night, when we got home, I asked him. It led to a long learning exercise, which involved getting in the car and driving to the YMCA.

"You have $108 in your pocket this week, so does Freddy, the guy I gave the money to," Dad said. "He's got to pay rent, he's got to pay for food, and he's got a wife and child; let's see how far $108 goes."

I had thought $108 was a lot of money, but as it turned out, I was able to use it to rent a room at the YMCA, buy some SpaghettiOs and some other staples, and then I was tapped. Dad explained that, unlike Freddy, I didn't have a wife and kid to support with my $108, and he was trying to make ends meet.

I thought I understood the point of the lesson—Dad was helping someone who needed a boost—but what he really wanted to show me was that Freddy's troubles had an impact on the company—and ultimately, on me.

"If you want to go to college someday, we have to get this guy Freddy through to payday," Dad said. "If Freddy doesn't make it through to payday, he'll leave the mill and find something else to do. If he finds something else to do, his job doesn't get done. If his job doesn't get done, the factory doesn't make the boots. If the factory doesn't make the boots, we don't get paid. If we don't get paid, you don't go to college. Are you following?"

I was following. While Dad was never one to preach philosophy lessons, the notion of interdependence—that you are your brother's or sister's keeper—was always part of our business model. You could see it at the mill every day. When the fire alarm went off, the mill shut down because our town's volunteer fire department was half staffed by people in our factory, but Dad never complained about an interruption. He knew that if the fire wasn't put out, the whole town would burn down. Even though this idea of the individual for the collective and the collective for the individual wasn't explicitly stated before I was asked to spend my $108, Dad had already graphically imprinted upon me a notion that our company was part of a social fabric.

While there's always been an organic element of civic service in our business, the pursuit became more formalized in the late 1980s when we became partners with a social justice organization called City Year. How that happened is an unlikely and funny story. In the summer of 1988, when I was working as the head of international operations, I got one of these standard badly written letters from the folks I liked to call the starving social justice people. You know the letters; you get them all the time. It went something like this:

Dear Friend,

We are young people in the city of Boston. We know that teenage pregnancy occurs during this time of the day, we know that violence happens at that time of the day, we know how to solve these problems. We have everything we need. We can save the world. All we lack for is 50 pairs of boots. You have lots of boots, we don't have any, please send some.

Love,
City Year

It was an inane fund-raising letter! I'm not even sure why I got it (maybe someone in the mailroom thought I needed a friend), but for whatever reason it landed on my desk at a time when I was willing to read it and respond. I thought—in a knighted corporate redistribution of wealth sort of way—it would be nice to do the right thing. (Disclaimer: the redistribution of wealth is not the right thing, but I didn't know any better at that time.) So, I sent them 50 pairs of boots.

Since I thought I had been enlightened enough to respond to the request, I expected to get a thank-you note. (My mom is big on Emily Post, and therefore very big on thank-you notes.) Well, these guys didn't send one. I did get a call from City Year, though, saying the cofounder, who is also from New Hampshire, was coming through and wanted to say hello. I thought he was going to come by to say thank you in person. (I was such an idiot.)

Let's fast-forward a few weeks: Alan Khazei, the cofounder of City Year, came to the office. I met him in the conference room (I didn't want to let a social justice person into my office. I was an entrepreneur and a red-blooded capitalist!)

Alan sat across from me. There was no thank you. Instead, he said, "You think your job is to make boots and shoes and that my job is to save the world. If you are willing to invest half a day— four hours—I'll show you how the two can be one."

It was an unusual sales pitch. I thought to myself that it was too intellectually wild an idea not to take a look at. I thought that I had to at least try. So, I did. I didn't do it by myself—if I was going to be a social justice person, somebody was going with me to hold my hand.

I brought 10 Timberland people and we went to the Odyssey House, a place in Hampton, New Hampshire, where young people deal with the end of their addiction to chemical substances. We painted the living room of the house. It was the cheesiest kind of corporate service you can do: paint a wall; take a picture—grip-and-grin stuff. At the time, though, I thought I was Mother Theresa. I thought, Calcutta must look something like this.

Later that day, as I was painting the archway between the living room and dining room, this young guy, who lived at the Odyssey House, asked me what I do at Timberland. I was very pleased to tell to him I was the senior vice president of international.

"But what do you *do*," he replied.

What do you mean, what do I do, I wondered. I was responsible for all the international operations of the Timberland Corp. I thought I was bigger than big, and larger than large. Yet, he was unimpressed. I didn't know what to say, so I asked him what he does.

"I get well," he said.

You can read an article, or see a story on TV, and it's just not the same thing. This sounds hokey and silly, but the Godfather was wrong when he said, "It's nothing personal; it's just business." Everything that matters in my life is personal, and this kid made that day very, very personal. In that moment, I got a connection to reality that was different from any reality I knew.

City Year opened a door and helped me across a transom into a place that was brighter and warmer and more full of possibility than anywhere I had ever imagined. That day, I left a caricature of me behind. I met me—a guy who was much more powerful than a title, a guy who could actually make a difference, a guy who could do something that you could see with your hands and feel with your heart.

The most important thing I realized was that this had nothing to do with me. Each and every one of us has the potential to make a difference. I went back to my desk at Timberland and decided two things:

1. We will partner with these guys because in four hours Alan Khazei showed me how making boots and saving the world can be the same thing.
2. I have to share this because it is so powerful. It's as close to truth as anything I had seen at that point.

For more than 15 years we have had a partnership with City Year and we've been sharing this truth with anybody who will listen to it. I don't like asking people for things, but I don't have any trouble trying to build the City Year/Timberland partnership. It's easy for me to ask another CEO for $50,000 for the right to sponsor a City Year team of volunteers because I know it will transform their company, and like me, they will get back 10 times more than they put in. If I sound like a snake oil salesman, it's only because I believe so desperately in this possibility of investing our work time and space with an underlying purpose that doesn't ignore, but transcends, the notion of profit.

Having a partnership with City Year doesn't mean that we just send uniforms, have our name on their stationery, show up for an occasional photo-op, or a chance to meet the President. I don't mean to sound flip, but a lot of so-called public/private partnerships get denominated like that. While that's better than nothing, we've structured partnership in a way that's more aggressive—and as a result, I think more valuable.

We have sought to design a boundaryless organization. That means when we negotiate our telephone contract, for example, we include City Year and treat them as a subsidiary. They pay their own bill, but they benefit from our purchasing power and get a lower rate. Additionally, we brought the for-profit accountability model to City Year. We showed them how we meet with our board, what our budget cycle looks like, and what our planning cycle looks like. Today, the City Year CEO's report has language and a format that relates to the Timberland quarterly review cycle—it's helped them better manage their organization.

We also provide each corps member at City Year New Hampshire with a mentor from the management team at Timberland. If someone signs up to mentor a City Year member, it's part of his or her performance and professional responsibility. If he fails to mentor successfully, it's as if he has failed to mentor an employee successfully. Equally, every Timberland mentor is going to have a say in whether or not the City Year corps member is rehired. Our partnership works because there is risk on both sides. I know that this is nontraditional, but by pushing partnership beyond the notion of transaction, we are really creating a sharing of strengths.

Partnership like this is difficult nitty-gritty stuff. It's a source of perspiration, but also of inspiration. Here's a good example: we provide every City Year corps member with a uniform. Male or female, everyone gets the same thing—a red jacket, boots, and a pair of men's khaki pants. We've been sending this to them for what seems like forever and, as you know, we would like a thank-you note.

Well, we got our thank-you note two years ago from 50 City Year women across the country. It came in the middle of a town meeting. "We love your brand; we love your boots; we hate your pants! We're not wearing these pants anymore!" one woman said.

"I beg your pardon?" I asked. "What's wrong with *free*? I'm the national sponsor, what are you talking about?"

"They don't fit—they are made for men. We're women and we are serving, how come you don't show us more respect?"

"What's wrong with the pants?" I asked.

She grabs the outside of both of her thighs and she tugs. There was enough material there to put another person in the pants. She looks at me and says, "Fix the pants!"

"No," I said, "You fix the pants." I didn't even know there was anything wrong with the pants, so I certainly didn't know how to fix them. Not only did this woman spearhead the project to fix the pants, she did it amazingly well. She taught us things about apparel that we wouldn't have paid attention to otherwise. She knew the way young people wanted to wear the pants. That's the women's pants we sell now.

I'll bet we invest $1 million a year in the City Year uniform. During the course of our relationship we've invested $20 million in shareholder funds in City Year. I say "invested" because we have earned—and continue to earn—a return from this relationship.

I know the economist Milton Friedman thinks it's immoral to redistribute shareholder funds, and that this type of effort would take value away from profits of stakeholders. I don't think so, though. There are different ways to value Timberland's performance. For the past eight years we've been on *Fortune's* 100 "Best Companies to Work For" list; last year we made the *Working Mother's* "100 Best Companies for Working Mothers;" and for the past seven years, *Forbes* magazine—"the capitalist tool"—has listed Timberland as one of the "400 Best Big Companies in America."

Can someone from the outside suggest that those achievements are because we make a better boot? Sure, we get paid for making a better boot, but *how* do you think we make a better boot? *Who* do you think makes a better boot? Do you think Timberland people are smarter than Nike people? Better dressed? Oh, it's the New Hampshire air as opposed to Oregon air! On what basis do you distinguish Timberland's performance for the past 10 years?

I'm not arguing that our superior returns are attributed solely to City Year either. What I am saying is that you can't reduce this to the absurdity of a formula that asks if we had invested $10 million instead of $20 million, would shareholders have $10 million more? Maybe they would, or maybe they have $50 million less.

Like all CEOs, I live for every 90 days in terms of corporate results. I'm accountable as the head of a publicly traded company. I'm also an undiversified investor—all of my wealth is tied up in Timberland stock. Of course my interests are aligned with the shareholders' interests. I am the shareholder! And, I defend our record. It is the recipe of what we invest in R&D, culture building, and community impact—and the milling together of those spices that makes Timberland unique.

Since our initial partnership with City Year, our interest in partnering with other organizations and community efforts has branched out extensively. When picking a partner we start from two screens. First, we ask, is it relevant to someone at Timberland? (Basically, somebody has got to bring the idea forward to make it happen.) And second, is it relevant to our consumer?

Examples of programs that would be relevant to our consumer include our "crib bootie" program, which highlights an issue of concern to many people—childhood hunger. For every pair of Timberland crib booties purchased, a portion of the money goes to Share Our Strength, an antihunger organization. Additionally, we invite consumers to participate in our community service projects on Earth Day, realizing that the environment is something many of them have an interest in. We have also partnered with the not-for-profit organization Clean Air–Cool Planet, which has helped us reduce our environmental footprint by 10 percent and put us on our way to our goal of becoming carbon neutral.

Let me give you a great example of what can be done when our employees find an initiative that is relevant to them. A few years ago, a neighbor of mine was serving as one of the chief fund-raisers for the Pan-Mass Challenge, a nearly 200-mile bike ride that raises money to fight cancer. It was a personal issue for him, one of his college buddies died of cancer, and every year he arranges a team to ride in his honor. I gave him money and outfitted his team in Timberland gear. In response, he told me to let him know if anyone I knew was interested in riding, and he would get them in. The fact that it would be difficult to get into a bike ride was news to me; I had never heard a word about this ride at Camp Timberland.

When I sent a note asking if anyone wanted to participate, I got back a trillion responses that people would love to. Apparently, it was very relevant to a lot of Timberland people and all of a sudden there's a Timberland team in the ride. This will now be the fifth year we have had a team in the Pan-Mass Challenge.

Some years after Timberland first got involved, Bonnie, a vice president who had been active in this effort, came into my office and told me that she was done with the Pan-Mass Challenge. Timberland is based in New Hampshire, she said, and she was going to create a ride in our home state. The next thing I knew, she put the entire building on its head, and with Timberland employees and residents of our state she organized the Granite State Quest, a 100-mile race to conquer childhood cancer. It was unbelievable, and perhaps more amazing is that recently Bonnie came to me and told me that she wanted to take a Service Sabbatical to focus on her next goal. "Do you know how many states in the union don't have a ride?" she asked me. "If I created a business model for this ride all across the United States, I can raise $1 million and put cancer out of business."

At Timberland our greatest strength is that we have a firm grip on the obvious. We know that the notion of service is innate and human. People want to be connected to something that is more powerful and noble than everyday ordinary stuff. This is not something we invented at Timberland. We simply created a vocabulary that says service is part of our business dialogue. By pushing that vocabulary into the language of everyday commerce, we have changed Timberland from the inside out in a profound way. Our employees care about their work here—it is not just their jobs; it is in their hearts. As a company it has made us more compassionate. It has made us more competitive. It has made us more powerful. The success we enjoy as a business is a reflection of the congruence between our values and our efforts.

I have been affected personally as well. I can easily imagine how, absent an experience like what I have had with City Year, one can become a hollow caricature. I'm grateful to City Year for the gift that gives to me humility, a true sense of integrity, and a challenge of real excellence. These are the values that we say we will be measured by at Timberland. In the context of being the CEO of a for-profit company, this partnership provides me with the most direct access to greatness I can ever imagine.

CHAPTER 4

A DIRECT APPROACH: DELL

Companies that plan to be in business for a long time have to act with a long-term view.

M ost people know the fairy tale version of Michael Dell's blockbuster success: a college student who rapidly built an empire that revolutionized the computer industry by making technology accessible and affordable to more people through "the direct model." What most people don't realize is that this seemingly overnight success had been in the making since Michael was in grade school.

At 12 years old, Michael worked washing dishes at a Chinese restaurant to raise money for his stamp collection and parlayed his investment into a company dedicated to stamp collectors and sellers. It did well (he made $2,000 from his first auction) and a few years later he bought an Apple II—the PC of choice at the time—with his earnings.

Unlike most people who coveted a computer (and keep in mind Michael had to beg his parents to let him buy himself one), he didn't want to use it as it was, but to take it apart, see how it worked, and put it back together improved. It was a hobby that evolved into yet another for-profit venture as he started to upgrade computers and sell them to his high school classmates.

Around this time, he spent a summer selling newspaper subscriptions at the *Houston Post*, and quickly discovered that people who had recently moved or married were the most likely prospects to purchase a subscription. He found a way to find folks with that profile, and went to them directly. It was an object lesson in direct marketing (one he would call upon later), and it worked beautifully: In one summer 16-year-old Michael earned $18,000. He, of course, bought more computers.

It's difficult to understand why a computer savvy serial entrepreneur whiz kid veered off course at this point, but he decided to enter college as a premed student, and in 1983 Michael went off to study at the University of Texas. He attended enough classes to realize that his passion was building computers, so he turned his attention to growing his computer business, which he was now running out of his dorm room.

As Michael learned more about the industry, a picture of glaring inefficiencies began to emerge. Customers bought computers from dealers, who had bought the computers from distributors or manufacturers. The machines were sold at a fourfold of what the parts inside were worth, and worse, they were obsolete by the time the customer took one home. At the end of his freshman year, with $1,000 and a mission to boost efficiency, improve service, and lower costs, Michael left his premed courses and college for good and officially launched PCs Limited, which eventually became the Dell we know today.

At that time, PCs didn't come with hard drives, and Dell first sold kits that upgraded computers to include one. It grew from there—mostly by providing innovative solutions to the problems Michael saw as plaguing the industry. Instead of relying on retailers to sell his products, Michael went straight to the consumers. By dealing with the customers directly on the phone at first (and online later), the company was able to reduce costs for consumers as well as gain valuable insight about customer purchasing habits.

It built a computer only after someone ordered one, which kept inventory costs down, and introduced the idea of customization to the industry. (Previously customers had no say what they wanted in a PC). In another hallmark introduction, Dell pioneered the industry's first service and support programs—practices that won the company a loyal customer base.

Additionally, Dell made the shift to Internet sales before it was proven or popular, earning it the distinction of being the first company to record $1 million in online sales and its status today as the largest supplier of PCs over the Internet. Michael continued to build his reputation in business, and in 1992 he became the youngest CEO to earn a ranking on the Fortune 500 (he was 27).

In July 2004, Michael—the longest-tenured CEO in the computer industry—named Kevin Rollins, then Dell president and COO, to the CEO post. (Michael remains chairman.) Kevin had been involved with the company since 1993, when as a partner at Bain & Co. he helped develop Dell's global strategy. In the newly defined roles, Kevin leads company strategy and operations and Michael focuses on trends in technology and customer preference. They stress, however, they work closely together and, in a nod to their industry's lingo, describe the relationship as a "two-in-a-box" senior-management structure.

It's a system that is operating well—revenues reached $49.2 billion in 2004. In March 2005, Dell was named America's Most Admired Company by *Fortune* magazine and holds the number three spot on the global list. The success stems in part because of the common ethic the leaders share, which they have jointly infused into the company. Michael had founded the company with an emphasis on treating customers and employees with respect, and Kevin continued and formalized the pursuit a few years ago when he launched "the soul of Dell" initiative, which publicly established company ethics and ideals.

As part of the effort, Dell committed to a culture of sustainability and responsibility that goes well beyond legal minimums. They strive to reduce the company's environmental impact through product design, manufacturing and operations, and product end-of-life solutions. (Dell announced an aggressive aim of a 50 percent increase in global product recovery in 2004—making it the first company to publicly release a computer recycling goal.) In a true testament to its commitment, the company has put systems into place to measure and ensure compliance, including a Global Ethics Council, which defines and advocates the policies at facilities worldwide, and Regional Ethics Committees, which put the efforts into effect locally. It even appointed another CEO—a chief ethics officer.

While Dell has been widely recognized for its efforts—the U.S. Environmental Protection Agency has honored it for increasing the energy efficiency of computers and raising customer awareness, and *Business Ethics* magazine has given Dell its Environmental Progress Award for its work leading computer recycling initiatives—Michael and Kevin say public recognition is neither why they do this nor how they measure success.

"The number one reason to do this is it makes good business sense. We view our community contributions as investments," says Michael. "Companies that plan to be around for a long time have to act with a long-term view." This is what Dell refers to as its "sustainability" program, which defines how the company's corporate and social actions directly benefit both the community and the business.

THE RETURN OF LEADING RESPONSIBLY

Michael S. Dell, Founder and Chairman, and
Kevin B. Rollins, President and CEO, Dell

Acting responsibly on behalf of shareholders and on behalf of the community doesn't have to be mutually exclusive.

B usiness leaders and economists are paying more and more attention to corporate social responsibility efforts. Some even criticize the programs because they appear to be incongruous with creating value for shareholders. While there are a lot of good causes and it's easy to throw money at things, simply handing out funds reduces profitability and is just too one-dimensional a way to deal with a problem.

We believe in giving back to the community, but in doing it slightly differently. We created a Sustainable Business program in 2003 that integrates economic, social, and environmental responsibility into everything we do. We don't see it as spending shareholder money, but as creating long-term stakeholder value. Acting responsibly on behalf of shareholders and on behalf of the community doesn't have to be mutually exclusive. It's our philosophy that if we have happy employees, they will do better. If we have good community relationships, we will do better. If we find ways to help the environment, to help workers, to help raise the standard of living in third world countries, we all will do better. It's simple: by acting responsibly, the company is better thought of, revenues grow, and profits increase.

People often ask us how much it costs to run our sustainability efforts. We don't look at the program in terms of cost. You may be familiar with a well-known book by Philip Crosby called *Quality Is Free*. It explains that it doesn't cost more to produce something of quality, and in fact, it can be an extreme source of profit as well. We believe that theory can be applied to environmental and social efforts. If factory workers are provided with better working conditions, for example, we see fewer accidents, less absenteeism, and higher productivity—it's a cost savings in the long run.

A more important question to ask regarding the cost of a sustainable program is the cost of *not* implementing one. Think about it: What's the cost of not removing hazardous materials from products? What's the cost of not raising the standard of living? Not doing anything is intolerable, and, in the end, would result in something far pricier than the investment we make in building a healthier future.

A more important question to ask regarding the cost of a sustainable program is the cost of not implementing one.

Over the years we have been fortunate both as a company and personally, and we have inherited a greater opportunity to do more with what we have. As Dell has taken on more of a global presence, we've seen a need to create initiatives that would positively affect global communities. First, we approached this effort from an environmental standpoint, and later, from a social standpoint, wanting to improve the quality of life of people worldwide.

Our first environmental efforts started with recycling. Through our Reduce, Reuse, and Recycle (R3) initiative, we collect different materials, such as cardboard, office paper, plastics, foams, batteries, disks, and more. All Dell manufacturing facilities have permanent recycling operations that have resulted in significant waste reductions. After launching successful programs in the United States, our environmental and facilities managers from Austin have worked closely with other Dell regions to reduce the company's solid waste stream worldwide. At the European manufacturing facility in Limerick, Ireland, approximately 70 percent of site waste is now being recycled, and the facility recently eliminated the use of individual antistatic bags for system boards used in desktop computers. In Xiamen, China, a wastewater treatment plant was constructed and put in service, reducing the amount of chemical oxygen demand material discharged to the waterways by 63.5 percent.

In recent years, finding a solution for what to do with the growing number of used computers has become the topic of much discussion. Dell has offered U.S. business customers "take-back" services since 1991, and we estimate we have recovered more than two million computers worldwide in that time. We've recently expanded the program and now include home pickup of consumers' used computer equipment, and we offer donation or recycling options for any brand of used computer.

Perhaps the biggest challenge of this effort was to educate consumers that this type of program was available. A few years ago we did some customer research and realized that there was an extremely low awareness of any manufacturer's recycling offer. In an effort to change that, we sponsored consumer recycling days in markets around the country. We worked with local government, university, and nonprofit organizations to promote the events and mobilize local consumers. We organized 18 of these events in the first year and collected nearly two million pounds of used computer equipment free of charge. More importantly, through media coverage, grassroots outreach, and consumer participation, we were able to reach more than 40 million consumers with our message: "No computer should go to waste." We've continued with different types of education-based initiatives. In January 2004, for the first time, we devoted an entire page of our product catalog to information about asset recovery and recycling. The catalog was distributed to almost 36 million customers. We continue to support collection events through grants and partnerships with nonprofits such as Goodwill.

While these recycling programs are important, we know that creating a sustainable future really begins by reducing the environmental impact of our products at the design stage. We have a Dell environmental affairs team that works closely with product design teams and suppliers to ensure that the products we build will be as environmentally sound as possible. Currently, we use up to 25 percent postindustrial recycled plastics in desktop computer, notebook computer, and server chassis plastics. We aim to conserve product energy consumption (we've been involved in the EPA's Energy Star program to reduce power consumption since 1993), avoid the use of environmentally sensitive substances, reduce or eliminate materials for disposal, and prolong product life span.

We strive to reduce our environmental footprint in our manufacturing, production, and distribution systems. We find that these programs reduce costs as well. Some great examples include an initiative to reuse boxes for parts and components, which saved approximately 78 tons of cardboard boxes and packing foam in 2004. A reuse program for foam components and end caps will reduce landfill waste by approximately 290 tons annually. A new effort to recycle plastic and foam in our Nashville manufacturing facilities will reduce landfill waste by approximately 800 tons a year. We've also cut a battery washing process at the same plant, eliminating a hazardous waste stream. This year we are redesigning the packaging for our notebook computers—something that will save an estimated 230 tons of packaging materials annually.

In the Austin area, we've enrolled in the Green Choice Program offered by Austin Energy, the city-owned electric utility, so that 10 percent of our energy will come from clean sources of energy (primarily wind-generated power). Additionally, since we know that air transportation produces roughly eight times more harmful emissions than trucks, we have implemented and expedited ground transportation networks, moved manufacturing centers closer to the customer, and implemented factory planning systems to maximize our ground transportation opportunities. At a time when we achieved significant volume growth, we reduced our use of air transportation from 25 percent to 14 percent.

Dell participates in philanthropic programs through the Dell Foundation, the charitable arm of the company. The foundation provides grants to nonprofit agencies in the locations where our employees live and work. Even at the foundation, though, we don't rely on simply giving money away: we place a strong emphasis on employee gift matching programs and volunteerism. To that end, in 2004 one in three of our employees worldwide gave their time to volunteer in their communities. The activities ran the gamut from employees in Denmark cleaning the Copenhagen canals, the U.S. legal team helping at the Humane Society, and Dell India employees conducting an AIDS telethon. In addition, the foundation's volunteer match program uses the Internet to connect and mobilize thousands of Dell employees worldwide in support of community needs.

One particularly innovative program that we support is the TechKnow Program, which gets technology into the hands and homes of young people who normally wouldn't have access to computers and training. The program is run as an after-school, 40-hour, hands-on, self-paced program that teaches kids the twenty-first-century technology skills they need to know. As part of the program students take a computer apart and learn to put it back together. We know firsthand how empowering that is. In addition to teaching these skills, the program provides students with a chance to earn a home computer, and nearly 5,000 middle school students across the United States have taken home a free Dell desktop (that they refurbished themselves) after completing the program. Now that it's proven a success, we're rolling this program out in more regions.

Another effort we support is the Student Tech Corps, a program that trains middle school students to run a help desk. Students are trained in the latest technologies, giving them excellent real-world skills. We see awarding these grants as a way to empower young people. It's also an investment. We know that these kids are the talent of the future, and we want them at Dell.

Programs like these have helped build a culture that emphasizes giving back. Our employees continue to amaze us through their creative and compassionate actions every day of the year. The Dell Italy team has donated notebook computers to a children's hospital in Milan so that parents who give birth prematurely can check and monitor their babies remotely when they can't be in the hospital. In Brazil, Dell's Digital Citizen Program provides technical computing education to youth and teenagers from low-income communities through eight Information Technology Technical Schools. Dell employees financially sponsor students to attend the program and volunteer their time to teach Junior Achievement and job-transition courses.

While we are proud of the work we've done, there have been situations where we haven't done something that we should have. (This generally is not out of neglect, but more the result of ignorance and naiveté). When an environmental organization, social responsibility agency, or group of socially responsible investors approach us with concerns that we were not doing enough in a certain area, we address it with the same model of being direct that Dell is built upon. Being direct doesn't only mean cutting out the middleman. It means going straight to the situation at hand—whether it be getting a customer a computer system or addressing an agency's apprehensions about our environmental impact.

We had a situation where some university students raised concerns about the amount of recycling we were doing, and requesting that we make it free. We were getting letters highlighting the same concerns and making the same demands—we decided we needed to do something about it. We believed we'd arrive at a solution if we talked with the students directly, so we met with the student leaders at our headquarters, and we wired the meeting for a Webcast. We included 21 different university campuses around the country. It was an opportunity to address each of the student's concerns, listen to them, and tell them from a business standpoint (meaning, within the limits of reason and time) what we thought the right approach was. It proved to be a great way of engaging directly with them. It was also a real turning point in that debate—it ended the campus protests.

Unlike the way some companies approach their efforts to lead responsibly, we view each situation or problem—be it reducing our environmental footprint, increasing diversity, or improving workers' conditions—not as an add-on corporate social responsibility initiative, but as a business challenge. By doing that, we not only have the opportunity to best leverage our employees' talents, but solutions are created in the context of how to also best benefit the business.

Implementing any new policies or creating change is not always easy. We've had some programs that have been difficult to get moving. One area that presented difficulties was the performance of our global diversity program. This was in the late 1990s and the program didn't have the support or direction it needed. We realized the magnitude of the problem when we were hit with a core business challenge: Dell was growing and we didn't have enough talent.

It was in trying to find a solution for this business problem—where are we going to get the talent—that we bolstered our diversity efforts. To grow a global company we knew that we wanted the best and brightest from every diverse population. To do that, we fostered strategic relationships with community and professional organizations such as the Congressional Hispanic Caucus Institute and the National Society of Black and Hispanic MBAs. We committed over $2 million in cash and computer equipment to the Dell and United Negro College Fund Scholars Program, which offers undergraduate and graduate students training, scholarship money, a paid internship, and housing to prepare them for potential careers at Dell. We've also contributed more than $1.5 million to the National Urban League and its affiliates.

We got our whole team involved in this effort. We asked our leaders to sponsor networking groups, which offer a support structure to women and minority groups. These sponsors are our direct reports, and fostering one of these groups is one of their business responsibilities—and reflected in their performance reviews.

We have seen the impact of these initiatives. The Department of Labor honored us with the Exemplary Voluntary Efforts award for our recruitment, mentoring, career development, and community outreach initiatives; we were named the 2004 Corporation of the Year from the Minority Corporate Council Association; and we were No. 8 on the National Society of Black Engineers Top 50 "Companies to Work For" list. In addition, Dell was named one of the top 10 employers in the United States by *The Advocate*, the leading magazine for the gay, lesbian, bisexual, and transgendered community. Dell's culture is one where diversity is embraced and where we benefit from each person's talents, skills, and life experiences. While all of that helps us measure progress as well as attract more talent to the company, we are most proud of how our effort is now woven in the fabric of our company. Today, women and minorities represent more than half of our U.S. employment, one-third of our U.S. managers, and 26 percent of our executives at the vice president level.

Although we've come an extraordinary distance in turning the program around, our efforts are in no way completed. We must continually work to recruit and retain many of the nation's top women and minorities, and we do that by each year sponsoring professional conferences, career fairs, and community events with professional minority organizations. Through our University Relations Department, we cultivate relationships with universities across the country to access and recruit top talent among women and minority graduates. We also actively recruit candidates at historically black colleges, universities, and other schools with significant minority populations.

Seeing quantifiable results at our company is incredibly rewarding; it's also an effective tool to help us get others involved. We view it as part of our role as business leaders to act as a catalyst. We want to make a difference, and we know that we can't do it alone. We've worked with our suppliers to ensure that they meet our environmental requirements. But we also hope to awaken their own sense of responsibility and for them to integrate environmental, health, safety and labor management systems into their own operations. To do that, we've held a series of Webcasts with suppliers to share what we've learned. More than 230 supplier attendees have participated.

Recently, we've started to ask others in the IT sector to participate with us on a joint "code of conduct" targeted to benefit suppliers in developing countries regarding labor and environment issues. We are branching beyond our industry as well. For example, in researching an effort to use more recycled content in our catalog, we learned that we could actually use recycled materials and not increase costs. (Our catalogs use 10 percent recycled content, and our goal is to increase this to 35 percent in the future). That's a win-win situation for everyone, so why not share that best practice? We sent a letter to the top 20 catalogers in the United States, telling them about what we've done and asking them to join us. We are confident that other businesses will realize, as Dell has, that the return on investment for acting responsibly is priceless: a sustainable ecosystem of shared success.

PERSONAL GIVING

Michael Dell and Kevin Rollins have much more in common than being copilots at Dell. They share the same taste in music (rock and roll from the 60s and 70s), each has four kids, and they both give tremendously of their personal wealth.

Described as a leader in a new generation of "superphilanthropists," Michael and Susan Dell were No. 7 on *BusinessWeek's* list of the "50 Most Generous Philanthropists," after reportedly giving away an estimated $933 million between 2000 and 2004. In 1999 they established the Michael and Susan Dell Foundation, which focuses on improving children's health, education, and welfare and which currently has an endowment of more than $1 billion.

Kevin and Debra Rollins are intensely private about their giving. "We believe if we get that recognition from the public, then we weren't doing it out of the goodness of our hearts," says Kevin. "It's a little out of synch with the notion of what service means to us." They have, though, gone public when they thought taking a leadership position would encourage others. Among those efforts: they have established a Center for eBusiness at their alma mater Brigham Young University and pledged $5 million to Arts Center Stage in Austin. (Both have performing arts background: Kevin sings and plays the violin, and his former band, the "Gents," won a national battle of the bands when he was in high school; Debra taught dance and plays the piano). Kevin is also the technology chairman of the Juvenile Diabetes Research Fund.

CHAPTER 5

MANAGING THE MOST IMPORTANT ASSETS: CITIZENS FINANCIAL GROUP

The company gives at least 1 percent annually of pretax profits to support local initiatives.

If you were casting the next Wall Street movie and you needed a stereotypical no-nonsense bank executive, chances are you wouldn't pick Larry Fish. Watch Larry in action and you'll see him start his day by handwriting thank-you notes to the bank tellers, phone operators, and cleaning folks who work for him. As the day goes on, you'll likely see him hug a colleague ("with gusto and with gratitude," as he says). As if that weren't un-bank-ish enough, he actually suggests that employees should "hug the customer" as well.

Larry, the chairman, CEO, and president of Citizens Financial Group, may not be your typical bank head honcho, but that makes sense since Citizens, by its own admission, is "not your typical bank." Here, being atypical yields spectacular results. The bank is revered as one of the best places to work, and it has earned a stellar reputation with its customers as well. Larry is known not just as the employee-hugger, but as a "ferocious on performance"[1] genius who has steered the bank to 12 straight years of record profitability and has grown Citizens 25-fold since he first arrived in 1992.

Citizens—now a $137 billion commercial bank holding company with more than 1,600 branches, 2,800 ATMs, and 26,000 employees—originated in 1828 as the High Street Bank in Hoyle Square, then Providence, Rhode Island's bustling market center. Years later, the directors of High Street Bank obtained a second charter and established Citizens Savings Bank—a mutual savings bank that opened with its first official deposit (made by the bank vice president's daughter) in 1871. By 1947, Citizens purchased stock in the High Street Bank and gained complete control of its original parent. It started opening branch offices and it became a member of the FDIC in 1950—the first mutual savings bank to do so.

Citizens continued to grow, and in 1986 demutualized. Two years later, it was acquired by the Royal Bank of Scotland Group (RBS), one of the largest banking groups in Europe, which viewed Citizens as the "flagship for the company's expansion in the United States."[2]

Backed by RBS, Citizens Bank became one of the most strongly capitalized financial institutions in New England and spent the next decade gobbling up other regional players. Although acquiring companies like Pac-Man was a trend that Larry would continue (he's orchestrated more than 25 takeovers for Citizens), he was also interested in growing Citizens organically. Shifting away from a "supermarket for financial services" mentality, the bank turned its attention to taking deposits and making loans. Citizens determined that the wealthiest customers weren't the best; it was the middle class customers who gave the bank the biggest bulk of its business. One of the bank's advertising campaigns promised: "You don't have to be well off to be treated well."

Citizens focused on individual customers and small business clients and won them over with exemplary service. While many of the Citizens' competitors were outsourcing customer service,

Citizens made customer service a signature part of the bank's central structure. In 1998 it launched a customer satisfaction survey and an incentive system to have branches compete for the best service. In one year, customer satisfaction skyrocketed. And, by measuring and publishing customer service data, the bank realized that its colleagues raised the bar themselves. Furthermore, when a monetary incentive was added, the results also appeared in the bottom line—deposits grew by 20 percent, and later by 40 percent.

While Citizens was growing organically thanks to its improved service, it also continued with its acquisitions—it bought among others, the commercial banking business of State Street Corp. and UST Corp.—and eventually became the second largest commercial bank in the region. In 2001, it bought Mellon Financial Corporation's retail and commercial banking activities, extending it to the Mid-Atlantic states. In 2004, it made its largest acquisition to date when it purchased Charter One Financial, which expanded Citizens into the Midwest, and grew it to $131 billion in assets, 24,000 colleagues, and 1,550 branches.

As Citizens has exploded in growth—it's now the eighth largest commercial bank holding company in the United States by deposits—it has been steadfast in retaining its familylike culture. On the day the Mellon Financial deal went through, for example, Citizens, which kept all except 100 of Mellon's 4,235 employees, had its executives pound the pavement to introduce the Citizens' way. The bank sprung for free transportation in Pittsburgh and Philadelphia (cities where Mellon had the biggest presence) and the executives personally handed out free coffee and newspapers to passers-by. The effort aimed to show that Citizens cared about the community, and it paid off: deposits went up 7 percent and loans went up 9 percent.

At Citizens, community relations span far beyond the free coffee and papers, or free lollipops and dog biscuits, though. The company gives at least 1 percent annually of pretax profits to support local initiatives. It funds, for example, homeless shelters, community centers, and family clinics in areas where there are branches.

The bank also uses its role as a lender to effect positive change via programs such as the Citizens Job Bank. This program makes $100 million in loan funds available at a below-market interest rate of 2.5 percent to companies that agree in return to create one new full-time job for every $25,000 borrowed. In just one year, the program has lent nearly $34 million to local businesses and helped to create 1,353 new manufacturing jobs across Pennsylvania.

A similar program was designed to help increase the supply of affordable housing, the lack of which has become one of the greatest challenges facing New England communities. This $200 million dollar initiative, called the Citizens Housing Bank, will provide qualified nonprofit housing developers with below-market construction financing and is expected to generate 1,200 homes. Each year the bank selects a nonprofit developer in each state that has created more affordable housing and awards the so-called Housing Heroes with a $50,000 grant from the Citizens Bank Foundation.

In addition to the monetary gifts, the bank wants its employees to get involved. "I like to say that if you're not generous of heart, if you don't feel the need to contribute to life beyond just your own needs, if you are not a volunteering individual, you are probably going to be out of sync at Citizens," says Larry. It's not just talk; Larry is personally committed to the community via the family foundation he established as well as by chairing numerous capital campaigns, including an initiative to assist Rosie's Place, an organization that aids poor and homeless women in Boston and the Vietnamese Community Center, a facility for nonprofit agencies that provide economic development and social services to Boston's 20,000 Vietnamese refugee and immigrant families. "I think that leadership in the business community comes with the responsibility to give back," he explains. He adds that it helps him—and it helps Citizens: "The more you give, the more you get," he says.

In his essay, Larry describes his secret weapon—a document called the Credo—that has kept Citizens on course throughout its gangbuster growth and guided its interaction with its customers, community, and colleagues.

LIVING BY OUR CREDO

Larry Fish, Chairman, CEO, and President,
Citizens Financial Group

The Credo has really become the life, guts, and soul of the company. . . . People refer to it—there are now Credo meetings, Credo moments, and un-Credolike behavior.

In the summer of 2002 I was celebrating my 10-year anniversary at Citizen's Bank. The company had gotten quite a bit larger as a result of the acquisition of Mellon Bank's banking practice in Pennsylvania, Delaware, and New Jersey. The acquisition was well digested at that point, and I felt that I could take some time and refresh. I took five weeks off and I went to Japan with my family. We rented an apartment in Tokyo and each of my three children studied different Japanese arts. (I studied *Ikebana*, or flower arranging.) I didn't take my office with me: I accepted no mail and I was not reachable by e-mail or telephone.

While I was completely disconnected from the company, I did do a lot of thinking about the company. We had grown greatly, and I realized that it wasn't possible to run a company in a highly personalized fashion now that we had 15,000 employees. I wanted to retain the principles that have historically guided the company, though. I wanted new generations of colleagues and acquired companies to understand what matters to us. I felt that we needed to put down on a piece of paper what we are all about—something that would capture the essence of the company.

With that in mind, I wrote the Credo while I was in Japan. It is very simply what we believe in: to treat the customer the way we'd like to be treated and treat them that way all the time; to make this the best place to work in the world; and to give back to our communities and at all times behave with the highest ethical standards. The Credo has really become the life, guts, and soul of the company. People understand it. People refer to it—there are now Credo meetings, Credo moments, and un-Credolike behavior. In 2004 we completed another very large acquisition that increased our employment to more than 25,000 people and expanded us into six new states. I think that the Credo is really guiding us as we continue to get larger and it's also giving direction to our new colleagues so that they understand the culture of the company.

One-third of our Credo is about how we view our place in the community. We have a made it a public policy to give at least 1 percent of our pretax profit back, and most years we beat that by quite a lot. As we've grown, our communities have been enriched more and more. In 2005, our giving exceeded more than $30 million.

While we think that's a big number, we want to be clear: We don't do blockbuster philanthropy. We don't have a slick annual report of all our good deeds. We don't do social "ball" philanthropy. We don't fund national organizations, even if it's just a percentage of the money that goes nationally. We don't do a lot with higher education; we don't do a lot with major teaching hospitals. We don't have a matching gift program (in our experience those funds typically go to secondary and primary private schools).

What we *do* do is focus on communities of color and communities in need. To the extent that we support an art institution, for instance, it's in the institution's outreach to those communities. For example, in 2005, we gave a $1 million gift to the Museum of

Fine Arts in Boston as part of their capital campaign that was specifically directed for two purposes: first to make Martin Luther King's birthday free to the public, and second, to create a chair at the museum for community outreach to engage underrepresented neighborhoods to get them more access to the visual arts.

Our banks are predominantly in cities, and some of our fastest-growing branches are in the inner city. Those communities have needs, but they are not looking for a handout; I believe they are looking for a hand. We do thousands of little things all the time in many different ways, in many different areas, on a very local basis.

We have something called Community Champions, which recognizes and supports nonprofit organizations for their contributions to their communities. A new Champion is selected each quarter and receives a $25,000 grant in unrestricted funds from Citizens Bank, media coverage with local television, volunteer support, public relations support, and promotional support. We also highlight the Champion on our ATMs and put a link to its Web site on our Web site.

When we give the award it's like the Publishers Clearing House announcements. There are TV stations there to record it, the bank president attends, and people often start crying. The impact this has had on these organizations has been beyond our wildest imagination, and it has gone far beyond the publicity they have received by being named a Champion. Take, for example RAW Art Works, an art therapy program for at-risk youth in Lynn, Massachusetts, which wanted to purchase new office space, but was facing challenges as it tried to get financing at reasonable terms. One of our bankers helped them negotiate the terms and finally establish themselves in a permanent home. When one of our Champions, Neighborhood Housing Services of Greater Nashua in Nashua, New Hampshire, an organization that develops affordable housing, needed marketing materials but didn't have the funds necessary, we helped secure the pro bono service of a local PR agency to design their brochure. As a direct result of being named one of our Champions, TechACCESS, an organization that offers assistive technologies to help individuals with special needs, received volunteers from Citizens who helped with everything from painting (all of the necessary materials were donated), to procuring items for fund-raising events, to printing agency letterhead and envelopes. As you can see, it's much more than a $25,000 grant—we aim to really get involved.

While many of our philanthropic endeavors are funded with corporate dollars, we also have something called Credo dollars, which allows each branch—and we have over 1,600 branches— to give at a very local level. Each branch gets between $2,000 and $4,000 a year, depending on the branch size, to empower them to give back to the community. That means that if the Lion's Club is having a pancake breakfast for the blind and they want $50, the branch doesn't need to refer it somewhere. If there's a Little League program or a need for half a dozen soccer balls to do youth soccer in the community or the desire to send flowers to a customer who is sick in the hospital, the branch has an account with which to do that.

I'm passionate about having Citizens give back because I know firsthand the personal benefits of getting involved. I had an interlude in my career before I joined Citizens where my predecessor and I reached an agreement on my employment, but he wasn't quite ready to leave and I was quite happy not to come right away. I had six months off between jobs, so I went to work in the inner city. I told the organizations where I volunteered that I would do everything or anything—except strategic planning or fund-raising. I mentored young children; I scrubbed floors; I worked in the greater Boston Food Bank. I really got to see the community.

This personal experience led to the Corporate Service Sabbatical Award, where every quarter we send one of our colleagues off for three months with full pay and benefits to work in a community organization of their choice. We have granted sabbaticals to 43 employees over the past 10 years. Our current corporate service sabbatical winner is an assistant vice president fluent in the Indonesian language who is active on the ground in Indonesia doing relief and reconstruction work after the tsunami. This is our first international corporate service sabbatical. Each of our winners reports back to us via e-mail and, when they come back, they meet with the officers of the bank that they represent and the board of directors and describe their experience firsthand. I think that hearing about these experiences touches people very deeply. It inspires people in their own life to do more in their communities.

We see this happen every day. Take, for example, this story that occurred not too long ago. We have a branch in Needham, Massachusetts. We had a customer come in and open an account to help raise money for a disease that had taken the life of one of her children. Our officer in that branch opened the account and, after all the paperwork was completed, he wrote a personal check for $100—making the first deposit in the account. When something that beautiful happens at the most local of levels, it sends out a light. That customer went home and talked to her neighbors about that experience. You know how I know that? I heard about it from three different people—and I don't live anywhere near this community. Our colleague who made that gift helped the way we are thought of as a bank.

Banks are intimate with their communities. I don't think you can have a healthy bank in a sick community. I believe deeply that the more you give back, the more you relate your brand with your consumer, the more reason you give the consumer to bank with you. That's important for us. We are not in the packaged goods business; there's a difference between Cheerios and Frosted Flakes, but there isn't much difference today between checking account A and checking account B. Consumers process their banking choices on criteria like convenience and service, and when you stack up on those fronts and then you add a commitment to communities of need, I think you give the consumer an enormously powerful reason to consider you—and even select you.

Our Credo also outlines how we should treat our colleagues. We say in the Credo that we want our company to be the best place to work in the world. That means not only providing the fundamentals: a salary, an incentive program that rewards performance, and the mandatory social coverages (medical, dental, and a real retirement plan), but by doing things that makes life easier and better for colleagues. That is where a company can really differentiate itself.

We have many programs that do this. One of the best is the Home Buyers Assistance Program. We give employees that have been with us for more than one year $5,000 in the form of an interest-free, forgivable five-year loan toward the purchase of their first home. If the employee moves into a community of color, or a community of need, we'll up that to $8,000. More than 1,500 colleagues now own a home in part because of this program.

We also offer an emergency assistance fund to help employees through calamities, such as a fire, or death of a loved one, by giving them $1,500 tax free, no questions asked. For colleagues wanting to adopt a child—whether that adoptee is from Guatemala, China, Russia, or the United States—we will financially provide for that adoption, and we'll allow that to be uncapped. We also allow multiple adoptions. We have Citizens Scholar Program where we award 50 scholarships to two-year or four-year colleges to the children of colleagues who earn less than $100,000 a year. We award $600 camp scholarships to the children of colleagues at the lower end of the income level to provide them with the opportunity to enjoy a safe and productive summer program. This is especially important for single parents.

We've found that different colleagues need different things to enhance their lives; one good example of that is pet insurance, which we subsidize. While the majority of people don't want pet insurance, for the approximately 300 people in our company who use it, it really matters. I met a woman in Detroit several months ago who has canaries—lots of canaries—and for her, the biggest thing we could offer was pet insurance.

At the moment, we have 17 colleagues in Iraq. We bridge the salaries of these colleagues and we self-insure for their life insurance (because death in the event of war in not an insurable event). We've had three colleagues who have lost a child in Iraq. We try our best to take care of these colleagues. For colleagues that have a child or grandchild being dispatched to Iraq, we give a week off with pay and an airplane ticket to be with that child for a week before he or she is sent off. I could go on and on, but the point is that by offering benefits that make a difference in people's lives, we have become a great place to work.

People ask me why we invest in doing all of this. The answer is simple, really: you can't have happy customers if you have unhappy colleagues. Have you ever been to a store where you were served by someone who didn't like the place where they worked? Did you like shopping there? The happier the people are that work here, the better we'll do. Our employees are happy, and so are our customers.

We've had lots of examples of companies like Enron or World-Com that made lots of money but lost their way on the value front. They are not around anymore. A great company doesn't just make money. A great company makes money and it has values at its core—it has some deep, passionate essence of what it's all about. For us it's taking care of customers, being a great place for our colleagues, and giving back to our communities.

THE CREDO AT CITIZENS BANK

Customers: Hug the customer. Smile. Say thank you. Return phone calls and e-mails in a timely manner. Do whatever you can every day, in every way, to provide world-class service. Consistently exceed customer expectations. Always honor our commitment to customers. Give customers a reason to say, "Wow, I love these people." In short, treat the customer the way you would love to be treated all the time.

Colleagues: We want our company to be the best place to work in the world. The environment will be extraordinarily caring, like an extension of your own family. We will be supportive in time of personal difficulty, create opportunities for professional growth, and always make an effort to listen and act on your ideas. Every colleague will be treated with dignity and respect at all times.

Community: We believe great companies have a moral core. We care deeply about our communities, and we demonstrate this commitment every day by volunteering where there is a need. We respect the law at all times, and always conduct ourselves with integrity. All of our work at Citizens must be ethical and honest. By giving back, and conducting ourselves with integrity, our customers and colleagues will be proud of us and our company.

Citizens Bank colleagues are expected to live the Credo every day and let it guide our actions. We are expected to be honest and ethical in all that we do. And, we are expected to make a difference, to think outside the proverbial box to deliver "Wow" customer service.

CHAPTER 6

GIVING BACK IN THE GOOD TIMES AND THE BAD: LEVI STRAUSS & CO.

Although corporate giving was in the DNA of the company since the earliest days, it made the Levi Strauss Foundation an official entity in 1952.

I magine the most popular clothing in the world—blue jeans— and no doubt a pair of Levi's jeans come to mind. The company invented the clothing staple, which was favored by image-makers like James Dean, and established itself as one of the most recognized trademarks in the world. Perhaps that's why it's so hard to believe that when Levi Strauss began 153 years ago, he stumbled on jeans pretty much by chance.

Levi Strauss (yes, there was a real person) emigrated from Bavaria to New York and then to California during the Gold Rush and set up a wholesale operation selling dry goods to small stores across the American West. His business sold blankets, underwear, and clothes, including pants made of denim. Levi's gold miner clientele had a need for pants rugged enough to endure the gritty work of gold panning, and when a Nevada tailor named Jacob Davis approached Levi with his idea to use rivets to make the men's denim work pants stronger, the two men struck upon their own golden opportunity.

They joined forces, protected the innovative rivet idea with a patent, and created the phenomenon that we call "blue jeans" today. By the 1870s, jeans became the standard outfit of the Western miner. Originally called the XX (the pants were made of 9-ounce. XX blue denim), the "501" lot number, or category number, was created to describe the popular work pant to customers in 1890. The 501 attracted enough of a following that by the end of World War II Levi's family members who had inherited the business after his death decided to quit selling wholesale goods (still the majority of the business) and focus exclusively on blue jeans. Production expanded to include jean jackets, shirts, and preshrunk jeans. Originally the uniform of gold miners, laborers, and cowboys, Levi's jeans were soon adopted by a generation of teenagers who branded them antiestablishment, irreverent, and cool. (Marlon Brando wore Levi's in the movie *The Wild One*—a godsend for the brand.)

By the 1950s Levi Strauss & Co. was selling jeans nationally. Ten years later, the jeans became part of the permanent collections of the Smithsonian Institution in Washington, DC, and Levi had established a distribution network in Europe and set up overseas production facilities. It was one of the first U.S. apparel companies to use radio and television to market its products. In 1986 it introduced Dockers as a way to bridge the gap between suits and jeans—offering a new way to dress for work. At the same time, the company continued to rework its traditional staple, creating custom-made jeans for women in 1994, and the first ergonomically designed jeans in 1999.

While Levi Strauss & Co. is revered as the inventor of jeans, it is equally respected as a leader in the corporate social responsibility movement. From the very beginning, Levi Strauss felt that it was important to give to the community. When he came to San Francisco in his twenties, he donated $5 (equivalent of $100 today) to a local orphanage immediately after his arrival. He later provided the funds for 28 scholarships at the University of California, Berkeley. In 1926 the company advertised in Spanish, Portuguese, and Chinese—showing its dedication to oft-neglected consumers. The company also revealed its commitment to its workers when during the Great Depression it decided to install new flooring in the plant as a way to keep employees busy and on the payroll.

Although corporate giving was in the DNA of the company since the earliest days, it made the Levi Strauss Foundation an official entity in 1952. By the 1960s Levi Strauss & Co. owners Peter and Walter Haas (fourth-generation descendents of Levi Strauss) determined they would supply the foundation with 2.5 percent of annual pretax earnings—regardless of profit. Some of the foundation's money was to be earmarked for community programs each year, while the rest fueled a reserve—a foresighted decision that would later allow Levi Strauss & Co. to continue giving despite the company's own financial hardships. The foundation, like the company, has always been progressive and innovative.

In addition to the usual programs such as funding disaster relief efforts, matching cash donations by employees, and providing grants to local community organizations, the Levi Strauss Foundation boldly commits to programs seen as more controversial. It was the first corporate foundation to give to AIDS-related programs—an effort it began in 1982 when a group of company employees came to senior management asking for help to increase awareness about a new disease, then called gay-related immune deficiency.

Over the past two decades, the company has given more than $27 million in grants for AIDS-related initiatives. Recently, the foundation has focused on prevention through improving syringe access in the United States. (The lack of clean needles is one reason why HIV is increasing, explains Theresa Fay-Bustillos, executive director at the Levi Strauss Foundation.) In addition to more than $1 million invested over two years to the Syringe

Access Fund, the foundation works to address AIDS stigma and discrimination, which the foundation believes to be the biggest single obstacle to slowing or stopping the pandemic.

The foundation also focuses on economic development in the communities in which it operates, specifically enhancing self-sufficiency for disadvantaged women and youth through micro-lending and asset building. The EARN Savings Program, for example, encourages the working poor to open bank accounts and provides an incentive by matching their savings at two dollars for every one dollar saved until the accounts reach $6,000. The initiative, which was originally designed to help people buy a home or start a business, has been expanded to assist students to save for college.

As a clothing company that operates worldwide, the management at Levi Strauss & Co. is well aware of the sweatshop conditions that exist. In 1991 it was the first multinational company to develop a comprehensive code of conduct for manufacturing contractors to ensure that working conditions at overseas factories were safe and fair. The terms of the code are guided by local laws and the company's own convictions based on U.N. conventions (when local and global laws differ, Levi Strauss & Co. adopts the more rigorous standard). While the company has a strict inspection system to ensure that the terms are adhered to, it will not simply pull out and leave workers jobless if the terms are violated. Instead, the company tries to use some sort of pressure to force change. ("The first reduction in production order usually motivates suppliers to quickly address the problem," says Michael Kobori, director of the Global Code of Conduct.) Kobori says in the past four years there have been fewer than five situations where they have had to pull all business from a supplier.

Levi Strauss & Co.'s groundbreaking code has earned it America's Corporate Conscience Award for International Commitment from the Council on Economic Priorities. An even bigger reward is knowing that Levi Strauss & Co.'s leadership has effected positive change; codes of conduct have become an industry best practice, and similar guidelines have been put in place by companies such as Nike and Reebok.

In addition to what Levi Strauss & Co. achieves at the factory level through its Code of Conduct, the Levi Strauss Foundation's Workers' Rights Grants Program provides funding to innovative organizations dedicated to strengthening workers' rights and improving working and living conditions in communities where the company's products are made. It funds the Foundation for International Community Assistance (FINCA) in Latin America, to establish various asset-building and educational programs to create and expand community-based microlending programs for low-income women in areas of Mexico and Guatemala where garment industry jobs are being lost.

Through the Asia Foundation, the Levi Strauss Foundation funds programs that have educated hundreds of thousands of women workers in China about workers' rights, financial literacy, and community-based life skills. The Levi Strauss Foundation has also provided significant funding for the first legal aid organization focused solely on migrant workers in China's Pearl River Delta, where most of the nation's manufacturing occurs.

On the policy level, Levi Strauss & Co. actively advocates on behalf of workers' rights in Washington, DC, and around the world. It views trade agreements as an opportunity to put labor provisions and mechanisms for enforcement into place. The company works with governments, nongovernmental organizations, industry associations, and trade organizations, including the World Trade Organization (WTO) to secure basic rights for workers.

While Levi Strauss & Co. has remained one of the world's most recognizable and valuable brands, it was accused of losing touch with consumers, and the company paid the price in the marketplace. Baby boomers, who grew up with Levi's jeans as the epitome of cool, stayed loyal to the brand that recognized their desire for casual clothes. Many of their kids however, adopted fashions inspired by current pop culture, which favored looser and lower-riding fits and celebrity endorsements. In addition, competition from less expensive in-house brands, as well as designers such as Tommy Hilfiger and fashion jeans makers like Diesel caused major financial woes for the company. In 1997, Levi Strauss & Co. closed 11 of its U.S. plants, shut the majority of its stores, and laid off a large percentage of its work force.

In 1999, the company, still owned by relatives of Levi Strauss (it was public for a brief period, but was bought back through the then-largest leveraged buyout in U.S. corporate history), hired Phil Marineau, installing as its president and CEO a nonfamily member for the second time in its history. Phil was tapped to transform the manufacturing company into a successful con-sumer-driven marketing machine and came with the necessary experience. As president and CEO of Pepsi North America, he led the challenge to outgrow Coca-Cola in North America for the first time in years. At Dean Foods Company, he led the success-ful repositioning of milk as a beverage rather than a food item. At Quaker Oats Company, he built Gatorade into a $1 billion business and the most significant brand in the company's prod-uct portfolio.

Phil has already restored the financial strength of the company— the $4 billion corporation saw annual sales turnaround from a 14 percent decline when he first arrived to an increase of 1 percent in 2005—through innovative ideas like Levi Strauss Signature (a more affordable brand sold in Wal-Mart and Target). He has also had to make some difficult, and unpopular, decisions. With the need to be competitive in order to survive, Levi Strauss & Co.—once known for its "Made in the USA" association, closed the last of the U.S. manufacturing plants in 2004 and shifted production entirely over-seas. Although layoffs are always ugly, Levi Strauss & Co. has aimed to ease the difficulties by committing to taking care of its former workers and community. Since the 1990s, the company has offered benefits packages that are more generous than the competition's, including giving up to three weeks of severance pay per year of service, offering out-placement and career counseling services as well as training programs that focus on English language skills and getting a General Educational Development (GED) degree, and fostering entrepreneurship through microlending programs. The lending programs have led to the creation of restaurants, handicraft companies, and babysitting businesses. The company stays in the community for six months to two years after a plant closing. "We never close a plant and say good luck," says Fay-Bustillos.

At the same time that Levi Strauss & Co. has weathered years of declining sales, it has changed, but not stopped, its commitment to community giving. It has donated more than $217 million since 1952. Levi Strauss & Co. has been widely heralded as a model for corporations interested in responsible leadership. It has been recognized as a trendsetter by the U.S. Department of Labor because of its commitment to monitoring labor conditions in its factories. One of its initiatives, "Project Change," an ambitious program aimed at ending institutional racism, easing racial tension, preventing hate crimes, and promoting diversity in local government was recognized by former President Bill Clinton when it was given the first-annual Ron Brown Award for Corporate Leadership. And while its community efforts and international reach have received kudos, so has its treatment of its own employees: Levi Strauss & Co. has also been repeatedly ranked as one of "America's 50 Best Companies for Minorities" by *Fortune* magazine.

Throughout the up cycles and down cycles that impact any business (especially one that is more than 150 years old), Levi Strauss & Co. has stayed true to its heritage. And, in the same innovative way its founder turned blue work pants into possibly the world's most popular clothing item, the company has found a way to insulate its foundation—and hence its myriad beneficiaries—from Levi Strauss & Co.'s own financial performance. Here, Phil, who announced he will retire at the end of 2006, explains how the company and foundation have evolved their competitive strategies while maintaining their core founding values—and how Levi Strauss & Co. is in a better place because of it.

Profits Through
Principles

Phil Marineau, CEO, Levi Strauss & Co.

We have four core values that are at the heart of Levi Strauss &
Co.: Empathy, Originality, Integrity, and Courage.

It's no secret that when I came to Levi Strauss & Co. in 1999, the company was in the throes of a very difficult economic time. The brand, however, remained extraordinarily popular. It is still one of the top-10 global trademarks in the world. The Levi's brand remains the classic definition of what jeans are and continues to symbolize all the great things about America—frontier independence, rugged individualism, democratic idealism. I think that one of the reasons Levi Strauss & Co. has stayed so well regarded is because it had a commitment to being a great workplace and an emphasis on giving back to community and society.

Since its beginnings, Levi Strauss & Co. has placed an importance on being socially responsible and being a great place to work. It was something that drew me to the company, and I certainly wasn't alone. People want to work for a corporation that they can be proud of. This is what I call the "employment brand." I've learned at Levi Strauss & Co. and through my 23 years at Quaker Oats—which is similar to Levi Strauss & Co. inasmuch as both are originators in their categories, both are over 100 years old, and both have a commitment to fundamental values—that there's more for employees to be proud of than a company's products and services.

Employees can feel pride about the workplace environment, the culture of the company, and the corporation's community involvement. All of these factors are part of the equation for sustaining our employees' commitment to the company and for attracting great talent. (And ultimately, we all know the success of the company is driven by the quality of the people who are employed there.) Customers, too, care about a company's commitment to the community. Being a good corporate citizen can earn the trust of the consumer—it makes a huge deposit in the consumer's mental bank account of how they feel about the products or services that the company offers.

When I came to Levi Strauss & Co. many people asked me if the values of the company would still prevail as we tried to improve the company's performance. I told them that the values absolutely would remain the same. We have four core values that are at the heart of Levi Strauss & Co.: Empathy, Originality, Integrity, and Courage. They work together and throughout our history they have been the source of our success. Performance and great values reinforce one another and create a virtuous circle. We call this "profits through principles." While there are some critics who believe that performance and responsibility have nothing to do with one another, preferring to apply the Chicago School of Economics philosophy that "the business of business is business," we believe that business is much more complex than selling another pair of pants profitably. Business success is about how you attract people to your company and how people perceive your company and your brand as a result of these efforts.

While we have been through a very difficult business downturn the past several years, it has nothing to do with our core values and sense of social responsibility. We've been through a difficult

time because we took our eye off the marketplace and didn't anticipate and move with it in a timely manner. We have suffered
accordingly, and we have since done what's been needed to get
back on track. I believe that the goodwill people have toward the
company has allowed the brand to sustain its high regard around
the world. Without that bank account of goodwill—which has
been created by that social responsibility and commitment to community—we would have been in more serious trouble than we
were, and we might not have come out of it as well as we have.

In our effort to rebuild and reenergize the company, we have
relied on the beliefs at the core of Levi Strauss & Co. At the
same time, it had become clear that we needed to restate—but
not re-create—our values in a contemporary way that is reflective of today's marketplace. The senior management team got
together, addressed the issues that we faced, and discussed a way
to make successful decisions that would stay true to the values
of the company.

During this process, we did have to make decisions that were
difficult. One of the most agonizing was the decision to close our
own sewing factories. This was driven by the world of free trade.
In today's marketplace, if you are going to be competitive, you
have to be able to produce outside the United States in lower-cost
situations. I don't see any problem with creating jobs overseas—
there's no reason why somebody in Texas deserves a job more than
someone in Pakistan deserves that job—but when it comes to
someone losing a job, we have to work to reduce the negative
impact of that job loss.

We created a system to try to minimize the economic impact
to the greatest degree possible. When we close a factory, we offer
very generous severance packages. We also spend our corporate
money and our foundation money to fund economic development
and education programs. I'm unaware of other companies doing

this within the context of solving their own business problems. Even though we have been struggling financially and had a lot of debt, we decided that our core values of both empathy and integrity required us to consider the contributions that our employees have historically made to the company and to deal with them as generously as possible. Some people could say we were foolishly generous. We believe though, that over the long haul, being true to our values and true to what the brand stands for will allow us to win in the marketplace. While the economic impact to our bottom line may have been severe in the short term, we will benefit in the long term in the goodwill that it generates both for the company and for the brand.

We have stayed true to our core beliefs and steadfast in our community giving, but we have had to change the way that we have traditionally given. Historically, the company gave 2.5 percent of its profits to the Levi Strauss Foundation. We were forced to stop doing that in 1997, when the company began losing money. Quite simply, in a world of competitive business performance, it's hard to foresee making a formulaic commitment again. We will contribute depending on the fortunes of the company, and we will continue to be creative, competitive, and opportunistic in finding ways to give back.

There was a recent example that highlights how we continue to contribute on an opportunistic basis. One of the last plants that we closed was the original Levi Strauss & Co. plant in San Francisco on Valencia Street. (Again, we did the same things in closing that plant in terms of how we dealt with employees and the community.) We did something interesting with the proceeds of the sale of the facility, though. Rather than taking the proceeds and adding them to the bottom line, we contributed them back into the Levi Strauss Foundation. It was a way to ensure that the foundation could continue the economic empowerment and HIV programs that it is committed to.

Another difficult balancing act came in the form of health care coverage. Like most companies in the United States, we are faced with the medical costs crisis. Historically, most companies have provided retiree medical, but with the rising medical costs in this country, many companies have discontinued this benefit. We felt a commitment to our retirees—they had contributed to the success of this company for decades—and we decided that we couldn't take medical coverage away from them. We also felt a commitment to integrity, and the need to be true to what we said we would do. We determined not to eliminate retiree medical, like many companies did, but to cap it. (We had never, by implication or otherwise, said that the benefits would be of unlimited costs.) We structured the benefit in a way that wouldn't handicap the lowest wage earners, and we required the higher wage earners to pay a higher percentage of those medical costs in retirement. We discontinued retiree medical for new employees into the future, and we believe that's appropriate and competitive in the world that we live in today. We believe that we did the right thing in terms of our values for our former employees, and the right thing competitively to drive the company's performance into the future.

We have become more creative in devising ways to give back. In 1997 the foundation stopped getting gifts from the company, but we were able to continue giving to the community, thanks to the reserve that we had been saving. Today we have $71 million in the reserve and we give away about $10 million a year—there's a lot we can do with $10 million. Because we have had to refine our giving strategy I think that we are just as influential and innovative, if not more.

The company has always encouraged volunteerism. In 1968, Levi Strauss & Co. pioneered an employee volunteer effort called Community Involvement Teams (CIT); there are now 78 CITs bettering communities worldwide. One of the things that has been most exciting to me is something we started in 2000 called

Community Day. We all take a workday and go out into the community and give back. We started the program in the United States, where volunteerism is a much stronger cultural underpinning of the not-for-profit world. The interesting part is that we have seen the idea spread around the world. We see people in South Africa or countries in Asia or even now in Europe—where society expects the government to take care of issues like this—making a commitment to give back. In 2004, employees volunteered more than 50,000 hours to charitable organizations around the world and provided $1 million in philanthropic support to local nonprofit groups. What's amazing to me is that we're a company that is operating from Brazil to Mongolia with different cultures and different frames of reference, operating in world that is quite divided in its points of view and certainly about all things American. But here, on Community Day, we have a sense of cross-cultural unity and commitment; it's pretty inspiring.

It's incredible to see some of what our employees have accomplished in their communities. A few years ago I was in the Philippines celebrating the company's thirtieth anniversary there. The brand is very successful in the Philippines, but it's a tough market because the economy is struggling. We knew they had a great story to tell about the progress they were making, but as we got off the plane, the first thing that the management team and some of the employees did was take me to a microeconomic development spot that the company and our employees had sponsored.

This program was founded to lend $100 to women in Manila who wanted to start businesses. The Levi Strauss & Co. team took me to a fair where the women who had received a loan were displaying what they had created. They had built catering services, apparel, toy, and food businesses. It's amazing what $100 loans started in this community. What's equally amazing is that the repayment rate on these loans has been over 90 percent. This wasn't just a handout; these loans really did work, and they transformed lives in this impoverished community in Manila. Attending this fair wasn't the focus of my visit—we spent the rest of the time talking about the performance of the business and the marketplace—but it did set the tone that there was pride to be associated with the company, and it showed that in every way our company was committed to succeed in the Filipino market.

In addition to making an impact in the community, Community Day has made an extraordinary impact on our employees. I have never been involved in anything that was better in terms of corporate team building. Getting involved and volunteering requires that you go out with people you may work with but don't know very well outside a work context. It's an opportunity to see them in a totally different light. Whether the work is painting a school or cleaning up a park, we witness a dramatic difference from start to finish in how we operate together. There's more than a sense of commitment to the values of the company, there's a commitment to the team and to one another.

In addition to Community Day, we have institutionalized the notion that everybody who works here is entitled to take five hours a month of paid time to go do personal volunteer work. I don't want to overstate the initiative. We live in a world where we are all time-deprived. Companies, including ours, ask more and more of their employees, so whether people take those five hours can be debated. We are trying, though, to show our support of people individually being volunteers and giving back to the community. I think that as time goes on we will find ways to make this effort not only a policy, but a practice that we live by.

Our pants are sold worldwide in more than 110 countries. Their popularity is based on their egalitarian appeal and originality, and they transcend cultural boundaries. We have strived to ensure that we implement this egalitarian philosophy in our business practices. Our commitment to equal employment opportunity and diversity predated both the U.S. Civil Rights movement and federally mandated desegregation. We opened integrated factories in California in the 1940s. In 1960 we led our industry by sending the strong message that we would not locate new plants in towns in the American South that imposed segregation. We continued this tradition with our workplace practices. In 1992, we became the first Fortune 500 company to extend full medical benefits to domestic partners of employees. While controversial at the time, this action led to the widespread acceptance of this benefit and positioned us as a progressive employer with prospective talent.

We have a rich history of being forward-thinking and we don't rest on it. When we set up our plant in South Africa after apartheid restrictions were lifted 10 years ago, we faced the issue of segregation all over again. There were people pressuring us that people of different races didn't want to work together in South Africa. True to the history of the company, the person setting up the plant there said, "We don't do business that way."

I recently went down to South Africa to celebrate our 10-year anniversary there. If you go to the plant today, you will see a group of employees that reflect South African society: people of all different colors working together in a highly collaborative collegial environment. There are 50 people in that 300-person workforce that have been there since the day we opened. The employees are extraordinarily proud and committed not only to the success of the brand, but to being involved in community activities, whether it's HIV/AIDS, economic empowerment, or visiting homes for the elderly and performing unbelievably beautiful African songs.

We have a lot to celebrate in South Africa, not least of which is that we've built the number-one brand in the marketplace. The biggest problem we face has nothing to do with race relations and employee commitment—it's counterfeit brands. I see that as a sign of great brand health. We have a huge growth potential for South Africa. I also believe it's the stepping-stone to move upward through the continent of Africa. This is really one of the

last frontiers for the Levi's brand. We are going to get there—
and everywhere else we go—on the same values we started with
when we took on our first frontier more than 150 years ago.

SPOTLIGHT ON THE RED TAB FOUNDATION: EMPLOYEE-TO-EMPLOYEE GIVING

Commitment to giving back is embedded in the culture of Levi
Strauss & Co., and nothing illustrates that better than the Red
Tab Foundation—a nonprofit organization started by employ-
ees for employees.

In 1981, Jerry O'Shea—who began at Levi Strauss & Co. as
a stock boy when he was 17 and rose up the ranks over 42
years—retired, but he didn't leave his values or dedication at
the door. He understood the difficulties of the factory workers who earned hourly wages and had little stockpiled to fall
back on if something went wrong. With $100,000 of his own
money, and support from other Levi Strauss & Co. executives,
he started the Red Tab Foundation as a way to provide for Levi
Strauss & Co. employees or retirees.

The Red Tab Foundation offers tax-free grants and loans to
those of modest means—employees living check-to-check or
retirees relying on a fixed company pension supplemented by
Social Security. Since its founding, the Red Tab Foundation has
awarded more than $5 million to 6,000 individual recipients
worldwide. It's allowed the families of employees to start businesses, open matched savings accounts for education, pay for
unexpected medical expenses, and assist with routine health-
related costs such as eyeglasses, hearing aids, and dental work.
The Red Tab Foundation has been a steady support in the face
of emergencies, funding an employee's hotel stay after his house

burned down, assisting with the funeral of a customer service representative's child, and helping a woman, who'd put in over 25 years making 501 jeans, in making her bathroom handicap accessible so she could continue to live at home after suffering a stroke.

Jerry passed away in the late 1980s, but the Red Tab Foundation lives on. Like Levi Strauss, it shows the power of one person to make a difference—and build a legacy.

CHAPTER 7

A TRANSFERRING OF SKILLS: MICHAEL MILKEN

The Milken Family has donated more than $750 million over 30 years.

G rowing up in the California's San Fernando Valley, Michael Milken was sometimes called a boy wonder. He was bright and competitive and into everything: he sat on the student council, participated in the debate team, and ran track. He also had a spot on the varsity basketball team, but at some point in high school he stopped growing, and was benched. What did Mike do? Well, it wasn't something that most teenage boys would have considered— he joined the cheerleading squad.

What this story shows, besides the fact that it isn't necessarily uncool for a guy to be a cheerleader (Mike was still voted prom king, and he dated the prom queen, Lori Ann Hackel, now his wife of 38 years), is that when faced with adversity, he never folds. And not only does he turn lemons into lemonade, he makes sure it's the best lemonade available. Mike wasn't just a cheerleader, he was the head cheerleader, and would tirelessly rally for his team (even when it was 42 points ahead).

"When things look their worst, you always have the seed of great improvements," Mike told *Time* magazine, when thinking back to those cheerleading days. It's an optimistic outlook and the strength that has carried him—and the many others he's worked with (it's said knowing Mike is like attaching oneself to the tail of a comet)—throughout his entire life. Anyone who thinks of Mike in terms of the headlines, remembering him as the "junk bond king," or the financier who was prosecuted in the 1990s, doesn't know him at all. He has spent his entire career dedicating himself to philanthropy, as evidenced by the fact that his family has donated more than $750 million over 30 years. More than just donating money, though, Mike has created positive change by improving problems from their core and systematically changing everything, from the way research is done to the way policy is written.

Mike's efforts to advance medical research, perhaps what he is most recognized for today, began when his mother-in-law was diagnosed with breast cancer in 1972, and it was bolstered in 1976 when his father was found to have terminal melanoma. When Mike discovered he had prostate cancer in 1993, he expanded his work by applying his understanding of best business practices, such as recruiting and retaining talent and fostering teamwork. Another debilitating event—the accusations of securities violations, the legal battle that followed, and the resulting decision that barred him from the securities industry—didn't stymie him either. His experiences and beliefs encouraged him to devote more of his financial genius and unstoppable energy to improving society—in particular education and health care, where he sees the biggest chance to make a difference.

Mike's dad was a lawyer and an accountant, but while he watched his father work growing up, it was the Watts riots of 1965 that led to his decision to go into business. Mike was 19 years old at the time, and amid the smoke and screams, he began to understand that civil rights wasn't just about being able to sit in the front of the bus. It was about being an active participant in our economic society—having the opportunity to own a business, not just to have a job. He found that access to capital—oxygen for businesses—was restricted. And so, Mike began his lifelong quest to create a "global democratization of financial capital." It inspired a similar interest in "human capital"—the idea that people and their talents are what possess the greatest value—a theme that would later reverberate in every initiative he would undertake.

As a student at the University of California at Berkeley in the 1960s, while other students were protesting or partying, Mike (who didn't even drink carbonated beverages) focused on his work. He saw business as a way to make a difference. Wall Street was his "battleground for improving society," he said. He majored in business, managed some investors' portfolios, and researched data sheets. (He was obsessed with data sheets; he was later known to read them during the wee hours of his morning commute with a miner's headlamp). He uncovered one study showing that high-yield bonds, also called "junk" bonds (loans to noninvestment-grade businesses that carry higher interest rates), were actually valuable investments. It was the beginning of his financial work that would eventually change the way the markets operate.

After earning an MBA at Wharton, Mike went to work at the investment bank Drexel Burnham (called Drexel Harriman Ripley at the time). Although he didn't fit in entirely with the East Coast buttoned-up firm at first, his mark on the company was obvious from the beginning. Early on, he organized the overnight delivery of securities—something that saved the company a half million dollars annually. He also had a hand in reworking the structure of the firm. Mike saw the existing hierarchy that placed sales at the top, traders in the middle, and researchers on the bottom as ineffective. Research, not sales, was what yielded new products, and ultimately, a bigger market, he thought. Before long, research became the top priority.

Unlike his colleagues, Mike was interested in convertible bonds, preferred stock, and real estate investment trusts, where he saw real buying opportunities. His eye for these distressed investments made the company (and Mike) a fortune. Starting with a trading account of $2 million, he doubled it his first year, and by 1976 he reportedly made $5 million in income. He was 30 years old.

By the mid-1970s, crisis ensued when Mike's father was diagnosed with an aggressive cancer. Mike moved his immediate family and his department at Drexel from New York to California so his children would know their grandfather. Working from the X-shaped trading desk in his Beverly Hills office, and employing sophisticated trading tools and databases, Mike continued his work raising money for noninvestment-grade companies.

Over the next decade, Mike raised funds for more than three thousand companies, including MCI, CNN, Safeway, and Chrysler. American Motors and Mattel were saved through high-yield finance. He financed a number of then-small companies that included MGM, News Corp., Viacom, and Time Warner. He also provided access to capital for women. (Previously no woman had ever headed a publicly traded company that she had not inherited.) Mike funded minority-owned businesses too—something that made him the target of hate mail and even a death threat.

In the early eighties, Wall Street began to view junk bonds as an important source of financing, and by the end of the decade the investment tool became the center of controversy. In 1988, the Securities and Exchange Commission filed securities fraud charges against Drexel and against Mike. Drexel pleaded guilty to six felony counts, and Mike pleaded guilty to five securities and reporting violations. He was incarcerated for 22 months and assessed a $200 million fine. It was conduct that had never before (or since) been subject to criminal prosecution.

In 1993, a few days after he was released from prison, Mike went for his regular medical checkup and asked his doctor to do a PSA test (a blood test that measures a protein called prostate-specific antigen that can reveal cancer). He was only 46, and his doctor thought he was being overly cautious, but Mike had just lost a close friend to the disease. "Humor me, I can afford it," he remembers saying. The test, and the biopsy that followed, revealed that Mike indeed had prostate cancer—and it had spread to his lymph nodes. He was given less than 18 months to live.

Mike first dedicated his energies to staying alive. He did hormone therapy, radiation, practiced yoga, and the self-described junk food addict who used to have dreams about chocolate pudding, cut out all fats. "I was willing to try anything that had the potential to work," he said. The regime did work; in the fall of 1993 Mike's PSA count went down to zero and the cancer was in remission. (Mike admits that he's not sure exactly what specifically made him better, but he has stuck to his healthy diet and evangelized its merits by sharing his favorite soy-based, low-fat recipes in the best-selling cookbook *The Taste for Living*.)

After watching his father succumb to cancer and drawing from his own experience as a patient, Mike decided that the way cancer research was done had to be changed. He was already familiar with the nonprofit world. In 1982 he had cofounded and endowed the Milken Family Foundation, which was designed to advance education, youth programs, inner cities solutions, pediatric neurology, and treatments for cancer. He wanted to apply what he learned there, as well as the intelligence he gained from the thousands of companies he'd worked with, to the world of medical research. At a time when there was little knowledge about the disease (the word *prostate* wasn't even in Microsoft Word's Spell-Check database), he started the Prostate Cancer Foundation (originally called CaP Cure) with a mission to find and fund promising scientific research, attract talented scientists to the field, require everyone to collaborate, and increase awareness. It's already had such a significant impact that *Fortune* magazine put him on the cover and titled the story, "The Man Who Changed Medicine."

Since its creation, the Prostate Cancer Foundation has raised more than $260 million and has become the world's largest private funder of prostate cancer research. Research supported by the Prostate Cancer Foundation has led to more than 80 treatments now being tested in human clinical trials. The National Cancer Institute reports that there has been a 26 percent decline in deaths that result from prostate cancer. The drop in the prostate cancer death rate is four times the decline in overall cancer rates during the past decade, according to the cover article in *Fortune*.

At the same time that he was initiating a revolution in health care, Mike and his family continued to invest their energies in the Milken Family Foundation. Now in its twenty-fifth year, the foundation has worked closely with more than 1,000 organizations around the world. The program's National Educator Awards, which was established in 1985, is the largest teacher-recognition program in the United States. It's been called the "Oscars of Teaching" by *Teacher Magazine*.

After success with these organizations, Mike started Faster-Cures: the Center for Accelerating Medical Solutions, a Washington, DC-based think tank dedicated to shortening the time it takes to find cures and improve treatment outcomes for all deadly and debilitating diseases. There's also a goal when it comes to the organization's work fighting cancer. "In ten years cancer will no longer be a cause of death and suffering," Mike says. He's so confident that he says he has already chartered a cruise ship for January 2015. He plans to take a month off from work and go around the world celebrating with all the people who helped make beating cancer a reality.

Not only has Mike has been widely recognized for his efforts to advance health care and education, but the financial theories he developed in the 1960s, and for which he was demonized, are now considered mainstream. *The Economist* said his financial innovations "are credited with fueling much of America's rampant economic growth by enabling companies with bright ideas to get the money they need to develop them." His use of equity-based securities, bonds, and hybrids to build the right capital structure for his clients helped to create millions of jobs. (Small- and medium-sized companies have created 62 million new jobs in the United States since 1970, while at the same time, Fortune 500 companies, although they have increased revenues, have decreased workforce levels.)

On a recent Saturday at 8 a.m. (Mike still works 15-hour days), a few hours before his good friend and fellow cancer survivor Lance Armstrong, the seven-time Tour de France winner, was coming over to visit, Mike met with us to discuss his mission to develop health care and education—and how investing in these efforts is our best shot at bettering our economy and our lives.

AN INVESTMENT IN HUMAN CAPITAL

Michael Milken, Financier, Philanthropist, Chairman,
The Milken Institute

In order to ensure a prosperous future, we must make a significant commitment to building human capital. The way to do that is through investing in the two things that drive people's ability and productivity: enhancing their skills through education and keeping them alive and well through good health care.

It's my view that all organizations—whether they be nonprofit, for-profit, or government—are defined by the people who work for them. It is their ideas, their talents, their skill sets, their vision that is any organization's greatest asset and that has the ability to make it great.

In the past century, the value of people—what Gary Becker, Nobel Laureate in Economics, calls "human capital"—has become even more important to building our economy. Eighty years ago the most valuable businesses were the heavy industrial companies; none of the top 100 companies were in technology, services, healthcare, or medicine—the sectors that are driven entirely by people and that make up 60 percent of the largest companies today. Eighty years ago the power of the individual wasn't as important; in 1920 the leading product was the automobile. Some 60 percent of the cost of an automobile was in the raw materials, such as steel, and only 40 percent of the costs were related to people. By 2000, though, the computer chip emerged as the leading product—an item that only has 2 percent of its value of in raw materials. That means that 98 percent of the product's worth is in the skills and experiences of individuals.

I've come to understand the growing importance of human capital through my work financing and advising thousands of companies, but these theories have also been put forth by some of our country's leading economists. In 1992, the University of Chicago's Dr. Becker, who won the Nobel Prize for his work on human capital, estimated that the skills and experiences of our people are worth more than half a million dollars per person.

Recently, Kevin Murphy, another economist at the University of Chicago, who in 1997 was named the most outstanding American economist under the age of 40 by the American Economic Association, suggested that number is too low. He marked it at $5 million. Whatever number you use, it is fair to say that less than 25 percent of the national balance sheet is in so-called traditional assets and somewhere between 75 and 98 percent of all the assets in this country are in the productivity and the capabilities of the people.

Yet, not only do we omit this asset from the balance sheet, we don't invest nearly enough in caring for it. In order to ensure a prosperous future, we must make a significant commitment to building human capital. The way to do that is through investing in the two things that drive people's ability and productivity: enhancing their skills through education and keeping them alive and well through good health care.

We've been involved in efforts to support and empower individuals through education since the 1970s. We believe that educators have the most important job in this country—every person remembers a teacher that changed his or her life—yet there was never recognition for the profession. For years we've had the Academy Awards for actors, the MVP awards for athletes, and the Grammy Awards for musicians, yet there was nothing for teachers—the people who educate all of the other award winners. In an effort to change that, the Milken Family Foundation, which is now headed by my brother, Lowell, created the Milken National Educator Award, an Academy Award of sorts for outstanding educators. Since the mid-1980s, we have honored teachers throughout the United States by gathering them together in a gala event and presenting each of them with a $25,000 award.

It's essential that we find and honor the right educators; we're looking for teachers, principals, and administrators who have been willing to try something new, who have helped students perform better or who have positively affected their environment. We've worked with the Department of Education in 48 states to search for these individuals anonymously. After the final selections, we hold an award ceremony in each recipient's school. It's an amazing event—especially because it's a big surprise. We make it appear as if there is a school assembly planned for another purpose, such as a visit from the governor, or a discussion with the superintendent of education. Then, we announce that the Milken National Educator Award is about to be awarded to someone in that school. We make sure there are TV cameras and newspaper reporters; we want these educators to get the recognition they deserve. Although these people never entered the profession in search of kudos, they are incredibly touched when their efforts are recognized. There are always a lot of tears at the ceremony.

Later, we get all the educators together for a celebration. In addition to giving each educator a $25,000 check, we offer continual education and enrichment. They also become part of a network that advises their state superintendent or governor on education issues. We believe that these awards have helped energize and lift the prestige of the profession. To give you just one example, we once gave the award to a principal in the state of Illinois, who later moved to a different school district. People actually sold their homes and moved to another part of the city just so their children could go to his high school! Our program isn't designed just to motivate teachers, principals, and superintendents, though. We want every student in the assembly to remember the event. It's our hope that maybe they'll decide to be a teacher themselves one day.

It's interesting to try to measure the value that has been created by recognizing and supporting excellence in education. Over the years, we've given the award to more than 2,000 teachers and invested more than $200 million in this program (when you include the ceremonies, the continuing education, and the infrastructure costs). Let's be conservative and assume that each of our 2,000 award recipients only influenced 10 teachers—now we have 20,000 teachers who were impacted. If we say that each of them has over his or her lifetime influenced 1,000 kids (and it's probably a lot more) we are looking at 20 million people who have been affected. When we look at those 20 million individuals who have benefited from the program and assign a value to it in terms of human capital, we find that we have built $10 *trillion* in human capital. It's a pretty impressive return on our original investment.

We've learned a lot from that program, which we've been doing since 1985, and we began to apply what we learned from our work in education to create a similar effort in the field of medicine. I initially got focused on cancer research in the 1970s when my father was diagnosed with melanoma. In an effort to help save his life, I met with medical school deans and physicians who deepened my understanding of the reality of medical research. I had learned from my father's case that no matter how talented I was, or what I could try to make happen, there simply wasn't enough time to find a solution to melanoma that would allow my father to survive. I came to this conclusion in 1976; he passed away three years later.

While the impetus for my involvement was because my family has been so deeply affected by cancer—I've lost 10 close family members to the disease—I've stayed so focused on it because every family is affected. One in two men and one in three women will get cancer in their lifetime. Cancer has just passed heart disease as a major cause of death for people in the United States under 85 years of age. I know firsthand that the suffering of cancer patients and the grief of their families and friends are beyond calculation. What many people often don't consider is that this disease has a staggering economic impact on our entire society. If we take the economist Kevin Murphy's average valuation of $5 million per life, and multiply that times the number of individuals who will die from cancer, we would add $47 trillion to the U.S. economy—a number that exceeds the entire household assets of the United States. Of course, these figures only amplify cancer's already astounding annual morbidity and mortality costs.

We've known since we first got involved in learning about the medical research system that to successfully accelerate medical care we needed to have the best and the brightest scientists working to find a cure. One of the major problems we found was that there wasn't a large enough effort focused on that: while $100 billion was being spent annually in the United States on cancer, only $2 billion was dedicated to finding a cure. ($98 billion was spent on patient care.) It just didn't make any sense. Can you think of any example in private industry where a company would spend 50 times as much to deal with the consequences of a problem as it would to solve the problem? It would never happen!

We wanted to solve the problem. But another factor we found was that the best young research physicians were tempted to leave low-paying jobs at the lab in favor of the more lucrative clinical practices treating patients. Although these young investigators hadn't entered the field of medicine to get rich, they were heavily burdened by medical school loans, the financial pressures to pay a mortgage, save for their children's college tuition, and plan for their own retirement. We established a competitive research awards program to encourage promising researchers to stay in the lab for a few more years.

This initiative would ultimately impact millions of lives. Take for example, Dr. Dennis Slamon, a researcher who received an award from us in the 1980s and who went on to later discover Herceptin, a revolutionary breakthrough in treating one type of breast cancer. One out of every eight women in America will get breast cancer at some time in her life, and one out five have a particular genetic profile that causes a certain cancer. Herceptin has the potential to save the 2.8 million women who will be affected by that cancer. Since the average person dies from cancer 16 years less than their life expectancy, and we can gain all those years back by this cure, we can add 44.8 million years of productivity. Imagine what we can achieve as a society with 44.8 million more productive years on our side?

There are myriad other examples as well. We all know the story of Lance Armstrong, the seven-time Tour de France winner, who had testicular cancer that spread throughout his body and into his brain. He was cured thanks to a highly successful chemotherapy regimen for testicular cancer, which virtually cures a disease that previously was almost always fatal. The treatment was developed by Dr. Lawrence Einhorn, a brilliant scientist, who has been supported by the Milken Family Foundation. The Foundation's support has also led to Dr. Bert Voglestein's pioneering work on the p53 gene, whose mutant form is believed to be involved in more than half of human cancers. Then there is Dr. Owen Witte, whose later work provided the basis for the development of a groundbreaking drug Gleevec, which is now used for patients with chronic myelogenous leukemia. There are many others as well.

Although I had been involved in a quest to improve medical research since the 1970s, I was shocked to learn how little I actu-

ally knew about prostate cancer—the most common nonskin cancer in America—when I was diagnosed in 1993. Even though one
in six men get prostate cancer and 35,000 American men were
expected to die from the disease that year (I had been given 12
to 18 months to live), there was little work being done to battle
the disease.

The thought at the time was that there wasn't any money available for prostate cancer research. The National Cancer Institute
had given up on it. One young investigator, Dr. Jonathan Simons,
was told going into the field of prostate cancer research would be
"career suicide." I knew that first I had to fight to stay alive long
enough to make a difference, and then I had to jumpstart research
in prostate cancer and change the current model that crippled our
chance of finding solutions.

We set up the Prostate Cancer Foundation (then called CaP
CURE) with the goal of making the medical research process
increasingly efficient and effective by first attracting the best scientific and medical graduates to enter research careers, and then
requiring multiple institutions to collaborate—something
unheard of at the time. (There was a zero-sum-game mentality;
because there was only so much money to go around, the
thought was that if Sloan-Kettering won a grant in a particular
area there wasn't an opportunity for M.D. Anderson or the other
cancer centers.) We also learned that scientists were spending as
much as 50 percent of their time writing grant applications
instead of doing research, so we decided to limit the applications
to just five pages. We knew that time was of the essence, so we
committed to making decisions about what research would be
funded within 60 days. (And, a commitment to pay within 90
days.) We encouraged some other nontraditional ideas as well,
such as encouraging for-profit companies to collaborate with
academic institutions and building public awareness through
advocacy.

We have raised more than $260 million, and grants have been distributed to more than 1,200 researchers at 100 institutions worldwide. We have seen results. In 1993 we offered grant money to Dr. Simons, the doctor who was told prostate cancer research was "career suicide." He used a PCF grant to develop an anti-prostate cancer vaccine called GVAX, which is currently showing promise in late-stage clinical trials. Now the head of the Winship Cancer Institute at Emory University, Simons and his colleague Leland Chung have received a $10 million grant from the U.S. Department of Defense Prostate Cancer Research Program to create a "Manhattan Project" to address the problem of prostate cancer. The program involves researchers at 13 universities. and it's the first U.S. cancer research grant that uses Web-based video conferencing for daily and weekly research meetings. We have also been advocates for greater awareness, and we have seen the results in government funding: the NIH budget has more than doubled and the National Cancer Institute budget has more than tripled. We have come a long way in a short time, and the new synergistic collaboration is what gives us hope at finding a cure for all cancers.

Today we have an organization called FasterCures. We believe that science is moving very quickly, but it is being held back by the current system. We have designed an Acceleration Agenda, which is composed of four key areas:

1. Bring the information revolution to medical research.
2. Address changes in laws and regulations.
3. Promote innovative financial models to support drug discovery and development.
4. Take a patient's eye view of the social and ethical issues at stake.

While we have been involved in running foundations and bringing the best practices of business, such as investing in finding solutions, recruiting the best talent, fostering teamwork, and using sophisticated financing tools, to the world of medical research and education since the 1970s, we have similarly long understood the importance of businesses playing an integral role in effecting positive change in the community.

Dating back to my business at Drexel, we knew that our employees would be better employees if they better understood the needs of society. We started a program where our employees and their children all over the country would spend a day with children who had challenges, such as physical disabilities, learning disabilities, or psychological problems. We teamed up with Variety Children's Charity; they would identify the groups they support. We would put on an event and pay for it.

It was a program that had long-lasting effects that I never would have been able to anticipate. In the mid-1980s we sponsored an event at Universal Studios with the Help Group, a school for children with special needs. Many of these kids had suffered great tragedies; some were subjected to extreme abuse by their parents and were wards of the state, others struggled with autism, or severe learning disabilities. In the middle of the event, one of the young men had a seizure. I rushed over to help this boy at the same time another person rushed over, the head of the school, Dr. Barbara Firestone.

This experience forged a personal relationship between Barbara and me that started that day and grew. Initially, I wanted to know what we could do to help these kids, and we used our skills to help them finance and build her organization. The first key to success was Barbara's talent and passion. I believe that if you don't have passion for something it's impossible to encourage others to be passionate about it, and fortunately we had no shortage of passion with Barbara Firestone. The next step was to get folks personally involved. It's not just writing a check that builds something great, but rolling up your sleeves and using your skills, whether it be financing, marketing, or communicating to help build solutions. We worked on fostering teamwork between her foundation and our staff, which increased all of our interaction and skills. We then worked on transferring those skills to others. Finally, we got Barbara to think big. I used to tell her, "If we build it, they will come, so think big."

Today, the Help Group is the largest organization in America taking care of children with special needs. There are 3,500 children with physical and emotional problems who are there. It grew from one building to several campuses around Los Angeles. While the numbers speak volumes, looking at the impact on a microlevel is where you can really see how the organization has made a difference. There was one young man whom I became close to. His life was like a horror story: His mother died and his father went off the deep end. His brother committed suicide; he was living in a car. Eventually, he landed at the Help Group. It changed his life: he went into the Marines; he traveled the world; he got married. Today, he and his wife have a child and he has a great job. He is productive member of our society, rather than being a negative cost to society. It's incredible to think that this was the result of the Festival for Youth program that started 20 years ago.

This program that we started at Drexel had a huge impact on our employees as well. Today they are some of the most philanthropic individuals leading charities throughout America. The initiative has deeply impacted my life, too. I started teaching at the Help Group, which led to a program called Mike's Math Club. (Today my sister and brother-in-law run that program and we've had more than 50,000 inner city kids involved. Some of the kids who were with us at the beginning are math teachers today!) My mother started spending time at the Help Group and so did my wife Lori and our kids. I started spending the holidays there. Slowly, the ties became tighter and tighter. Barbara's family became intertwined with my family. Our children all went to the same school in Los Angeles and then to the University of Pennsylvania. My brother's oldest son, Jeremy, and Barbara's daughter, Sarah, fell in love and got married. I have the cutest great-nephew in the world. Jake is the first child of the next generation.

I tell this story to make the point that these things change you. By building human capital we have increased the assets in this country's balance sheet by trillions of dollars. It has changed millions of lives—and, it has changed mine.

Five Keys to Building Effective Philanthropic Organizations

1. **Follow Your Passion.** The most effective patrons begin the process of giving by asking what they care about passionately.
2. **Get Personally Involved.** There is more to giving than writing a check; roll up your sleeves and work together to make a difference.
3. **Foster Teamwork.** By turning competitors into collaborators we can accelerate the process.
4. **Transfer Skills.** The impact of a monetary gift is magnified when the giver also contributes his or her skills, be it in finance, communication, technology, etc.
5. **Think Big.** Don't underestimate what you want to set out to achieve. Small organizations, when managed right, can impact a great number of people.

CHAPTER 8

INGREDIENTS FOR SUCCESS: SAFEWAY

What we've found is that when you give someone a job that might otherwise be hard to get, they are enormously appreciative and do a tremendous job and are successful.

Y ou may know Safeway, one of the largest food retailers in North America, by names such as Vons (if you live in southern California), Dominick's (in Chicago), or Carrs (Alaska's largest retailer), but chances are you wouldn't recognize the supermarket chain by its christened name—Skaggs Stores.

Pleasanton, California–based Safeway, now a Fortune 50 company that operates about 1,800 stores in the United States and Canada, dates back to 1915 when a young man, M.B. Skaggs, purchased his father's Idaho grocery store for $1,089. He called it Skaggs' Cash Stores and tapped his five brothers to help him grow the company. M.B. employed a strategy of giving customers value and expanding by keeping a narrow profit margin. The approach proved to be a stunning success: by 1926 Skaggs had 428 stores in 10 states.

That same year, the business practically doubled in size when Charles Merrill (the innovative investment banker who would later go on to found Merrill Lynch & Co. with friend and former soda-fountain-equipment salesman Edmund "Eddie" Lynch) engineered a merger between Skaggs and another supermarket chain, Seelig, which had 322 stores in Southern California. The newly merged company became Safeway and two years later listed on the New York Stock Exchange.

Running any business during the Great Depression was not without hardship, but M.B. never lost his focus on providing value for customers. The company not only survived during these economically challenging years, but M.B. came up with advances that would revolutionize the supermarket business, including pricing by the pound, open dating on perishables, nutritional labeling, and some of the first parking lots.

Thanks to the financial backing of Charles Merrill (who was the first investment banker to recognize that chain stores would eventually dominate retailing), the company had the capital to expand by acquisitions and it snapped up a bevy of regional grocery stores, including the West Coast Piggly Wiggly stores, the country's first self-service grocery store (previously clerks shopped for the customer) and the first to provide shopping baskets, checkout stands, and prices on every item in the store. By 1931, Safeway owned 3,527 stores and had expanded into Canada. Over the next several decades it would gain control of stores in countries as far-flung as Germany, Australia, and Kuwait.

In 1986, on the heels of a hostile takeover bid, Safeway was acquired for $4.8 billion by legendary LBO powerhouse Kohlberg Kravis Roberts & Co. (KKR) and taken private. As part of the transaction, the company took on tremendous debt (KKR had borrowed 97 percent of what the deal cost)—something it paid back by selling, among other parts of the business, the U.K., Kansas City, and Little Rock divisions. Over time, almost half of the stores in the chain were sold. Safeway's once national presence was reduced to Northern California, several Western states, and Washington, DC.

The company went public again in 1990 and in 1993 tapped Steve Burd, who was a consultant to KKR, as CEO of Safeway. Steve came to Safeway at a time when the company was battling slow sales and increasing operating expenses. He engineered one of the most dramatic business turnarounds in the entire retail sector, resulting in a nearly eightfold increase in the company's share price and 30 consecutive quarters of operating expense reduction. In the late 1990s the company acquired several regional chains including Randall's in Texas, Carrs in Alaska, Genuardi's in Pennsylvania, and Dominick's in Illinois. Under Steve's leadership, the company also exercised its option to acquire control of Vons. (Safeway had previously sold most of its stores to the Southern California–based Vons in exchange for a 30 percent interest in the company.)

While Safeway's gangbuster growth under Steve secured its place as the number-three supermarket in the country (in 2004, it did $35.8 billion in sales), the company, along with the rest of the unionized retail grocery sector, has had its challenges. In recent years, cut-price operators like Wal-Mart as well as smaller niche players such as Whole Foods and Trader Joe's have grabbed market share from conventional grocers. It's a climate that has required severe cost cutting in the already penny-pinching supermarket business. (The supermarket industry has notoriously low margins, with only a few cents on the sales dollar.) The industry's focus on labor cost control, which Steve called "a matter of survival,"[1] sparked battles with organized labor, including a four-and-a-half-month strike over benefits in Southern California in late 2003.

For the past several years, Safeway has worked hard at re-inventing the way it goes to market. It launched a new "lifestyle" format by redesigning and remerchandising its perishables departments. It also added more organics and freshly prepared meals;

full-service bakeries; floral design centers; sushi and olive bars; along with its line of proprietary brands Sweetest of the Season fresh produce, Rancher's Reserve beef, and Signature soups, salads, and sandwiches, and its "O" line of organic products. It supported the effort with a $100 million "Ingredients for Life" advertising campaign, something that's been called the most notable of big box retailers trying to create a distinctive impression.[2] Steve reports that the new strategy is already paying off. "We will be the most successful conventional supermarket for at least the next five years," he says. "And, we have plans that we are putting into place that will extend that out well beyond five years."

Although low margins in the supermarket industry make it challenging, Safeway has long been committed to giving back to the communities in which it operates—something that differentiates it as one of the most generous companies in its sector. Each year, Safeway raises and donates nearly $150 million (money as well as merchandise) to nonprofit organizations.

As a food retailer, it makes sense that Safeway has long dedicated itself to efforts that reduce hunger. The company is one of the largest supporters of America's Second Harvest, the nation's largest network of food banks. In 2004 it donated more than $100 million worth of merchandise to local food banks and hunger relief programs. It is also committed to funding education as a way to build strong communities, and in 2004 it contributed more than $20 million to local schools.

In the health and human services area, Safeway supports women's shelters, health screening, and childcare. It is also one of the largest breast and prostate cancer research fund-raisers and over the past four years has donated more than $20 million toward those causes. During the past 10 years, it has raised more than $12 million for the Muscular Dystrophy Association. The company has also had special focus on agencies that help people with disabilities and other special needs—something that has resulted in raising more than $65 million for Easter Seals since 1985.

Safeway has also made it a policy to hire people from different backgrounds (it was recognized for this in *Fortune* magazine). In addition to employing people of all races and religions, the company gives jobs to people with various developmental disabilities. Steve explains that the company has several thousand such employees who work in a range of different store-level jobs. "What we've found is that when you give someone a job that might otherwise be hard to get, they are enormously appreciative and do a tremendous job and are successful," he says.

Since its early days, the company has tried to act as a steward of the environment. It has been recycling cardboard since 1960. It has also encouraged customers to join its environmental efforts— something that has resulted in the recycling of several million pounds of shopping bags. Recently, the company replaced ozone-depleting chlorofluorocarbons (CFCs) in its store refrigeration systems. Safeway is also one of the largest buyers of green energy and recently announced that it would power all of its San Francisco stores and its fuel stations nationally with 100 percent renewable wind energy.

In his essay here, Steve, who came to Safeway 13 years ago and considers it the best business decision of his career, talks about the company's specific programs, its impact on the community— and on the company.

MAKING A DIFFERENCE— AN INGREDIENT OF LIFE

Steve Burd, President and CEO, Safeway

This philosophy of selecting charities at retail has led us to partner with organizations we'd never have found any other way.

Safeway operates under a fairly simple philosophy when it comes to community involvement, and it's a philosophy that has changed very little since our earliest days. To us, being the neighborhood grocery store means you occupy a privileged place in the lives of your customers. You become, essentially, a partner to your customers in feeding their families. That's a very special role to fill, and it carries with it an obligation to be involved in our communities, working to make life better everywhere we do business.

Of course, it's also good business for us to be seen as a responsible citizen of the community. We have competitors virtually everywhere, and consumers face an unprecedented level of choice when it comes to grocery shopping. Customers have come to expect—rightly—that the companies that serve them also serve their communities.

A great deal of the corporate giving we undertake flows naturally from the business we're in. For example, each year, we give more than $100 million in food donations to local and regional food banks. Although we have become much more skilled at inventory control and product flow, our stores end each day with a certain amount of food that, while still perfectly wholesome, no longer meets our high standards for sale. This food—perhaps sliced bread that has reached its "pull" date but is still fresh— goes to a food bank, where it is served or distributed the same or next day.

Through the years, we've become better at controlling inventory and reducing waste. Part of that growing sophistication has included becoming skilled at coordinating with food banks to make sure nothing goes to waste. Our stores work with large, highly organized food bank operations with elaborate distribution systems, and with local churches that might send over a van to pick up a few cases of lettuce or some dairy products.

This is more than inventory control to me. Growing up, I remember my father going to the bakery each morning to get the day-old bread for a dime. It was what our family could afford and it made a big difference to us. I'm committed to helping those who continue to make food available for families who need it.

If our work with food banks is a natural extension of the grocery business, much of the rest of our charitable work is a natural extension of the generosity of our employees and our customers. We've been amazed through the years at how responsive our customers and employees are when given an opportunity to help those in need.

In 2001, we established the Safeway Foundation to make the most effective use of our charitable efforts. Through employee contributions and special fund-raising events, our foundation raises money that goes to local charities. We're mindful that grocery shopping is a local endeavor—most customers stay within a mile and a half of their homes when choosing a store—and that we're expected to help make a difference in each of our 1,800 store locations.

This philosophy of selecting charities at retail has led us to partner with organizations we'd never have found any other way. In

Colorado, for example, we're proud partners of Joseph's Journey, an organization that grants "wilderness wishes" to terminally ill children. In Texas, we're helping "Stuff a Bus" with school supplies for needy school kids. In Chicago, we help sponsor a summer camp that lets children with disabilities forget about limitations for a few weeks each summer. There are similar stories of partnership at each of our 1,800 stores, thanks to employees who understand what it means to be involved in their communities.

Other efforts require a divisional or national focus. For example, we sponsor two Ladies Professional Golf Association (LPGA) tournaments each year, raising more than $1.5 million for regional charities in Portland and Phoenix.

Of these centralized efforts, none is more important to Safeway than the work we do to raise awareness and research funds for prostate and breast cancer. Our focus on these particular diseases stems in part from their prevalence (as many as one in six men will be diagnosed with some form of prostate cancer; breast cancer affects one woman in eight) and in part from the opportunity we see to eradicate them. I share the view of Mike Milken and others leading the war on cancer that we can cure this disease within our lifetimes.

Each year, Safeway dedicates the month of June to raising funds for prostate cancer research. We donate the funds—which last year alone totaled more than $4.4 million—to the Prostate Cancer Foundation, which supports more than 1,200 researchers at 100 institutions worldwide.

Every October is devoted to the same kind of fund-raising on behalf of breast cancer efforts. Last year, we raised more than $5 million for organizations conducting research into breast cancer cures or providing services and treatment for breast cancer patients.

Here's an important fact about the grocery business: profit margins are low. On a dollar of sales, we might make 2 cents. That's not a complaint, because our company does very well. It is, however, something that can't be ignored when we determine how best to support the causes that matter to us. We can't necessarily match the check-writing power of a technology company, which might clear 60 cents on a dollar of sales.

But no one in any industry can match our power for reaching people and for mobilizing the natural goodwill of our customers and employees. Our work with prostate cancer and breast cancer efforts provide perfect examples of this.

We see about 30 million customers a week and in June, every one of them hears about Prostate Cancer Awareness month and gets an invitation to contribute. Customers are invited to "buy" a blue ribbon or blue wristband signifying their support for the cause. In 2005, we partnered with singer Jeff Austin Black to sell a special CD of Black's songs for $2, with all proceeds going to the Prostate Cancer Foundation.

In October, customers are asked to donate at each checkout stand and receive a pink ribbon or wristband indicating their support for Breast Cancer Awareness Month. Other events include contests, special product sales, and special events. In 2005, we were proud to team up with Grammy winner Melissa Etheridge to sell her greatest hits CD, *The Road Less Traveled*, in our stores. Etheridge, a breast cancer survivor herself, recorded "I Run for Life" on the new CD, and the song quickly became an anthem for women whose lives have been changed by the disease. Outside our stores, Safeway sponsors 10 Susan G. Komen Foundation races, each known as the "Race for the Cure" in a local community.

But our work with cancer groups isn't just about raising money. It's also about raising awareness and helping our customers and their families reduce their risk of breast or prostate cancer. Facts about the diseases, including the importance of early detection and the need for periodic screenings, appear in our weekly sales circulars throughout the United States. Similar messages are carried on the packaging of some of our most popular items and private label products. During the awareness months, shoppers even hear the facts they need to know over our in-store broadcast system. In June, our pharmacies sell a specially priced self-screening kit that tells men if they are at elevated risk for prostate cancer.

And throughout the year, we remember that we aren't alone. Our business partners—big companies who supply our stores with the products we sell—hear from us frequently and understand we expect them to join us in making a difference. We're privileged to associate with generous vendors who share our vision of community involvement. Last year, for example, Kimberly-Clark and participating partners donated $250,000 to the Safeway Foundation for the Breast Cancer Awareness program.

Nowhere was this ability to partner with our customers and others better illustrated than in the aftermath of the 2004 tsunami in south Asia and eastern Africa. Very shortly after the tsunami hit, we implemented a way for our customers to donate to relief efforts, using every checkout stand at every one of our 1,800 stores. In extremely short order, we were able to deliver a check for $3.8 million to the American Red Cross.

The help we were able to give to tsunami relief efforts demonstrated an important fact about corporate philanthropy: we can offer an extremely effective vehicle for funding charitable causes. By tapping into systems already in place, we are able to raise a great deal of money without sacrificing a significant share of it to maintaining an administrative structure. To us, this ability translates to a responsibility to help when we're needed.

If we needed another reason, we'd find it on the bottom line of our balance sheets. I'm convinced that giving as we do ultimately helps our business. In a business as competitive as ours, we spend a great deal of time trying to create and maintain the right image. We want our customers to feel like they've made a good decision when they walk in our doors. A lot of things go into this: the look and feel of our stores, the lighting we use, the way oranges or avo-cados are displayed, the friendliness of our staff—and whether people perceive us as caring about the things they care about. To me, giving back to the communities where we do business has become an essential part of our ability to identify with our cus-tomers and remain their choice for grocery shopping.

I got a nice reminder recently of how that can work. Last sum-mer, during the last week of our June fund-raising, I was at an event at someone's home when someone pointed out a gentleman across his yard. The gentleman, he said, had just come back from his local Safeway store. Recently diagnosed with prostate cancer himself, he was overwhelmed to see all the efforts under way in our store to increase awareness of the disease and raise funds for a cure. From this day on, he said he would "never shop anywhere else."

That's not why we do what we do, but it certainly is nice to hear someone notice and appreciate it. It's a reminder that our company can do well by doing good.

CHAPTER 9

HEALTHY CHOICES: GLAXOSMITHKLINE

GSK has gone beyond that inherent mission [improving the lives of its customers] to ensure that more and more people have access to their products—regardless of what they can pay.

Jean-Pierre Garnier, the CEO of pharmaceutical giant Glaxo-SmithKline (GSK), is known as simply as "JP" in the industry. He's also reportedly known as "Dr. Gloom and Doom" by his colleagues. That's why when upon meeting the dynamic French-born CEO, you can't help but be surprised by the way he generously peppers his sentences with words like "wonderful," "phenomenal," and "spectacular."

The fact that JP's vocabulary reveals an optimistic outlook, and at the same time he's branded a pessimist by his peers is reflective of the complexity that plagues the pharmaceutical industry today. While Big Pharma is revered for creating drugs that improve and save lives, the industry is simultaneously crucified over the escalating cost of medicines and the way it reports clinical trials.

There's no doubt the pharmaceutical business is a tough industry through which to steer, but despite the issues, JP isn't feeling too gloomy these days. Long worried about the rising costs of research and development as new product releases remained stagnant (this concern is what originally dubbed him Dr. Gloom), JP, who became CEO of GSK in 2001, streamlined the company's R&D operations, while building what is now the largest pipeline of new drugs in the industry. While JP has paid close attention to growing profits, he has also committed to growing the company's commitment to the global community. Although by design all pharmaceutical companies are dedicated to improving the lives of its customers, GSK has gone beyond that inherent mission to ensure that more and more people have access to their products—regardless of what they can pay. This philosophy has established GSK as one of the brightest examples of corporate social responsibility. In 2004, its investment to the community was valued at $600 million—some 5.4 percent of the company's pretax profits.

It's amazing to think that GSK—a company that now employs 100,000 people in 116 countries, distributes more than 35 doses of vaccines every second, and spends more than $450,000 each hour to find new medicines—began in 1715 with a single London-based pharmacy called Plough Court, which specialized in items such as cod liver oil, malt extracts, and throat pastilles. The company's growth is the result of dozens of mergers and acquisitions (including the purchase of Plough Court) and most recently the merger of two giants SmithKline Beecham and Glaxo Wellcome. While the firm has been reconfigured and renamed myriad times, its founding fathers have left their indelible mark in the tradition they established for innovation, quality, and community caring.

The Smith in GlaxoSmithKline honors John K. Smith, who in 1830 opened a small drugstore in Philadelphia. Mahlon Kline joined the company as a bookkeeper, but soon took on sales and expanded his knowledge of medicine. Under the name Smith, Kline & Company, the firm became the largest wholesale drug business in the Philadelphia area and established many now-customary practices including filling orders and delivering them in a timely fashion (Smith Kline was the first company to have orders received in the morning sent out by late afternoon); having laboratory chemists screen products for quality and purity standards; and sending pharmaceutical samples by mail to doctors across the United States.

Smith Kline eventually increased its attention to research and developed drugs that alleviated scores of ailments. The tranquilizer Thorazine, launched in the 1950s, revolutionized the treatment of mental illness. In 1952—after more than seven years of research and more than 35,000 hours of work—it introduced the first time-released medicine. It used this method for a number of other sustained-release preparations, including the cold remedy Contac, which became the world's leading cold medication. The company was also responsible for the development of Tagamet, which changed peptic ulcer therapy, earned one of the firm's scientists a Nobel Prize, and became the first drug to achieve sales of over $1 billion a year.

While Smith and Kline were working in Philadelphia, Thomas Beecham founded the Beecham Organization in northern England. His product, Beecham's Pills, a brand of laxative, was an immediate success and reached faraway markets in Africa and Australia. By 1885, Beecham's son Joseph ran the company and created new standards in hygiene, ensuring that the staff dressed in white coats and that the working environment was dust free. After having placed ads in more than 7,000 newspapers around the globe (each ad was translated for the language of the publication), the company saw production of Beecham's Pills laxative reach one million a day. Two decades later, the company went on an acquisition binge, adding consumer products to its lineup in the form of toothpaste, energy-replacement drinks, and a men's hair application.

Beecham Research Laboratories (BRL), created in 1943, focused on basic pharmaceutical research and yielded the important discovery of the penicillin nucleus, which allowed Beecham scientists to produce a wide variety of antibiotics, including the first semisynthetic penicillin. BRL discovered amoxicillin in 1972, which later became the most widely used antibiotic. In the 1980s it made an acquisition that added Tums antacid tablets and Oxy acne treatments to its product portfolio.

In 1989 the Beecham Group merged with SmithKline & French to form SmithKline Beecham, one of the world's biggest research and development organizations. In the 1990s SmithKline Beecham launched new drugs such as Paxil for the treatment of depression and Havrix, the world's first hepatitis A vaccine. In 1996 the company created a corporate social responsibility program called Community Partnership to formally focus its philanthropy on community-based health care.

The Glaxo part of the GlaxoSmithKline story begins in 1873 with the New Zealand–based Joseph Nathan and Company, which produced milk powder for infants. (When considering brand names, they selected Lacto, but similar names were registered— by changing the order of the letters and adding some new ones, they came up with Glaxo.) The company became involved in the production of penicillin, and by1944 it was responsible for 80 percent of the United Kingdom's penicillin supply. Glaxo went public in 1947, and in the 1950s it launched a bevy of new products, the most significant being cortisone, used for rheumatoid arthritis and dermatological and allergic respiratory conditions. It created the antiulcer treatment Zantac, which became the world's top-selling medicine by the end of the 1980s and represented 40 percent of the company's turnover for many years.

As Glaxo was establishing itself in New Zealand, Henry Wellcome, a salesman and marketing maven (he sold his first product, "invisible ink"—really lemon juice—at age 16) and his pharmacist friend Silas Burroughs created Burroughs Wellcome & Company. They introduced the selling of medicine in tablet form (previously medicines were sold mostly as powders or liquids), and their patent on the equipment that compressed powdered medicines into tablets made them millionaires almost overnight.

Burroughs passed away shortly after, and Wellcome continued to build the firm with a special attention to investigating tropical diseases. He set up several research laboratories, including one in Sudan with a floating laboratory on the Nile River that enabled medical teams to reach regions that were not otherwise easily accessible. Research at Wellcome yielded the introduction of new forms of diphtheria vaccines and the development of a yellow fever vaccine. Wellcome, who was knighted by the Queen of England, passed away in 1936 and through his will created the Wellcome Trust, a charitable foundation to support medical research worldwide. Today, with an endowment of around £10 billion, it is one of the world's largest nongovernmental sources of funds for biomedical research.

The company's focus on research has earned several of its scientists Nobel Prizes. It has discovered important drugs including Purinethol, one of the first effective anticancer treatments, and Daraprim, which provided a new standard for protection against malaria. It also created Retrovir (AZT) for AIDS, the antiherpes drug Zovirax, and cough medicines Sudafed and Actifed.

In 1995 Glaxo and Wellcome merged to form Glaxo Wellcome. And, in 2000 Glaxo Wellcome and SmithKline Beecham joined forces to become GlaxoSmithKline. Today, the company produces more than 1,400 different brands including best sellers such as asthma medication Advair and antidepressant Wellbutrin. It's grown its over-the-counter offerings as well, producing an incredible nine billion Tums tablets, six billion Panadol pills, and 600 million tubes of toothpaste a year.

While community investment and giving back has been a piece of the DNA of the founding companies, the commitment has grown much more powerful as the firms have been woven together. "The pharmaceutical industry today sells 80 percent of its products to 20 percent of the world's population," said JP when he became CEO after the merger. "I don't want to be the CEO of a company that only caters to the rich. . . . I want those medicines in the hands of many more people who need them."[1]

With a mission to increase access to medicines, JP, a Fulbright scholar who originally intended to spend his career in research, launched initiatives to provide medicines to people who can't afford them. In addition to offering prescription savings cards in the United States, for example, GSK was the first to lower the prices of HIV/AIDS drugs to patients in Africa. JP also encourages GSK scientists to search for vaccines and cures for diseases such as malaria, which strike a patient population that can't pay for the drugs.

In addition to supporting increased access to its own medicines, GSK is involved in myriad programs that have created healthy changes in our communities. By funding the Rosalynn Carter Fellowships for Mental Health Journalism, for example, GSK has helped to improve the American public's negative perception about mental illness. It has established dozens of international projects, including one of the first projects in China to work directly with people living with HIV/AIDS in the provinces Yunnan and Xinjiang, where more than 50 percent of people living with HIV/AIDS in China are located. Through its support of the Ovarian Cancer National Alliance, which came in the form of the largest grant ever gifted to an ovarian cancer group, GSK has heightened the awareness of ovarian cancer—the fifth leading cause of cancer death among women in the United States—and increased patients' survival rates.

GSK is also involved in many programs that focus exclusively on improving the lives of children. Science in the Summer, for example, is a free science education program held in local Philadelphia public libraries designed to get kids excited about studying science with hands-on experiments. Zippy's Friends is a 24-week school-based program aimed at helping very young children cope with issues such family breakups, bullying, and bereavement. (The program is taught through story-based lessons starring a stick insect named Zippy.) Already deemed effective in Denmark and Lithuania, the program has been expanded to the United Kingdom, India, and Canada. GSK was also a founder of the Barretstown camp in County Kildare, Ireland, which offers seriously ill children a fun and safe environment. The first camp of its kind in Europe, it now provides therapeutic recreation for more than 1,500 children each year.

Employee involvement is part of the culture at GSK, with thousands of GSK workers worldwide donating their time. In Germany, for example, in September 2004, more than 500 employees from six GSK sites gave their time to 60 community projects, including building a bowling alley at an elderly care home, painting rooms in a women's shelter, and helping a local charity develop a marketing and PR plan. In addition, the company motivates employees to get involved by making cash donations to the charities where they have donated their time.

During 2004, for example, the company's Making a Difference program in the United Kingdom provided grants of £269,000 to more than 400 charities based on employee involvement; in the United States, GSK's Investment in Volunteer Excellence (GIVE) gave grants to 700 charitable organizations where employees volunteered, totaling more than $350,000. The company also matched employee and retiree donations to the value of $4 million and gave another $1.3 million to match what was donated by employees to the United Way campaign.

GSK has received a range of awards for its community investment activities. In 2004 it was a finalist at the Committee to Encourage Corporate Philanthropy awards. Its Personal Hygiene

& Sanitation Education (PHASE) program, which teaches the importance of hand-washing and other hygiene practices to improve the health of 200,000 children who live without basic sanitation, won a World Business Award organized by the UN Development Program and the International Chamber of Commerce. It has also been widely honored as a great work environment: GSK Belgium received a national award for being the most desirable place to work, GSK Poland won the Supportive Employer award, and GSK U.S. was named one of the 100 Best Companies by *Working Mother* magazine.

JP, who has been a leader in global pharmaceutical industry for 30 years—and who during that time has championed the search for treatments for HIV, tuberculosis, and malaria—has been the recipient of several prestigious awards as well. President Chirac of France awarded him the Chevalier de la Légion d'Honneur—the country's highest civilian honor (roughly equivalent to being knighted in England). The Cancer Research Institute honored him with the Oliver R. Grace Award for Distinguished Service in Advancing Cancer Research. *BusinessWeek* named him one of 50 "Stars of Europe" and presented him with the Marco Polo Award for GlaxoSmithKline's commitment to China. He is also the recipient of the Humanitarian Award from the Sabin Vaccine Institute and the Fulbright Association's Lifetime Achievement Medal.

In his essay here, JP discusses the new avenues he's pioneered to increase access to medicines, and how he's helped to create new and innovative partnerships so GSK doesn't have to take on the risk alone. He also discusses the company's most significant effort—and why it's worth $1 billion to him.

GOING BEYOND
COMMERCIAL TRANSACTIONS

Jean-Pierre Garnier, CEO, GlaxoSmithKline

Companies have to go beyond their zone of comfort and try to help with resolutions—in our case major world health problems.

At GlaxoSmithKline we say the mission of our company is to improve the quality of human life by enabling people to do more, feel better, and live longer. Although our products deliver clear benefits to patients around the world, that's not our whole story. I think that anyone sitting in my seat, seeing the millions of people affected by tragedies such as HIV and malaria, would ask: What can I do besides enriching my shareholders and protecting my employees?

Companies are expected to act responsibly, and for us, people's lives are at stake—that's the bottom line. Ensuring that our medicines and vaccines are available to as many people as possible, and developing medicines for diseases that strike patient populations that won't be able to pay for them, is not only the right thing to do, it's completely congruent with our mission to help people. This is what transforms a good company into a great company.

We have long been committed to communities around the world. Our total community investment in 2004 was valued at more than $600 million (that's a mixture of money and product donation, which we calculate at the wholesale price). It's an amount that equals more than 5 percent of our profits, which is a lot more than the average 1 percent given by most Fortune 500 companies.

Ensuring that everyone has access to medicine and that nobody falls through the safety net is one of the most essential issues in our industry today and the one that I am most passionate about. At GSK, we are confronted all the time with patients who need our medicine, who would see great benefits if they had it, but who can't get it because they can't afford it. This is a problem that exists worldwide, and is particularly tragic with diseases like malaria, TB, and HIV/AIDS in Africa. It's also a problem that exists in the United States—the richest country in the world. To make sure that all people have access to our products, we have had to come up with innovative solutions that go beyond traditional commercial transactions.

One program that illustrates this effort is the Orange Card, which we started in late 2001 as a discount card to help senior citizens pay for their medicines. At the time, an estimated 80 percent of retirees used a prescription drug every day, and about 30 percent—23 million seniors—didn't have any kind of drug coverage. They were forced to pay out of their own pocket, which for some was extremely difficult. Many patients found alternative means such as going to Mexico or Canada to try to buy the drugs cheaper. Others went through the Internet. A recent inquiry has revealed that roughly 80 percent of the drugs bought through the Internet were not in compliance with the FDA requirements.

The Orange Card—which gave 20 to 40 percent savings off the usual price of prescriptions—served as a real solution for disabled people and low-income seniors (singles who make under $30,000, or a couple who earns $40,000, or less) who did not have public or private insurance programs or other pharmaceutical benefit programs.

When we began this effort, we invited the rest of the industry to join, but many companies were hesitating, so we just went ahead. Hundreds of thousands of seniors signed up right away, and before too long, other companies began to realize that it was a good idea. Within six to nine months of the Orange Card launch, pharmaceutical companies decided to join forces and we created the Together Rx Card. It's the same concept, but now in addition to medicines from GSK, it included products from AstraZeneca, Sanofi-Aventis, Novartis, and more. This effort really shows the benefits of an industry banding together; until we ended the program when the new Medicare prescription drug coverage took effect in January 2006, we had several million people on Together Rx who were able to access 155 of the most common prescription drugs for less.

Based on the success of the program, we have begun to replicate the Orange Card elsewhere. One place that had a particular need for such a program was Lithuania. Patients in Lithuania must contribute toward the cost of prescription medicines, and many senior citizens don't get the treatment they need because they can't afford to pay and do not have private medical insurance. The Orange Card, which we launched in Lithuania in July 2004, helps to tackle this problem by giving all senior citizens a discount of up to 100 percent of the patient's contribution on all GSK prescriptions. The card was an instant success, by February 2005, only months after we launched it, thousands of patients had applied for an Orange Card, and 107 pharmacies had registered to participate.

While the Orange Card, and later Together Rx, has helped increase patient access to medicines, we know that there still are people who can't afford to buy drugs—even with the discount. For that patient population, we simply give the drugs away for free. I know this is something the media never likes to cover, but the fact is we give away more than $1 million in medicines each day to U.S. patients as part of our Patient Assistance Program. In addition, our international humanitarian product donation program provides essential medicines such as antibiotics to impoverished communities in over 100 countries and for disaster relief such as the Asian tsunami. In 2004 this was worth $90 million ($250,000 each day).

The biggest and most spectacular of our donation programs is the international effort to rid the world of the disfiguring and disabling tropical disease lymphatic filariasis (LF) by 2020. LF is a terrible disease that is spread through mosquitoes and can lead to arms and legs swelling to five times normal size, scaly elephantlike skin (giving the disease the common name of elephantiasis), and serious fevers. While you may not have seen the effects of this disease (except in documentaries), it is a major problem in Asia, Africa, and Latin America and one of the principal causes of permanent disability globally. There are more than one billion people who live in areas endemic to the disease, and there are over 120 million people who have it. LF is not curable, and sufferers are handicapped, unable to work, and become social outcasts in their villages.

In the 1990s it was discovered that one of our drugs, albendazole, which is used for various conditions associated with tropical diseases, could be taken as a prophylactic treatment to protect against LF. Tropical disease scientists have shown that communities that take, per person, one albendazole tablet plus another antifilarial medicine once a year, every year, for five years, can eliminate transmission of this disease—protecting them for life.

With the encouragement of former President Jimmy Carter and the Carter Foundation, we helped found the Global Alliance to Eliminate Lymphatic Filariasis, which now includes the WHO, the Ministries of Health of LF-endemic countries, and more than 40 organizations from public and private sectors, academia, government bodies, and nongovernment organizations. We committed to donate as much albendazole as required to treat the one billion people in 83 countries who are at risk. We also provide significant financial support for coalition building, workshops, and communications.

It's an enormous program, and the truth is that it's a daunting task. To interrupt transmission of LF, it's necessary to treat more than 80 percent of the entire at-risk populations. Many of these people live in the most inaccessible of places, which require teams of health workers and community volunteers to venture into secluded rural communities, jungle villages, and overcrowded urban shanty dwellings to administer the medicine. They also have to ensure that people actually take the tablets, which means that the community needs to understand the disease and the global plan to prevent transmission. Working with very different cultures, we have had to learn about the best ways to work with the head of the village or the medicine man so that together we can end this disease. The sense of scale on this project is huge. In one day in Sri Lanka, 50,000 volunteers dispensed this free medicine to 10 million people! We have just built a new plant to make the very large quantities of medicine that will be required over the coming years.

The incredible thing is that the program is working. Since the effort began in 1998, we have given away more than 350 million tablets—more than 100 million people are being reached by receiving the preventative treatment. What is really exciting is that some of the first countries to start have now completed five years of treatment. The preliminary results are fantastic. In Egypt, 80 percent of the villages with LF are now clear of the disease. We are optimistic about the countries where the program is not yet finished, such as Bangladesh and Sri Lanka plus many countries in Africa.

It's been a wonderful adventure, and through this program we have the rare opportunity to eliminate a disease. As more people join the program, fewer people will carry the parasite in their blood, transmission by the mosquitoes will cease, and the disease will die out. Our contribution is worth more than $1 billion over 20 years. This is our most significant program and will be a great victory for the billion people at risk of getting LF. It will be a great victory for us as well; GSK will be proud of its part in eliminating a disease.

As a for-profit company, simply giving away our products obviously isn't always the answer. We have several programs where we make drugs and sell them at no profit. In 1997 we became the first company to lower our prices for HIV/AIDS products in Africa. In 2004, we tripled shipments of Combivir tablets to help alleviate the disease in the developing world. Although we are the number-one supplier of HIV medicine to Africa, we don't make any profit there.

In fact, there are many drugs that we need to develop and distribute, from which we will never make a profit. While these medicines are important for saving lives, they are not a business priority because they have little commercial appeal. We don't want to tell our scientists *not* to look for those drugs for rare and difficult diseases just because there's little commercial incentive, though. At the same time, we know that we can't charge our shareholders for it. We believe that public-private partnerships are a creative solution to this conundrum, and we have developed a number of these with funders such as the Bill and Melinda Gates Foundation.

Bill Gates has been staunchly committed to combating malaria, one of the world's biggest killers, and we were able to show him our prototype malaria vaccines and medicines that we were interested in moving ahead to test in human trials. This type of testing is very expensive (it could easily be several hundred million dollars), and we didn't feel that we could invest that amount since we knew we would never make a profit from the vaccine. Bill and his team of experts believed what they saw had promise and agreed to fund the trial.

We are ecstatic about this kind of partnership because everybody wins. It has already led to a scientific breakthrough with a malaria vaccine called Mosquirix (named after mosquito and for Rixensart, Belgium, a small town where we did our research).

The vaccine, which was tested in large trials in Africa, protected a significant percentage of children against malaria. It also reconfirmed the vaccine's safety in one- to four-year-old children. Further studies are needed, and we still have several years of work ahead of us, but the vaccine shows great potential at helping to prevent malaria—a disease that kills more children in sub-Saharan Africa than any other infectious disease. For us, behaving responsibly isn't just about what we give away; it's also about what we get back. We live in a time where the public believes that companies should do more because governments are not able to solve the big problems of the world anymore. There's a strong feeling in society that most multinational companies are more powerful than countries. (They are certainly richer than some countries.)

We've determined that companies have to go beyond their zone of comfort and try to help with resolutions—in our case major world health problems. That is what has encouraged us to enter into the single largest donation program for LF, provide HIV drugs at cost in Africa, and to enter in the malaria vaccine discovery and development program. We believe there is a need for our company to go beyond the narrow and common dictum that a business must turn a profit every quarter and return everything to the shareholders.

Shareholders can be very critical of everything that you spend money on; they mention everything—even the printing costs for the annual report. "Why don't you stop doing that, you are wasting money," they say! I have, however, never had a shareholder tell me we are giving away too much, or comment negatively on our efforts to increase people's access to our medicines.

Shareholders understand that although these efforts cost money, being recognized as generous in our communities is of great benefit. Our company's reputation improves; people trust the company more. It helps foster a relationship with our consumers, and it helps with our international and domestic business dealings. It also helps with our employees. Our scientists, who are by nature idealistic people, are motivated to work with a company that has this kind of attitude toward people who have nothing and nobody to defend them.

When we started these efforts, we knew we could have a hand in improving the health of our communities. As we have become more involved, as we have broadened our goals to help people live better longer, and as we have seen firsthand what a modest investment, hard work, and passion can accomplish, we have also improved the health of our company.

CHAPTER 10

PREDICTING— AND CHANGING— THE FUTURE: INTEL

Intel has made its contribution not only in ushering in the Digital Age but by advancing social causes as well.

Craig Barrett, the chairman of Intel, says when he was a kid he wanted to be a forest ranger, but since there was no School of Forestry at Stanford (where he attended university), he settled on becoming an engineer. Although Craig, a Fulbright Fellow with a penchant for lizard-skin boots and cowboy hats, has never publicly professed to wanting to be a rock star, that alternative aspiration made itself clear in 2005 when the then-65-year-old CEO joined Aerosmith's Steven Tyler for a live version of "Walk This Way" at the International Consumer Electronics Show in Las Vegas.

The audience was warned that Barrett can't carry a tune, and he reportedly proved that point, but the idea he was really aiming to get across—a demonstration of new software that allows users to mix their own music—was well received. It was another example of how Craig ensures that Intel, the company behind memory chips and the microprocessor—two of the most important building blocks in modern technology—stays on the cutting edge of the computer age. It was also a reminder that despite the sexier career choices Craig may have desired, he found his real calling merging his mind for material science and his talent for leadership.

Intel, which was founded in 1968 and did $38.8 billion in sales in 2005, is the leading semiconductor maker in the world. Intel's chips are found inside 90 percent of the world's computers and populate products from Internet servers to cell phones to antilock brakes. For its contributions to our increasingly technology-dependent society, the Santa Clara, California, firm has been called "the essential firm of the digital age."[1]

Intel is the brainchild of chemist and physicist Gordon Moore and physicist Bob Noyce. Both had defected from Fairchild Semiconductor (which they had founded and which was one of the first Silicon Valley companies). At 39 and 40 years old, respectively, they had already established themselves in the semiconductor industry. Bob received notoriety (and several patents) for coinventing the integrated circuit (a piece of silicon with more than one transistor), an innovation upon which modern computing, communications, manufacturing, and transport systems are all dependent. Building upon this development, in 1965, Gordon predicted that the number of transistors that could fit on a piece of silicon would double in power and halve in price every 18 months. Now known as "Moore's Law" (although that name reportedly makes the modest Gordon cringe), the idea has proven itself time and again, and—as Gordon also predicted—led to the proliferation of products from personal computers and cellular phones.

The two scientists planned on naming the start-up after themselves and calling it "Moore Noyce." They quickly determined however, that the name wouldn't best suit an electronics company inasmuch as noise is associated with bad interference. They momentarily settled on NM Electronics before switching to Integrated Electronics, which immediately became "Intel" for short. They hired one of their former colleagues, chemical engineer Andy Grove, as the director of operations. The so-called Dream Team—whose one-page business plan simply stated they wanted to "work in silicon and do interesting things"[2]— set out to produce the world's first semiconductor-based memory chips.

The first year the company did revenues of about $3,000— the "interest on the money in the bank," according to Gordon Moore.[3] In 1970, Intel developed the dynamic memory (DRAM) chip, called the 1130. It was the first that was inexpensive enough to be used for memory in mainframe computers. A year later, Intel was turning a profit and became a publicly traded company.

The company's next big breakthrough came thanks to the increasing popularity of scientific calculators. It was a tough market to crack because big companies such as Texas Instruments and Casio had already teamed up with the established semiconductor companies. Then opportunity struck for Intel when Busicom, a Japanese start-up with a desire to build a set of high-end products, took a chance on hiring the fledgling Intel to create the chips.

At the time, all logic chips were custom-designed for each customer's product and were used to perform calculations and execute programs. Unlike memory chips, they didn't store instructions and data. One Intel engineer, Ted Hoff, decided that instead of designing 12 custom chips as Busicom suggested, he would build a set of four chips with a central processing unit, which could be used for logic and memory. With this innovation, Intel birthed the first general-purpose microprocessor chip. (Of course the term *microprocessor* would not enter the lexicon for many years.) Most exciting about the invention were the possibilities beyond calculators—it became clear that the microprocessor had the ability to power everything in our daily world, from elevators to traffic lights.

There was one major problem for Intel, though. It didn't own the rights to its new technological invention, Busicom, the company that paid for it, did. In a somewhat amazing twist of fate for Intel, Busicom, which was poorly financed, began running out of cash and sold the invention back to the company for the production cost. For $60,000 Intel gained the complete rights to the microprocessor.

Bolstered by its new technology, Intel introduced the model 4004 microprocessor in 1971. The chip, which was the size of a thumbnail and squeezed 2,300 transistors on a sliver of silicon, could deliver the same amount of computing power as the first electronic computer. A year later, the model 8008 microprocessor had 3,500 transistors. Driven by Moore's Law, Intel engineers constantly reduced the size of transistors within chips to fit more on a single silicon wafer and simultaneously reduced each chip's cost and increased its speed. By 1981, Intel's 16-bit 8086 and 8-bit 8088 processors were more powerful than anything previously imagined, and the company won an unprecedented 2,500 design awards in one year.

In 1986, IBM selected the Intel 8088 microprocessor to run its first desktop personal computer. With the PC revolution, came the necessity to produce tens of millions of chips a year—something the prophetic founders of Intel hadn't even anticipated and something that changed the direction of the company. With the new demand, then-Intel CEO Andy Grove decided to exit the memory-chip market to focus on microprocessors. It was a move that positioned the company to become one of the largest and most successful businesses in the world.

In 1997, *Time* magazine named Intel's Andy Grove "the person most responsible for the amazing growth in the power and innovative potential of microchips," its Man of the Year. Putting the accomplishment into a societal context, it wrote, "The microchip has become—like the steam engine, electricity and the assembly line—an advance that propels a new economy."[4]

Today, despite issues including several charges of antitrust violations, and an unlawful monopoly allegation by competitor Advanced Micro Devices, Intel remains the largest microchip maker and is just as relevant in its role of powering the world with its tiny silicon chips. And, as the company continues to embrace its previously planned future with more transistors on each chip, it has also expanded into new lines of business that are representative of today's age. In one of its newest partnerships, the number-one chipmaker joined forces with Oscar-winning actor Morgan Freeman to form a digital entertainment company that will allow consumers to watch movies online before they come out on DVD. As in the past, Intel continues to demonstrate a keen ability to predict—and advance—the future.

Intel has made its contribution not only in ushering in the Digital Age but by advancing social causes as well. The company, deemed one of the most generous, has been named one of the "100 Best Corporate Citizens" by *Business Ethics* magazine and one of "The World's Most Socially Responsible Companies" by *Global Finance*. It gave nearly $107 million in donations in 2004. Although Intel is focused on environmental stewardship and safety, diversity, and community building, it is most deeply committed to education (in particular strengthening math, computer science, and engineering programs). "We like to say of the external priorities we have at Intel, the top priority is education, the second priority is education, and the third priority is education," says Craig. "We don't do golf tournaments, we don't sponsor football games. We think doing the right thing is helping to prepare young people—in the United States or wherever they are—to become contributing members of society."

The company offers a myriad of education-bolstering programs, many of which Craig discusses in depth in his essay later in this chapter, all of which have achieved tremendous impact. Take for example, "Connected to Schools," which integrates many of its education, diversity, and volunteer programs, and the success that program has achieved in the state of Arizona. In 2002, 20 percent of K-12 schools in Arizona were underperforming academically. Intel selected two urban schools in Phoenix, and in less than a year it trained 89 percent of the faculty in the Intel Teach to the Future program, which aims to aid teachers in integrating technology into the classroom. The company helped both schools receive computer labs valued at $50,000 each. Both schools have now moved off the state's underperforming list, and their students showed an average of 25 to 29 percent improvement on the state's proficiency exams.

In addition to bringing modern technology into schools, the company strikes up unique partnerships with various types of organizations to find new ways for technology to improve people's lives. It has, for example, created a consortium—the first of its kind—with the Alzheimer's Association to fund more than $1 million in research to develop new models of Alzheimer's care based on current and evolving technologies in computing, communications, and home health care. In addition, it's working with Seattle's Fred Hutchinson Cancer Research Center to create ways to use semiconductor equipment, previously used to detect microscopic imperfections, to search for early stages of cancer. Also in the health care arena, it's working with the Clalit's Schneider Children's Medical Center of Israel to use wireless LAN technology to provide instant access to patient records from anywhere in the Clalit network and at any point within the hospital.

Intel also places great effort into reducing its environmental footprint. Its global waste recycling teams exceeded their goals for 2004 by recycling more than 63 percent of the company's chemical waste and 73 percent of its solid waste worldwide. The company also favors using renewable resources wherever possible. In fact, Intel, which has a research and manufacturing center near Portland, Oregon, is that state's largest retail renewable power user and one of the largest purchasers in the western United States. It also implemented power management on enough laptop displays and desktop monitors to save 9.65 million kilowatt-hours in 2004, which is equal to enough electricity to light 11,000 U.S. homes for a month. In addition to the environmental benefits, Intel saw a monetary upside as well: the effort saved $482,000 in 2004.

Of course much of Intel's responsible approach shows up closer to its core—with the people who work in its very own headquarters, offices, and laboratories—something that has earned it a spot on *Working Mother* magazine's "100 Best Companies for Working Mothers" and a consistent ranking on *Fortune's* "100 Best Companies to Work For" survey. The company has always promoted an egalitarian philosophy (no one has an assigned parking spot, and everyone—even Craig Barrett—works from a cubicle). All employees are given stock options—something that has produced thousands of millionaires. The company also offers flexible work hours, telecommuting, and three-month paid sabbaticals for every seven years of service, and a few years ago, it gave a free computer for every employee to take home for personal use. The result is not just happier but also more loyal employees. More than half of Intel employees have spent 5 to 20 years at the company, and more than 30 percent of new hires were referred by current employees.

The health and safety of its workers is considered a top priority, and the company has established itself as a leader in reducing injury rates. In fact, Intel's safety performance and practices are so highly regarded that the Columbia Accident Investigation

Board turned to the company for information in the aftermath of the Space Shuttle tragedy.

By making injury reduction a corporate priority (for every lost-day case, Craig receives a written document or e-mail within 24 hours that describes the situation, the corrective action, and any other follow-up activities), the company has slashed its recordable injury rate. Again, it's not just the right thing to do: this diligence has increased the number of productive workdays companywide in 2003 and achieved a cost avoidance of $14.4 million, a 43 percent improvement over 2002.

In May 2005, Craig—who had been at Intel since 1974 and served as the company's CEO since 1998—was elevated to chairman, succeeding Andy Grove. Following company policy, at 65 years old, he also relinquished the CEO title to Paul Otellini (another longtime Intel vet, who in 1989 worked as a technical assistant to Andy Grove and reportedly taught him how to use a PC).

As chairman, Craig will stay committed to preparing Intel for the future. He will also stay active in improving education both from inside and from outside the company. Craig will continue to contribute as a board member of Achieve, Inc., a partner with the Education Trust, and the force behind the Barrett Honors College at Arizona State University. (Established thanks to a $10 million gift from Craig and his wife Barbara—the largest personal gift ever given to Arizona State at that time—it was one of the first honors colleges in the United States and recently ranked one of the top eight honors programs in the country by *Money* magazine.) In his essay here, he talks about the importance of improving educational programs and how that will have a real impact on the future of Intel—and the future of the United States.

TEACH TO THE FUTURE

Craig Barrett, Chairman, Intel

Sometimes I think we need another good punch in the eye, like the one we had in 1957 when the Soviet Union launched Sputnik, the world's first satellite.

At Intel we've always included in our mission statement our basic business philosophy that we should be good citizens in every community in which we operate. There are lots of ways to interpret that charter. The simplest is the understanding that a company's primary job is to make money for its shareholders and to provide jobs for its employees. We've always taken a somewhat broader attitude, though. In addition to the traditional responsibilities of making quality products that meet the needs of our customers, there are new expectations such as practicing uncompromising integrity, being an asset in our communities, sharing knowledge with developing economies, and continually improving environmental performance.

For many years we've kept and refined a Corporate Code of Conduct for employees. This document continued to grow and grow as it became necessary to add additional potential situations and interactions with suppliers and customers. It eventually evolved into something that was 400 pages long. Ultimately, we sat back and said, "This is nonsense. What we need to convey to employees is something simple: Intel is all about doing the right things the right way." We realized we didn't have to be hyper-specific about this, and we were able to fit our philosophy of doing the right thing in a short pamphlet.

Of course, as a responsible company, we must try to maximize shareholder value—we must, however, approach it with a long-term view in mind. Part of the long-term maximization of shareholder value is having and running a profitable business, and the other part consists of investing for the future. There are a variety of ways to invest in the future. It requires investing in the research and development of new products, investing in the future in the brand, investing in recruiting the best employees, and providing them with professional development opportunities.

At Intel, we also view investing in educational programs as essential not only to our future growth and success but also to create long-term sustainable change in our education systems. As the chairman of a U.S. flagship company—and as a father and grandfather of kids who live in this country—I'm troubled by the future competitiveness of the United States. Education is the fuel that drives the global economy, but our K-12 system has broken down. While other countries are revving up their education engines, our students are falling far behind. In one recent study American 15-year-olds ranked twenty-fourth out of 29 industrialized nations (behind South Korea, Japan, Canada, and most of Europe) on practical math applications. In another test, fourth-graders in Taiwan and Singapore outperformed their peers in the United States in both math and science. In Singapore, 44 percent of eighth-graders scored at the most advanced level in math, and 38 percent of students in Taiwan reached that level, compared to just 7 percent of American students.

More troubling still is a report released by Achieve, Inc., which reveals one reason that explains why we're lagging behind: we've institutionalized low performance through low expectations. Our high schools only expect a small number of students to take the advanced math and science courses that all young people need.

Currently, not a single state requires every high school student to take a college-and-work-preparatory curriculum in order to earn a diploma. In math, only four states (Alabama, Arkansas, Mississippi, and South Carolina) require that all students complete four or more math courses for graduation, and just three states (Arkansas, Texas, and Indiana) require the key subjects Algebra I, Geometry, and Algebra II. Even more alarming, several states, concerned about their high school passing rates, are considering easing up on their graduation standards—even though their exit exams are pegged below the tenth-grade level (and similar to material that foreign students cover in the eighth-grade).

When it comes to higher education, the picture is also bleak. Although college enrollments have been booming in the United States, China graduates twice as many students with baccalaureate degrees and six times as many engineering majors. India and Singapore have started pumping out scientists through top-notch undergraduate programs. In 2001, India graduated almost a million more students from college than the United States, including 100,000 more in the sciences and 60,000 more in engineering. And, for the first time, foreign nations are set to overtake the United States in annual production of U.S. patents. And the U.S. share of published papers in science and engineering is declining, with Europe now ranked first and Asia's share rapidly increasing.

These trends should give any American chairman or CEO pause—and they certainly bother me tremendously. Science and technology are what drive economic growth and national security in the United States, and our educational system is no longer producing enough qualified graduates in these fields to keep up with the demand. Our corporations are going begging for talent, as foreign scientists and engineers choose to stay at home, realizing that they can find exciting, well-paying jobs on their own doorsteps. Already, the balance of innovation has begun to tilt eastward, as China and India begin taking their own products to market.

If this isn't addressed, we are going to find ourselves in a period of weak or negative economic growth. We are going to find ourselves in a period of a decreasing standard of living (that is, decreasing real wages compared to the rest of the world). And, we are going to find ourselves in a position where the United States is no longer leading as an industrial power, setting global standards and having an international reach. The United States will look much more like some of the Western European countries that are effectively retreating—where the economies are a little bit like glaciers in a period of global warming.

Sometimes I think we need another good punch in the eye, like the one we had in 1957 when the Soviet Union launched Sputnik, the world's first satellite. Jolted by the competition, the United States shook its complacency and pushed for excellence in mathematics and science, resulting in dramatic increases in enrollments and a subsequent rise in the number of scientists and engineers. In turn, these workers created whole new generations of technology and commercial applications that led to the nation's unprecedented prosperity and preeminence in the global economy.

I'm not sure what it will take to shake the United States out of its current complacency, but we have committed to investing heavily (about $100 million a year, almost $1 billion overall) to improve education and to help us remain competitive for jobs and growth.

Some of the education programs that we sponsor are targeted at individual students; some of them are targeted at teachers; some of them are targeted at research and development activities at universities. All of our future employees—and all the young children in today's world—need to have a comprehension of math, engineering, and science.

Perhaps the programs that have had the biggest impact on me personally are the Intel Science Talent Search in the United States and the Intel International Science and Engineering Fair, both of which reward young children for their accomplishments and competency in math and science and engineering. We sponsor these programs to demonstrate to young children that they don't have to be an all-American basketball or football player to get recognition. The Science Talent Search is considered the "junior Nobel Prize" and is a 64-year-old program that has been sponsored by Intel since 1998. We recently had more than 1,600 students apply for the prize. The International Science and Engineering Fair recently brought together more than 1,400 young scientists from around the world who shared ideas, showcased groundbreaking projects, and competed for $3 million in scholarships and prizes.

I'm always in awe of the students who participate in this competition. When I meet with these finalists at our annual event, I feel optimistic about the future of American ingenuity. These young researchers are destined for great things in mathematics, science, engineering, and other fields. Like previous finalists, some of them no doubt will win Nobel Prizes, Fields Medals, National Medals of Science, and MacArthur Foundation "Genius Grants." They may be teenagers, but the brilliance of their work makes my own PhD dissertation look dim in comparison.

I know, though, that these students are the exceptions. We have a lot of work to do to foster the development of the majority of young people. One of the greatest challenges in education—not just in the United States, but all over the world—is getting K-12 teachers knowledgeable about math and science and technology. That's why we began a program called the Teach to the Future, which trains teachers. We run this program in 33 countries, including Australia, Chile, Turkey, the Ukraine, and Vietnam. In the past five years, we've trained some three million teachers, and more importantly, we're seeing an impact: evaluations have confirmed positive results in the classroom.

We also have a program called the Intel Computer Clubhouse Network. These are clubhouses that go into economically deprived (read that *poor*) areas to give kids after-school opportunities not just to learn how to use computers but to learn how to use computers to do something that they are interested in doing that will stimulate them and may even spark an interest that might lead to gainful employment. We've expanded these clubhouses around the world, with sites launched in Ireland, Ramallah/West Bank, and South Africa. We recently inaugurated our one-hundredth Computer Clubhouse in Washington, DC.

It shouldn't come as a surprise that government relationships play a crucial role in our education efforts. Such relationships have helped us reduce our costs for teacher training, while continuing to grow our program offerings. We can't simply depend on help from the governments, though. Changes of the scale we need cannot occur without significant support from the business community, which must be more involved in efforts to improve American education. For business, this is not just a "nice to do"—although it certainly is the right thing to do. In a very real sense it is a "must do" because the success of our enterprises depends on the quality of the education in our classrooms. The success of our businesses is tied to the quality and quantity of the teachers in our classrooms and their ability to create a deep pool of highly skilled people at home who can keep pushing the boundaries of knowledge and innovation.

From a personal standpoint, outside the company, my wife and I both believe that the most valuable gift you can give any young person is a good education. We both received scholarships for higher education, and neither one of us could have afforded the education activities we had without scholarships and fellowships. We are strong supporters of giving back primarily at the university level to facilitate those activities.

It's important to be successful. If you are successful, it's important to give something back. It's important to recognize that the resources in the world are finite and you have to leave a small footprint when you pass through the world, whether it is in your personal life or in business. If you set up your value system, and then you adhere to doing the right thing the right way, you can achieve great results. What I've found is that the system knows what to do, the people know what to do, as long as you give them those very simple guidelines. People know how to behave as long as you put them in a position where they can exercise responsibility and judgment. I know this to be true because of what I've seen from our 95,000 employees at Intel. They have made Intel's accomplishments possible, and I find they nearly always do the right thing.

CHAPTER 11

SERVING PEOPLE FIRST: STARBUCKS

One impressive fact is that Starbucks is also committed to communities where it doesn't have a presence.

W hen Jim Donald became the CEO of Starbucks in March 2005, his first day on the job didn't look like what you'd expect of the top brass at one of the world's most influential brands. At 3 a.m. the Starbucks CEO began working the third shift at the company's Kent, Washington, coffee roasting plant. And, he didn't cut out for lunch (which takes place at a time that looks a lot more like breakfast); he sat down for Texas barbecue with the rest of the employees—or "partners" in Starbucks parlance. "I like barbecue," he said by way of explanation. "So do they."[1]

Jim, who replaced former Starbucks CEO Orin Smith, brings a lot more to his new post than a love of barbecue. He's spent the past two and a half years training for this job in the role of president of Starbucks North America. That assignment had him running operations at a time when the company's net income skyrocketed approximately 85 percent and worldwide sales climbed to $5.3 billion.

While Jim is the first nonhomegrown CEO to run Starbucks, and this is his first gig in coffee, he's hardly a stranger in the food industry. Jim previously spent 35 years in the supermarket business, a career he started when he was 16 years old bagging groceries at Publix. From there he went to Albertsons, where he became valued as a turnaround guy and was sent from one distressed store to the next. (He took 15 years to finish his undergraduate degree because of the constant moving and his commitment to the supermarket chain.)

Jim's down-to-earth style and comfort level with all types of people—from supermarket executives to store clerks—was apparent as he rose through the ranks. In 1991 Sam Walton, the famed founder of Wal-Mart, personally tapped him to help expand the giant discounter into the supermarket business. Later, Jim moved to Safeway, where he managed 130 stores and 10,000 employees. By 1996, he was named CEO, president, and chairman of Pathmark, a regional supermarket chain in New York, New Jersey, and Philadelphia, which was struggling with declining growth. Under Jim's leadership, Pathmark emerged from bankruptcy proceedings to become a public company.

Although Jim is lauded as a turnaround specialist, it's well known that Starbucks isn't—and never was—broken. Since its beginnings, in fact, Starbucks has enjoyed gangbuster growth. Maintaining that energy, though, requires the same skills that Jim honed in the supermarket business.

As Howard Schultz, the brains behind the modern Starbucks and the company's chairman has said, "The people who operate grocery stores are the best at what they do because they have to operate within a set of disciplines, because of the competitive nature of the business, the commodity nature of the business and how low margin it is." Howard has also said he was also drawn to

Jim's "limitless energy" (when not volunteering for 3 a.m. shifts, he's known to work from dawn to midnight), which Howard believes can help take the company to 30,000 stores across the globe.[2]

It's odd to consider that the Starbucks we know today for its grande green tea Frappuccino, venti vanilla cappuccino, or tall soy no-foam decaf latte, began without a prepared drink in sight. The original Starbucks was the brainchild of three coffee aficionados, English teacher Jerry Baldwin, history teacher Zev Siegl, and writer Gordon Bowker. The three friends invested $1,350 and launched a company to sell fresh-roasted gourmet coffee beans and the brewing and roasting equipment so that customers could do it themselves. The first store, which opened in 1971 in Seattle's Pike Place Market (a place originally designed in 1907 to bring farmers and consumers together), quickly garnered a word-of-mouth following, and Starbucks became a destination for coffee lovers.

By 1980 Starbucks had six retail stores and established itself as the largest roaster in Washington State. To keep up with demand, Starbucks was snapping up merchandise such as plastic drip coffee makers in large enough quantities to attract the attention of New York-based housewares salesman Howard Schultz. In 1981 Howard went to investigate what the Seattle company was all about. Legend has it that he drank coffee that was better than any he'd had before and he spent the next year trying to convince Starbucks to expand across the country—and to hire him to execute that plan.

Starbucks did hire Howard in 1982, and although he sometimes felt he didn't fit in (he wore suits when mostly everyone else wore Birkenstocks), he loved his job. Before long, he went on a business trip to Milan, which would change his life—and the direction of Starbucks. While in Italy, Howard became intrigued with the Italian coffee culture and its espresso bars, where customers lingered long after their cups of coffee were completed. He had his first cafe latte and a big idea: "Starbucks could be a great *experience*, and not just a great retail store."[3]

While Howard became obsessed with Italy's communities built on coffee, his bosses back home were hardly as enthused. After all, their plan was to sell whole beans, not enter the risky restaurant business. Still, Howard pressed them, and in 1984 he was given the opportunity to test a small espresso bar in the corner of a Starbucks store. It proved to be an immediate hit: almost 400 customers passed through the store on opening day, and after two months in business the bar was serving 800 patrons a day.

The founders of Starbucks weren't convinced of the new direction however, and in 1985 Howard left to open his own coffee house, Il Giornale (it was named for Italy's largest newspaper), which sold coffee drinks made with Starbucks beans. Howard always wanted the Starbucks name, though, and in 1987 opportunity struck when the coffee company was put up for sale. Howard raised $3.8 million by convincing investors of a bold plan: 125 outlets in the next five years.

Now under Howard's helm, Starbucks' mermaid logo got a makeover (let's say she was more "exposed" in the early days) and the six existing Starbucks' roasting shops were converted into Howard's version of Italian-style coffeehouses. Over the next five years, Howard's vision for the company was realized. The coffeehouses achieved "a neighborhood feel" and customers became "regulars." The company also exceeded its growth goal: by 1992 there were 165 cafes in operation and Starbucks was a publicly traded company with an even more ambitious expansion plan.

Starbucks, and Howard, never slowed down, and today the company is the leading retailer, roaster, and brand of specialty coffee in the world. There are cafes in more than 35 countries in North America, Latin America, Europe, the Middle East and Asia Pacific. In addition to selling coffee drinks, Starbucks produces and sells a wide variety of consumer products including Tazo's teas, and it licenses its brand on grocery store products from packaged drinks to ice cream.

The coffee empire also includes Seattle Coffee Company, which runs the Seattle's Best Coffee and Torrefazione Italia coffee brands in the United States. The company is involved in some less linear extensions as well, including a successful foray into the music business by selecting music for its XM satellite radio station and selling CDs at its stores. (More than a quarter of the three million copies of the Ray Charles' CD *Genius Loves Company* sold in the United States were bought in Starbucks cafes.)

These days, it seems like Starbucks are everywhere—from Tallahassee to Tokyo—something that's made the company a target of antiglobalization activists. But while Starbucks, like most multinational companies, has its share of critics (Google "Starbucks" and see that the fourth link is a site called ihatestarbucks.com), there's overwhelming evidence that Starbucks actually makes a positive difference in the areas it calls home.

Take, for example, how Starbucks has benefited the city of San Francisco alone. In 2004, Starbucks employed more than 1,000 local residents and paid them $19 million in wages and benefits. And, going a step beyond the call of normal business duty, the company contributed $98,000 in grants and product donations to local nonprofits. By encouraging its employees and customers to volunteer, it was able to give another 400 hours of service in the community. (That's the equivalent of one person working full-time for 10 weeks.)

Perhaps more impressive is that Starbucks is also committed to communities where it doesn't have a presence. Consider Harlem, where Starbucks opened its second location in 2001, and subsequently closed the store after three years of poor performance. While Starbucks left its economic stake in the community, it never stopped investing in bettering it. In April 2004, for example, a team of 85 Starbucks employees and community members volunteered more than 400 hours beautifying St. Nicholas Park by spreading compost, planting perennials, and clearing brush. Starbucks also contributed financially by donating thousands of dollars to the community's parks and to the area's annual film festival.

While much of giving back at Starbucks is on a local level, the company also has a foundation, launched in 1997, which formalizes the contributions on a national scale. In 2004, Starbucks donated $14.6 million, or 2.3 percent of the company's before-tax earnings. The foundation is dedicated to improving the lives of young people in underserved communities through literacy programs such as America SCORES, an initiative that combines soccer and creative writing to inspire teamwork. The foundation also has a partnership with Jumpstart, an organization that pairs trained college students for one-on-one tutoring to at-risk preschoolers. Funding from Starbucks has enabled the program to expand to 57 sites across the United States. Starbucks staff also offered their creative talents to develop new brand identity and marketing materials—something that has helped raise the visibility of the organization.

The company has also given significantly—and encouraged employees and customers to do the same—in instances of emergency. The most recent example is the company's $5 million five-year commitment to the victims of Hurricane Katrina. (Howard's family foundation pledged an additional $1 million.) In addition to the financial commitment, Starbucks has donated more than 30,000 pounds of ground coffee; 235,000 bottles of water; and 9,600 bottled drinks to the relief workers. Starbucks employees have volunteered to deliver brewed coffee, pastries, bottled water, and ground coffee to police and fire rescue personnel, local emergency service providers, and utility workers who are working in the affected areas. Through a program called the CUP (Caring Unites Partners) Fund, the company and employees are able to help other employees cope with the effects of natural disasters or other catastrophes with cash grants. In another effort to help its employees, the company committed to extending benefits, pay, and assistance to employees who were affected by the disaster.

Every time Starbucks opens a new store, an average of 16 new jobs are created. What matters most, though, is that they are good jobs. (For the past six years, in fact, Starbucks has been named on *Fortune*'s list of the "100 Best Companies to Work For.") Howard has said that he built Starbucks with the goal to create "the kind of company that my father never got the chance to work for, in which people were respected."[4] In 1988—the year Howard's father died (with no savings or pension)—Starbucks began the unusual practice of offering comprehensive health benefits to all employees, including part-time workers.

Starbucks has also stepped forward as a leader in trying to improve the health care crisis, where more than 43 million Americans don't have health insurance and the rising costs of health care coverage are making it more difficult for individuals and employers to purchase affordable policies. (Starbucks itself has reported double-digit increases over the past four years for the health care coverage it provides to employees). In an effort to effect change, Starbucks has sponsored Cover the Uninsured Week, an annual campaign focused on expanding access to affordable quality health care coverage.

Starbucks' commitment to those who work there extends beyond the folks who work in the corporate offices or coffeehouses to the farmers who produce coffee for the company. Starbucks doesn't own coffee farms, grow its own coffee, or employ growers, but it does treat the farmers with whom it works with care. Starbucks has always paid top dollar for coffee—almost twice as much as other buyers (it paid $1.20 a pound in 2004)—to get the highest-quality coffee and ensure that coffee farmers can cover their production costs and earn a profit. This is especially significant considering the current crisis in coffee production. Since the late 1990s, an oversupply of low-grade coffee has flooded the market and suppressed prices—something that hurt business for all coffee farmers. Starbucks, in an effort to lessen the problem, launched the Farmer Support Center in San Jose, Costa Rica, in 2004, which provides agricultural expertise to farmers (it houses a team of experts in soil management and field-crop production) and builds relationships with coffee farmers and their communities.

Recently, Starbucks expanded beyond improving communities through the coffee sold at its stores to improving them through the water it sells as well. In 2005, the company acquired and began selling Ethos Water, a natural bottled spring water business founded by social entrepreneurs Peter Thum and Jonathan Greenblatt as a means to raise awareness and funds to bring clean water to children around the world. (Lack of clean water is one of the world's greatest health problems. It's a problem that's fixable, though; in some regions a mere $25 could enable access to an adequate amount of clean water for one person.)

Under the simple concept "water for water," five cents from every bottle of Ethos Water purchased at Starbucks is donated to nonprofit organizations that are helping to alleviate the world water crisis, such as UNICEF, CARE, WaterAid, and WaterPartners International. Through the sale of Ethos Water, Starbucks is currently supporting humanitarian water projects in Bangladesh, the Democratic Republic of Congo, Ethiopia, Honduras, India, and Kenya. The effort is expected to raise $10 million by 2010 to help children and their communities get clean water. It's also expected to raise awareness about the world water crisis and encourage others to work toward finding a sustainable solution.

Today, there are more than 10,000 Starbucks coffeehouses scattered across the globe, and the company has achieved great financial success. (The stock has split five times since its IPO in 1992.) At the same time, the original store in the Pike Place Market still exists. (Howard reportedly still keeps a key from the store in his pocket.) While Jim may not have been at Starbucks since the earliest days, he says that the first store serves him as a reminder of the ideals the company was built upon. "We like to say around here that our mandate is to grow big but to stay small," says Jim. Here, he talks about fostering a "human connection" with the company's employees (Jim personally calls 15 to 20 of them a day, including weekends), coffee farmers, and customers—the secret ingredient in the company's house blend.

GUIDED BY PRINCIPLES

Jim Donald, President and CEO, Starbucks

If I were to go back to the business today . . . I would take a look at just how important it is for a retailer—or any type of business—to interact with communities, to interact with customers, to interact with the people who are its neighbors, to make itself a part of that landscape. To me, that's the real secret of doing business and being successful.

Giving back at Starbucks goes back to the early days of the company when Howard Schultz and Orin Smith and others decided they wanted to create a company with a heart and a conscience. It was their dream to build a company that could achieve balance between fiscal responsibility and doing social good. The company was to be a reflection of their personal values, which led to the establishment of the Starbucks Guiding Principles—the foundation that still governs our company today.

Our Guiding Principles break from the traditional thinking that businesses should only be responsible to their shareholders. Instead, it underscores the responsibility we have to all of our stakeholders: our employees, customers, coffee farmers, communities, the environment, and of course, our shareholders, too. Everything we believe is baked into our Guiding Principles, including treating people with respect and dignity, contributing positively to our communities, embracing diversity, and developing enthusiastically satisfied customers.

One of our most important ingredients for success is how we treat the people who work at Starbucks. We say that we need to treat our partners with respect and dignity. That's not enough, though; we'd prefer to treat them like family. There are a few ways we try to do that. The first is health-care benefits, which we provide to eligible full-time and part-time partners, despite the escalating costs.

The second is stock options, what we call "bean stock." Since 1991 Starbucks has shared ownership of the company with its partners, including part-time folks. Some years it amounts to as much as 14 percent of base pay. It's made a big difference in bettering our partners' lives. Recently, I met with Denise, a store manager in New York City. She told me, "Jim, because of bean stock I have been able to move out of the city, buy a home, pay off my car, and really provide great service for our customers and provide a wonderful life for my family." We've seen the impact of sharing company ownership with our partners: it attracts and retains partners (Denise has been with us for nine years), and they do everything in their power to make sure that the company is successful.

A benefit that we started more recently is tuition reimbursement. We decided to do this after receiving feedback from our partners. In the two months the program was active in 2004, 807 partners were approved for this benefit. In 2005, we explored starting similar programs in other countries.

We've launched programs to give back to our coffee farmers as well. We want them around for the long haul, so we need to do things to sustain their communities and their coffee farms. Since 1992 we have been working with CARE International, a global humanitarian organization, to help alleviate poverty and create long-term solutions (such as sustainable community health services, primary education programs and village banking net-works) in coffee-growing communities. In addition to offering funding to the organization (which is expected to benefit 4,600 local residents), we get involved on a more integrated level as well.

Deidra Wager, a Starbucks executive vice president, spent a year as an "executive on loan" to CARE. Deidra's 25 years of cor-porate experience was tapped to help improve collaboration between CARE and its corporate partners. The organization also set up a two-year pilot project in the remote Guatemalan munic-ipality of San Pedro Jocopilas. Another great program that we support is Coffee Kids, a nonprofit organization established to help improve the lives of women and their families in coffee-growing communities. We provided $25,000 in 2004 for micro-credit projects—something that has benefited more than 3,500 women and their families in Veracruz, Mexico, and Matagalpa, Nicaragua.

In 2004, we contributed nearly $1.8 million for 35 social proj-ects to help provide adequate housing, health clinics, schools, good roads, and fresh drinking water. We contributed more than $1 million to improve housing for coffee-growing families in the Colombian state of Nariño, an area of extreme poverty and polit-ical unrest. Since the housing project's inception in 1999, approx-imately 2,300 people have benefited. Guatemala Starbucks contributed $79,000 to help build and equip a health clinic and kindergarten facility in Ayarza, a remote coffee-growing village in the highlands of eastern Guatemala. (What was especially amazing was to see how contagious giving is: our supplier, a cof-fee exporter, matched our contribution.) Today, the village has its first doctor and a kindergarten facility. Approximately 50 people visit the clinic daily and 80 children attend the kindergarten annually.

Over the years, we have built strong relationships with many of our coffee suppliers. The relationship has been based on two things: the coffee farmers provide us with the highest-quality coffee in the world, and we pay premium prices so that they make a profit and their farms can be sustained. This effort is summed up in a program we have called C.A.F.E. Practices, which stands for Coffee And Farmer Equity. We partnered with Conservation International, an environmental nonprofit organization, to develop C.A.F.E. Practices, which aims to promote equitable relationships with farmers and employees, enhance the environment, and ensure the future supply of a high-quality coffee. (Yes, it's a lot; we're really reaching out and trying to hit all the buttons at one time.)

Starbucks buys coffee on a preferential basis from coffee farmers who meet the C.A.F.E. Practices requirements and who score high in environmental and social criteria. In 2004, we purchased 43.5 million pounds of coffee under the pilot program guidelines (out of 299 million pounds purchased)—this was an amount that exceeded our target of 30 million pounds. By 2007, though, we expect to purchase 225 million pounds of C.A.F.E. Practices verified coffee—that's the majority of all coffee that Starbucks purchases.

While we're pleased with how the program is going overall, it's most rewarding to see how farmers and communities are personally affected. One great example is the Santa Teresa farm in beautiful Chiapas, Mexico. For years, Santa Teresa did well enough by producing regular extra-prime coffee rather than higher-quality specialty grade. Everything changed when world coffee prices hit rock bottom several years ago, though. Ervin Pohlenz Cordova, the son of the farm's owner, wasn't earning enough for his crops to cover the farm's expenses. The farm nearly went bankrupt.

Then, Ervin was introduced to Starbucks through his exporter and realized that he could earn more if he switched to producing higher-quality coffee. To work with us, Santa Teresa needed to improve the quality of the beans and implement sustainable farming practices. It was a commitment that Ervin was willing to make, although his father, a man of a different generation, was skeptical.

It took three years before the coffee grown on Santa Teresa reached our quality standards. In 2003, we signed a three-year contract to buy all of Santa Teresa's high-quality coffee at premium prices. We also added a provision that earmarks funds for social improvement and environmental protection projects to benefit the farm. Santa Teresa is now far from the bankruptcy that threatened the company a few years ago, and the farm operates under sustainable conditions. With the impact on the farm and the community, even Ervin's elderly father has changed his thinking and embraced this new way.

A big part of giving back at Starbucks is dependent on the generosity of our partners—and to this extent, we've been in awe of their commitment and contributions. Four years ago we started something called Make Your Mark, a program that encourages partners to volunteer in their neighborhoods and rewards their efforts by providing cash contributions from Starbucks to the organizations where they volunteer. Starbucks matches $10 for every hour volunteered. Even better, our partners can enlist their friends, families, and customers to participate on a team project, and we match those hours too.

To see this program in action is incredible. Not too long ago, I had to drop my son off at crew practice and I had about two hours to kill, so I went to a store that I normally don't go into. It was raining out, but the store was busy. I asked one of the partners, "Where is the store manager?" The store partner told me the manager and the assistant and two partners were across the street. I looked across the street and there was a tent set up with about 30 people surrounding it. There were 30 volunteers—customers and partners—there to clean up the park. "The rain isn't going to stop us," the store partner told me. "Today is the day we picked and we are going to do it."

That one example probably adds up to three hours times 30 customers who were helping improve their own community with 90 hours of service and $900 for the effort from Starbucks. Last year this program led to 214,000 hours donated to help local nonprofits.

Before I came to Starbucks, I spent 35 years in the supermarket business. Much of my time was spent looking at growing sales and reducing costs. If I were to go back to the business today—which I'm not—I would do things entirely differently: I would take a look at just how important it is for a retailer—or any type of business—to interact with communities, to interact with customers, to interact with the people who are its neighbors, to make itself a part of that landscape. To me, that's the real secret of doing business and being successful. You just can't exist on a stand-alone basis where everything is all about the company. You have to give back to the organizations, to your partners, to your customers who help make you successful. It's not just the right thing to do; it makes good business sense. Customers see the company as a place they don't mind investing in, knowing that they are going to get a great product and a great service—and that some of what they spend is going to come back to them.

What I've learned since I've been here is that what makes Starbucks coffee special is that we pick one cherry at a time. It's not stripped; it's not taken out by machines. Last year we picked more than 4.4 billion coffee cherries that way. This is the same approach we use to operate our business. We have close to 100,000 partners; we don't look at it as 100,000 partners; we see it as one partner at a time. We have 10,000 stores. We don't see it as 10,000 stores; we see it as one store at a time. We have 34 million customers come in a week, but again, we have to look at it one customer at a time.

This is what makes Starbucks special. People often ask me what at Starbucks has had the biggest impact on me. The answer is always Michelle. A few years ago, I got a phone call from our store in Southcenter Mall and one of our partners invited me to come celebrate Michelle's birthday. I didn't know Michelle, but I had the time slot open, so I went 20 miles down the road to attend this birthday party. When I walked into the store I saw Michelle immediately. She is bound to a wheelchair and not able to converse, but her eyes light up the entire restaurant. Michelle has been a partner at the store in the Southcenter Mall for eight years. She motors around in her wheelchair delivering beverages to all the managers in the mall. Meeting Michelle was a day that I could never forget.

Last November I got a call from the store saying that it was Michelle's 10-year anniversary. I dropped everything to go celebrate it. It seemed like a lot of other people did too. That store has a capacity of 25 people, but there were 125 people there. Store managers, friends, family, relatives—all of them were there to celebrate this success. When I look at what has changed me the most, I look at Michelle. What Starbucks means to Michelle and what Michelle means to Starbucks is really what Starbucks is all about.

THE STARBUCKS SIX GUIDING PRINCIPLES

These principles were established with the creation of the company, and they are what Jim describes as, "the foundation that still governs our company today."

- Provide a great work environment and treat each other with respect and dignity.

- Embrace diversity as an essential component in the way we do business.
- Apply the highest standards of excellence to the purchasing, roasting and fresh delivery of our coffee.
- Develop enthusiastically satisfied customers all of the time.
- Contribute positively to our communities and our environment.
- Recognize that profitability is essential to our future success.

CHAPTER 12

CONNECTING THE COMPANY TO THE COMMUNITY: CISCO SYSTEMS

To mark the company's twentieth anniversary in 2004, it committed to giving back 20 years' worth of service to the community.

R ead anything about John Morgridge, the chairman emeritus of Cisco, and his unmatched work ethic and innate frugality are certain to come up. Growing up in Wauwatosa, a suburb of Milwaukee, John worked long hours at less-than-glorious jobs in construction, at a cannery, and at a brewery. Later, he managed a coffee shop while getting his MBA at Stanford. After benefiting from Cisco's eye-popping success (the company did $24 billion in sales in 2005), he hasn't strayed from what he calls his Midwestern values of working hard and being frugal. He takes the latter to an extreme: he once stapled a coupon for long-term parking—"Park here five times and get one free"—onto an executive's expense report, and Cisco employees have claimed he buys his suits at Costco.

When it comes to giving money away, though, John is anything but penny-pinching. He and his wife, Tashia, have made many generous donations to their alma mater, the University of Wisconsin at Madison, including a $50 million gift in 2006—the largest donation in history to the UW institutions. In 2005, he committed $10 million to the Cisco 21st Century School Education Initiative to help rebuild and improve schools in the Gulf Coast region devastated by Hurricane Katrina. And each year, his family foundation earmarks millions more to support environmental, public service, and educational programs.

John, who was named chairman emeritus in late 2006 after serving as Cisco's chairman since 1995 and CEO for the seven years prior to that, is credited not only for growing Cisco into an Internet superpower but also for infusing his philanthropic beliefs into the company and establishing it as one of the most generous corporations around. (Cisco, which gave away $68 million in 2005, was recognized with the Committee to Encourage Corporate Philanthropy's 2006 Excellence Award in addition to many other honors.)

Cisco's current CEO, John Chambers, recalls how it was John Morgridge who ensured giving back was embedded into Cisco's culture since its start. "I remember a day early on when John Morgridge came and asked me to make a contribution to Stanford University [where Cisco had been created]. I said fine—but the air went out of my lungs when he handed me the bill. [The amount he'd asked for] was equal to 10 percent of my net worth at the time!"[1]

San Jose–based Cisco, which makes routers and switches (devices that connect networks by enabling them to talk to each other) and employs 45,000 people globally, is universally recognized as one of the most outstanding businesses of the Internet Age. The company was founded, however, with a much more modest goal in mind. Cisco was started in 1984 by a group of computer scientists at Stanford University led by married couple, Sandy Lerner and Len Bosack.

Legend goes that Sandy and Len wanted to communicate with each other at work, but couldn't because their respective departments used different computer networks. (It may seem impossible to remember, but back then different computers such as Apples, IBMs and Unix machines couldn't talk to one another.) The couple came up with operating software, called Internet Operating System (IOS), which could route streams of data from one computer to another. Next, they loaded that software into a box containing microprocessors designed for routing and created what we now know as the multiprotocol router. The importance of the device is that it enabled previously incompatible computers to communicate using different network protocols—something that paved the way for the Internet revolution.

With their revolutionary technology, Sandy and Len established Cisco (an abbreviation for San Francisco) in their home in Atherton, California. Venture capitalists weren't interested in their start-up, and to make ends meet the founders borrowed $20,000 on their credit cards, mortgaged their house, and kept their day jobs for 18 months. They worked nights and weekends. Before very long they shipped their first product—the MEIS Subsystem, an Ethernet adaptor for DEC computers—and moved out of the house and into office space in Menlo Park in 1986.

In 1987 the company underwent a major change when prominent venture capitalist Don Valentine (he financed Apple and Oracle) invested $2.5 million in the company. (In return he got a whopping 32 percent stake.) As part of the deal, he insisted on new management, including a new CEO. He picked former Honeywell executive, John Morgridge, because he wanted someone who had "conservative instincts" and "a calming influence," and who would be able to handle Cisco's gangbuster growth.[2] He also wanted someone with an incredible drive to build a leading company and the tools to ready it for an IPO. John came on in 1988 as Cisco's 34th employee (for many years he wore a badge identifying him as such) and was compensated with stock options worth about 6 percent of the company at that time.

Under his leadership, Cisco's revenues skyrocketed from $1.5 million in 1987 to $27.7 million in 1989. The company went public the following year and was listed on the Nasdaq market. Shortly after the IPO, and once John Morgridge was leading the company, Sandy and Len left. (They received $170 million with which they set up a charitable foundation that supports, among other things, scientists and animal rights.)

In the early 1990s Cisco's technology—once cutting edge— began to become dated. (After all, what technology doesn't? Consider the typewriter or cassette players.) Around 1993, routers were still heavily depended upon, but two emerging technologies, one called switching and one called asynchronous transfer mode (ATM)—both are too complicated to warrant explaining—were being manufactured by smaller companies and generating interest. Cisco saw the changing future and quickly transitioned by expanding its business beyond routers. It bought a start-up called Crescendo Communications, a company that was beginning to make switches. (This company was also funded by venture capitalist Don Valentine.) The price was hefty, $95 million. Next, Cisco snapped up Kalpana, Inc., another expensive small company that made switches, and Grand Junction, a start-up providing Fast Ethernet (100Base-T) and Ethernet desktop switching products.

Although Cisco was criticized for spending so much on start-up companies, the strategy was an undisputed success. Virtually overnight, Cisco was in the switching business. As the next few years would reveal, switches didn't replace routers, but complemented them as computer networks used both routers and switches. Cisco had planted itself in the perfect place to take advantage of the trend.

The company continued to grow, and in January 1995 John Morgridge stepped down as CEO and became chairman of the board of directors at Cisco. John Chambers, a charismatic West Virginian with a law degree and an MBA, was named CEO of Cisco. Although John Chambers was not an engineer—something that made some people skeptical of his abilities to run Cisco—he is largely credited with taking Cisco to dizzying new heights.

Cisco continued its buying spree, acquiring dozens of companies that allowed it to sell sophisticated switches that won customers such as AT&T and MCI and made Cisco a competitor of companies including Nortel, Siemens, and Fujitsu. Later, Cisco purchased companies in the optical networking market, something that allowed it to offer customers a one-stop-shop for all of their networking needs. Next, the company added a new customer base. In 2003 Cisco acquired Linksys, a popular manufacturer of home networking gear, and continued its success as a leading brand for the home and end user networking market.

While many things have changed in Cisco's 20-year history (its founders are not only gone from the company, but divorced; it now offers more than 40 product lines instead of one router; and it has offices in 259 cities around the world), the company still retains many of the qualities John Morgridge infused in it. Attentiveness to customer needs, thriftiness (everyone flies coach and works in identical cubicles), and no assigned parking—except those for customers—are still values that make up Cisco's core culture. The company's ever-expanding new features and technologies continue to shape the future of the Internet.

Giving back is another tradition that remains just as strong. In fact, to mark the company's twentieth anniversary in 2004, it committed to giving back 20 years' worth of service to the community.

John Morgridge and John Chambers challenged every Cisco employee across the globe to volunteer one day to the community. The result exceeded the target 175,200 hours—equal to 20 years of service—by over 30 percent (235,000 hours were volunteered).

The company continues to offer assistance in times of disaster, such as contributing more than $5 million to the victims of the tsunami in Southeast Asia as well as donating its time to help set up IP and wireless communications systems in affected areas, which returned much-needed communications capabilities. Cisco responded in the wake of Hurricane Katrina by announcing a $40 million commitment to its 21st Century Schools (21S) project, an education initiative to aid in post–Hurricane Katrina rebuilding.

In his essay here, John, whose personal philanthropic passions include working with CARE, the Nature Conservancy, and Interplast, talks about the legacy of corporate giving at Cisco and the company's strategy of leveraging its business and technical expertise in addition to writing checks as a way to make the most powerful impact.

BUILDING NETWORKS IN THE COMMUNITY

John Morgridge, Chairman Emeritus, Cisco Systems

One of our most unique initiatives to get people committed to giving back is the Cisco Fellowship program, a program that leverages employees' skills and knowledge to help nonprofit organizations use the Internet to their advantage.

At Cisco, we believe that corporations and civil society are part of the foundation of the community—one of the pillars on which a community can thrive and grow. Everyone thinks that the contribution a company can make to the community is about money, but community involvement is about so much more. By leveraging talented people, reach, culture, innovative technology, and solid relationships, we've found that companies can make a more significant difference.

The concept of giving back has been part of Cisco's DNA since the beginning. Cisco's philanthropic roots date back to the early days, when times were lean. Early on, our offices were located in the middle of East Palo Alto, California, a city struggling to provide services for its residents. The many needs that were not being met were especially evident at Costaño Elementary School, which was located right across the street from our growing technology company. We were separated only by a fence.

Cisco employees found it difficult not to help; they literally jumped the fence and got to work to help improve the school. What began with painting walls and cleaning the schoolyard quickly grew into a partnership of mentoring and working with teachers and administrators to accomplish long-term objectives. Employees took the time to tutor students and donated computer and playground equipment. They became dedicated to help the school get up and running—in every sense.

Our company's early involvement with this school was a very rewarding experience for my family and me. My wife and I were able to build a personal relationship with the principal of the Costaño School, and I became a sponsor and enjoyed volunteering my time; I was frequently given the honor of being "principal for a day" at the school or speaking at graduation. We eventually moved Cisco headquarters to San Jose as the company expanded, and still today, we have continued the connection with Costaño School. The quality of education at the school has been directly affected by the efforts of many individuals at Cisco

Besides impacting me personally, our success with the Costaño School influenced our philosophy as a company going forward. We went on to create numerous programs aimed at improving access to education and technology—with an emphasis on working in disadvantaged countries and communities. One of our first programs was called "Take a Router" to School, in which we encouraged our employees to purchase a router, at a discounted price, and to donate it to a school of their choice.

In 1997 we made a more formal commitment to our community efforts by starting the Cisco Systems Foundation, which makes grants in communities where Cisco has a significant business presence. At the close of Fiscal Year 2005, the total value of the annual Cisco Systems Foundation endowment was more than $100 million. As Cisco's corporate philanthropy's primary cash investment vehicle, the foundation provides grants to organizations with long-lasting local or global impact. The Cisco Systems Foundation also empowers employees to give more through a matching gifts program. The goal is to establish a legacy of trust between the community at large and the foundation. We believe the foundation further establishes Cisco's commitment, as well as its longevity.

One of Cisco's key strategic investments is the Cisco Networking Academy, which provides people in developing countries with access to training on the latest technologies. At Cisco, there is a strong belief that it is the responsibility of those companies, countries, and governments that benefited from technology in the twentieth century to ensure that no one gets left behind as we move further into the twenty-first Century. In the United States, there is a direct one-to-one correlation between percentage of capital expenditures on IT and productivity increases. Over time, this correlation is also occurring on a global basis. Technology is bridging the gap between the world's developed and least developed countries and raising the standard of living through better health care and educational opportunities.

We believe that by improving access to education and the Internet—the two fundamental equalizers in life—the Networking Academies can serve as vital catalysts for international economic development. One of the most exciting parts of this workforce development program is the success we have had scaling it to be successful in multiple countries. Today, there are Cisco Networking Academies in more than 160 countries. We have seen the academies spur significant changes, especially in areas such as Africa and Afghanistan, where women were shut out of their country's public life for so many years. Thanks to the United Nations Volunteer program (UNDP), United States Agency for International Development (USAID), and the Cisco Networking Academy in Kabul, women are learning specialized skills in the dynamic and much-valued area of IT.

Another program designed to harness technology and boost development is the Jordan Education Initiative (JEI), which was launched in June 2003. The JEI is supported by 45 organizations, including international corporations, local companies, government ministries in Jordan, international donors, and nongovernmental organizations. Among its objectives are curriculum reform, teacher training, adoption of information and communications technologies (ICT) as an enabler of learning, and the improvement of ICT infrastructure in schools. Cisco provides funding, training, equipment, and other resources. Our support ranges from comprehensive online mathematics lessons for young people to providing technical and educational specialists for the JEI program management office. We are currently working to replicate this model in India and other areas around the world.

In addition to contributing resources such as time and money, we have found that we have a tremendous impact on community organizations through product donations and helping them to use applications effectively. Take, for example, our work with the Hearing, Speech and Deafness Center (HSDC), based in Seattle. This nonprofit has a simple mission: provide communications to its constituents.

A large part of their work involves using technology to put the deaf community on an equal footing. HSDC understands that people become more empowered with full access to e-mail, video, and communications technology. But with limited resources, the organization needed help. Everything they used to operate ran through one-and-a-half servers, and important applications used up bandwidth, causing continual network crashes. The unreliable network negatively affected staff and clients, often crippling HSDC's ability to do business. Through our product donation program, HSDC was able to provide reliable, consistent applications. The result: increased reliability, speed, and efficiency. HSDC is now able to provide its essential services over a reliable network. It has also allowed them to expand, increase staff, and offer more services.

Another good example of the contributions that can be made through increasing access to technology can be illustrated by our work with the Second Harvest Food Bank of Santa Clara and San Mateo Counties, a nonprofit organization that collects and distributes more than 27 million pounds of food each year to agencies that distribute or prepare and serve the food or to direct sites distributing to qualified recipients.

Cisco employees have been working with Second Harvest for more than 10 years, providing food, cash donations, technical expertise, and hours of volunteer time. Five years ago, Cisco Community Fellows—a group of employees who dedicate their skills to the community for a period of time—working at the food bank went about the task of improving the business processes.

They utilized Internet technologies, including developing and implementing a hardware and software network infrastructure. The food bank needed integrated data and reporting capability, as well as a way to evaluate third-party applications, including fund raising, inventory management, finance, payroll, and human resources software. They also developed longer-range strategies for Internet expansion. This relationship was recently enhanced with the donation and installation of an IP telephony system, increasing the efficiency and reducing the cost of communications between their Santa Clara and San Mateo county offices.

Also in Seattle, Cisco applied its technological know-how to Community Voice Mail (CVM), a nonprofit organization that provides voice mail boxes for the homeless and others who may not have access to phones—something critical to help them secure jobs and services (it's hard to secure a job or a place to live if people can't get in touch with you). Using Cisco's unity voice over IP (VoIP) technology, CVM has now strengthened the communications technology that drives the voice mail for thousands of homeless

individuals nationwide. The result is evident: the partnership with
Cisco to upgrade its voice mail technology has increased the
agency's impact and reduced costs for the organization.

When it comes to working to fulfill basic human needs—
another goal of our foundation—one of the most rewarding
efforts has been our relationship with Habitat for Humanity
International. Since 2000, Cisco has worked with the Habitat
organization around the world getting our partners, suppliers,
customers and employees involved.

Through the More Than Houses campaign, Cisco and Habitat
have built more than 420 houses. Cisco employees have worked
with local Habitat offices to find affordable and appropriate solutions for wiring houses for Internet access. Additionally, the Cisco
Foundation provides funds each year for distribution to Habitat
affiliates around the world, where Cisco employees engage with
them to provide housing in their communities. From volunteering time to offering technical expertise and much-needed products, employees of Cisco are working wonders in areas around
the world where help is most needed. Habitat for Humanity
volunteering is one of the favorite team-building activities for our
employees.

We've see the benefits of encouraging employees to give something back. The idea that they have a responsibility and an opportunity to make a difference in the communities where they live
and work—not just at corporate headquarters—can be valuable
and empowering for an employee. That's why promoting
employee volunteerism has been a central component of Cisco's
community involvement efforts.

What our employees around the world have taken on themselves and accomplished in the community has been incredible:
more than 250 employees from Cisco's offices in Korea spent an
entire day rejuvenating the Mt. Bookhan hiking area; Cisco has
over 3,600 employees worldwide helping Habitat for Humanity;

and everyone in the company (including leadership at all levels) is involved. For example, John Chambers and the Cisco senior executive team painted a building and expanded a playground at InnVision, a provider of housing and services to homeless and at-risk families and individuals in Silicon Valley.

One of our most unique initiatives to get people committed to giving back is the Cisco Fellowship program, a program that leverages employees' skills and knowledge to help nonprofit organizations use the Internet to their advantage. We began the program in March 2001, when Cisco had it its first-ever layoffs. This program allowed 81 employees affected by a workforce reduction to stay on Cisco's payroll, earning a partial salary and benefits, while working for nonprofit organizations. These employees were given the option of working for one year with one of 20 partner community organizations, such as One Economy, Public Allies, City Year, Save the Children, and Second Harvest Food Bank. The employees embraced the challenges, shared their considerable technical know-how, and helped the organizations take advantage of technology and the Internet to further their missions. For some employees, the experience was life-changing. After the year, many of the employees returned to Cisco (about 40 percent of the workers eventually returned to full-time work at Cisco), but several embraced the nonprofit world and forged new careers.

Due to the impact this program had on both the nonprofits as well as our employees, we have evolved this into a Leadership Development Program at Cisco—the Leadership Fellows Program. The individual impact our employees have made in their communities, through this program, is extraordinary. In the aftermath of Hurricane Katrina, for example, 10 Cisco Fellows embarked on a yearlong project to help restore the educational environment in the stricken areas of Mississippi and Louisiana. Working with superintendents, the state boards of education, principals, and teachers, the Cisco employees have been able to take our culture, process, and energy and apply their technology expertise to help rebuild and reform, with a goal to make the system better than it was prior to the disaster.

I am extremely proud of the people that make up this company. They have continually stayed focused on the things that are most important, both in good times and during the challenging times. This continued attention, execution, and ability to surpass goals— both within Cisco and in their personal lives—amazes me.

Recent research by the Walker Institute for the Council on Foundations finds that corporate giving can help businesses succeed. The research indicates that customers, employees, and community leaders who view a company's philanthropic programs as successful are more likely to conduct business with that company— even when faced with a better financial deal elsewhere. We have found that this is not just an academic theory, but a practical reality in the business world.

Our commitment to community involvement shows shareholders that we are in business for the long haul. More of our institutional investors look at socially responsible programs today. They want to know that as a corporation, we think holistically, have a 360-degree view of the world's communities, and are continually looking at ways to move forward. Last year we published our first Corporate Social Responsibility Report as a way to show that we take responsibility for the commitments we make to our customers, our shareholders, our employees, and our community and NGO partners. We believe that all of this strengthens Cisco and increases shareholder value.

Cisco's community involvement also makes a difference in our company's bottom line. When you become entrenched in a community, you inspire confidence, which works to your benefit when customers are seeking the best solutions for their own organizations. Customers want to know you will be there for them, as they grow and change their businesses. If they can see the programs and organizations that are gaining benefits from our solutions, it reinforces customer confidence, and favorably impacts our business.

Personally, there is no question that my life has been enriched by people whom I've met and the organizations with which I've worked. Along with Cisco, our community philanthropy partners have grown and changed through the years, and it is gratifying to see what ideas and cooperation have accomplished. I am especially proud of the impact we have made in post-Taliban Afghanistan, where we had an opportunity to partner with local government and international organizations to bring their educational program closer to the twenty-first century with the latest tools and technology.

That said, we cannot become complacent. There is so much more for us to do. I would challenge people to find ways they can help to further the collective mission of the organization, by leveraging our unique capabilities and those of our partners. I would hope that employees make careful choices, looking at opportunities where they can provide assistance, come up with better partners and better ideas, and think broadly. As we've seen, it is so much more than just money that makes an impact—it's the collective resources of the company including our employees' expertise and time, our products and technology, and our global reach that can make a difference.

Things have changed since the early days of Cisco Systems. That's part of the natural evolution of any corporation. But the early culture we established—one of employees breaking down the barriers and climbing the fence of the neighborhood school to offer help—remains a constant at this company. What hasn't changed is the enthusiasm I see when I talk to Cisco employees. If anything, it has grown through the years as we have partnered and invested even more.

JOHN MORGRIDGE'S FIVE STRATEGIES TO SUCCESSFUL CORPORATE GIVING

Look carefully at your employee engagement programs: The variety of programs you offer, how strongly you support them, and your willingness to encourage employee-originated ideas are essential for a successful program.

Get strategic about your giving: Just as in business, you can have greater impact by focusing on a few "markets" for corporate giving programs. At Cisco, we have focused our efforts in three areas: education, the Internet, and support for basic needs, such as food and shelter. This three-pronged focus allows us to leverage the energy, ideas, and strengths of Cisco employees and product solution areas.

Be creative: There are many other ways besides cash and equipment donation programs in which companies can contribute. We have launched more than 10,000 Cisco Networking Academies—many located in least developed countries—and U.S. Empowerment Zones—to help train the next generation of information technology engineers.

Partner with nonprofits that demonstrate success: Many nonprofits seek the business expertise and technical know-how that business can offer, while others are already highly successful and would receive greater benefit from ongoing counsel and support. When choosing a nonprofit in which to invest, assess your choice as carefully as you would a stock market investment: devote resources to organizations that consistently demonstrate success over time.

Make it a win/win: There are many ways that companies can contribute to the global community, but we've found partnering to be successful over the years. The best part-nerships, and those that are able to make the biggest impact, are those in which both parties benefit. Make any initiative a win/win situation for all parties involved.

Provide long-term commitment: Most programs are not successful overnight; they require an investment in time, money, and resources. By being committed for the long term, the initiative has a better chance of success. For example, Cisco's Networking Academy program is now 10 years old and Cisco continues to invest in this initiative.

Consider endowing a corporate foundation. There are more than 2,000 corporate foundations in the United States. Many of these foundations are funded as line items in annual company budgets. As a result, foundations are funded generously in good business cycles but suffer when business is challenging. By endowing a corporate foundation and diversifying its portfolio, you protect your foundation dur-ing tough times.

CHAPTER 13

BUILDING HOSPITALITY IN OUR COMMUNITIES: CARLSON COMPANIES

Carlson Companies was a pioneer and charter member of the
"Five Percent Club" (now called the Minnesota Keystone Club), an
organization of Minneapolis–St. Paul area corporations dedicated
to giving 5 percent of their earnings to nonprofit organizations.

Doing things differently is the modus operandi for Marilyn Carlson Nelson. Take her entrance to an annual meeting of Carlson travel agency owners and executives: she sailed up to the stage on roller skates, waving a Carlson banner. Sure, it was an unusual entrance for the new chief of the world's largest travel and hospitality business (and we don't recommend trying to keep up with her; she's also been known to enjoy power-diving in an F-16, pulling 9Gs with the USAF Thunderbirds). It does however, illustrate how Marilyn, the second generation in her family to run Carlson Companies—one of the largest privately held companies in the United States—is determined to bring her own style to the company that her father started the year she was born.

Today, Minneapolis-based Carlson Companies is the largest company in the world run by a woman. (For the past two years, she has been ranked on *Forbes* annual list of the world's most powerful women; for the past seven, on *Fortune* magazine's list of the

"50 Most Powerful Women in American Business.") The Carlson empire, which rang up $26.2 billion in sales in 2004 (a 25 percent increase from the previous year) owns, manages, and franchises more than 900 hotels under brands such as Regent, Radisson, and Park Plaza as well as a six-star luxury cruise line (Radisson Seven Seas Cruises). There are also restaurants (the 776-unit T.G.I. Friday's among them), travel agencies (Carlson Wagonlit Travel and Results Travel,) and marketing consultancies (including Carlson Marketing Group and Peppers & Rogers Group).

The story of Carlson Companies begins in 1938 when Marilyn's father, Curt Carlson, quit a promising job at Procter & Gamble (he was named the number-one salesman in 1938) and, with a $55 loan from his landlord, struck out on his own. Curt always had an entrepreneurial spirit—he started selling newspapers when he was 11 years old and soon organized a network of new routes and hired his younger brothers to make the deliveries. He later drove a truck delivering soda and sold advertising on fraternity and sorority bulletin boards to earn money for tuition at the University of Minnesota.

This time, Curt's entrepreneurial idea was to start a trading-stamp business—and to introduce a program for grocers to offer rewards to shoppers. (Curt's father was a grocer, so he had a sense of how this could benefit grocery store owners and customers alike.) Curt did not invent trading stamps; while working at P&G, he had noticed that a retail department store in downtown Minneapolis was successfully giving away red coupons in exchange for dollars purchased. The coupons could be redeemed for cash or merchandise at the department store. Curt decided that if the coupons boosted business in department stores, they would be a boon to grocery stores as well—after all, grocers truly needed a way to differentiate themselves inasmuch as they all sold the same products.

Curt and his wife, Arleen, poured their energies and passion into selling his trading-stamp idea to the small mom-and-pop food stores in the Minneapolis area. The stores expressed interest and in the fall of 1938 Curt's company—Gold Bond Stamps—was officially launched.

The Carlsons didn't have much money (Curt's salary as a soap salesman—albeit the best soap salesman—had been $110 a month), and investing everything into the company became the family's focus. Marilyn says that they gave up dessert to put more savings into the company. Before long, though, the idea of bringing trading stamps to the food industry became a hit.

The financially strapped folks of the Great Depression appreciated the simple system of filling out a Gold Bond stamp book from purchases at a local grocery store and redeeming it for $3. (Later, homemakers enjoyed selecting home furnishings from a Gold Bond catalog.) Grocers loved the new program too. Those who supplied Gold Bond stamps to their customers saw business increase by 60 percent.

In 1953 Curt sold Gold Bond trading stamps to one of the largest wholesale grocery chains in the nation, Super Valu, which operated hundreds of large supermarkets across the Midwest. With that introduction, Gold Bond became a household name virtually overnight. By the 1960s, 19 out of the top 20 food chains were issuing trading stamps, and 50 percent of all gasoline stations were giving stamps on purchases. ("It was an idea whose time had come!" Curt later said.[1]) Eventually, Gold Bond made it to Europe and Japan. Soon, the trading-stamp industry became a multibillion-dollar business—and reached close to saturation as 400 companies were vying for market share. Curt decided it was necessary to diversify the business, and the Gold Bond Stamp Company expanded into the hospitality industry with the purchase of the Minneapolis Radisson Hotel. Later it acquired T.G.I. Friday's restaurants and Ask Mr. Foster travel agencies. By the early 1970s, Curt's company was purchasing an average of four new businesses a year and enjoying a compounded annual growth rate of 33 percent. In 1973, in a move to recognize its new diversification, the company changed its name to Carlson Companies. It established four major divisions: Carlson Hospitality Group, Carlson Travel Group, Carlson Marketing Group, and Carlson Promotion Group (this included the original Gold Bond business.)

By 1977, Curt Carlson became Minnesota's first billionaire. The family that once skimped on dessert now had a vacation home in Wisconsin, a yacht, and an airplane. In addition to investing in growing his company and enjoying some new luxuries, Curt always gave back to his community—and established himself as a leader who encouraged others to give generously as well.

Carlson Companies was a pioneer and charter member of the "Five Percent Club" (now called the Minnesota Keystone Club), an organization of Minneapolis–St. Paul area corporations dedicated to giving 5 percent of their earnings to nonprofit organizations. The group, which was launched with 23 companies, has since expanded to include dozens of organizations and has spawned a sister group for companies that donate 2 percent of their earnings to community groups.

Curt always gave personally, too. In 1959 he set up the Curtis L. Carlson Family Foundation, which focuses its attention primarily on improving the lives of underserved children through mentoring and education. The foundation was also a way for Curt to give back to his alma mater, the University of Minnesota. Curt frequently expressed gratitude to the university for allowing him to attend at a reasonable cost and for preparing him to enter the business world in the late 1930s.

In total, the foundation has contributed more than $46 million to the University of Minnesota. It's contributions included a gift that enabled the school to build a new freestanding business school, eventually named the Carlson School of Management in Curt's honor. Curt also committed to improving the university by chairing committees and spearheading drives that have raised nearly $380 million—an amount that helped propel the University of Minnesota into one of the top five public universities in the United States.

For his community involvement, Curt has been awarded with *Town & Country* magazine's "Generous American Award." The same magazine later called him "a visionary with a different tactic . . . the man who has inspired the new philosophy of corporate giving." Carlson Companies has also been acknowledged through the Minnesota Keystone program's first-ever Honored Company Award, which recognized the corporation for its distinguished history of community giving.

In 1998—after running the company for 60 years—Curt relinquished his role as president and CEO to Marilyn, his eldest daughter. Curt was 84 at the time; Marilyn was almost 60. (Industry watchers called Marilyn's promotion "the longest-running succession saga in business history."[2])

One year after Marilyn was named CEO, Curt passed away. His values and ideas are still alive at the company, but they have taken on a definite Marilyn-like tone, reflecting her international view. (She graduated from Smith College with a degree in international economics, and attended the Sorbonne and the Institute des Hautes Etudes Economiques et Politiques in Geneva, Switzerland.)

Like her father, she has a gift for salesmanship—or saleswomanship, as the case may be. In 1994 she partnered with the French hospitality giant Accor to create Carlson Wagonlit Travel. Like her father, she has a penchant for acquiring companies, including the purchase of British travel firm Thomas Cook, which she sold off in only a few years at a record profit. She also restructured each business unit to achieve greater profitability.

To Marilyn—like Curt—doing good business isn't just growing profits, though. "My vision is to become the most-respected private company on earth. To create a great place where great people can do great work," she's said.[3] In fact, her first official acts as CEO were things that may not have fit into her father's philosophy, he having forged his empire in a different time. But they were things she determined were good investments, and she personally ushered into existence an in-house day-care center and a subsidized company cafeteria.

The number of women executives in Carlson has grown to 40 percent under her leadership; she's created a "surrogate stock" plan for executives; and written tuition reimbursement, financial assistance for adoption, flex work hours, and parental leave into the company's benefit plan. These types of programs and the company's deep commitment to its employees put the company on *Working Mother* magazine's list of the "100 Best Companies for Working Mothers" and *Fortune* magazine's list of "The 100 Best Companies to Work For." For her strong leadership style, *BusinessWeek* selected Marilyn as one of the "Top 25 Executives in Business."

Marilyn's commitment to create a company that achieves great financial success while also helping to create great communities surely has its roots in her father's philosophy, but it's been expanded based on her unique experiences and ideas. In 1985, Marilyn's oldest daughter, Juliet, was killed in a car accident at the start of her freshman year at Marilyn's alma mater, Smith College. Marilyn said that it became necessary to use her grief to impact the world in a positive way. "I don't know if I'll be here tomorrow. I know that today is a day I have and I've often said that what Juliet taught me was that each day should be a day I would sign my name to and that we should live as a kind of artist, because that may be the last day."[4] Today, Carlson Companies, whose brands provide employment for 190,000 people in more than 140 countries, is one of the largest privately held businesses in the nation. The company looks vastly different from the trading-stamp business it was built upon, but its origins have not been forgotten. (And, although Gold Bond Trading Stamps may no longer exist, the next version of consumer incentives—in the form of frequent flyer miles, hotel guest loyalty programs, and Gold Points Rewards—are a modern twist on what Marilyn's father started 67 years ago.

Founding Fathers

Marilyn Carlson Nelson, Chairperson, CEO,
Carlson Companies

*We aren't looking to get the highest possible return each quarter
at the cost of making investments in our community and doing the
right thing at our company. To us, this is smart business.*

One of the things my father believed in—and that he certainly taught us—was a real dedication to the free enterprise system. As long as we had breath, he believed we should fight to protect the free market system. This conviction came from his father and his grandfather who had left Sweden at a time when there weren't a lot of jobs, opportunities, or freedoms. My great-grandfather, with my grandfather in tow, came to the United States with the great Swedish immigration of the 1800s to pursue the American Dream—the right to succeed or fail, based on one's own ingenuity and energy.

While my father considered profit to be an essential and an honorable ingredient to a successful business, he gave considerably to his community. This was first through the economic growth of companies that provided jobs and good salaries with opportunities for advancement, education, and prosperity—and also through philanthropy.

In 1977, my dad became one of the founders of the Keystone Program, a group of Minneapolis businesses owners that committed to giving back 5 percent of their pretax corporate income to the local community. My dad was pretty decisive about what he wanted to do philanthropically and there were several other local families running successful businesses—the McKnights of 3M, the Pillsburys of Pillsbury, the McMillans of Cargill, and the Daytons of Target—who also had a strong drive to use corporate income to improve our city.

It was an especially interesting idea because at that time the national average of giving was less than 1 percent, so the idea that in Minnesota our "founding fathers" would suggest that we have two clubs, a 2 percent club and a 5 percent club, was just unheard of in the country. Also, at that time, the federal government was very involved in giving block grants to cities and states. The National Endowment for the Humanities and the National Endowment for the Arts were making great contributions to communities. Instead of simply relying on that federal funding, though, the founders of the Keystone Program saw power in combining funding so that there was more total funding available for cultural and social welfare organizations. The goal was to create a city with the quality of life that is second to none in the country. And in fact, during those years, Minneapolis did almost always rank at the very top of cities surveyed for the best quality of life.

The impact that the Keystone Program has had on our community is evident today. For seven consecutive years Morgan Quitno, a national publishing and research company, has named Minnesota as the country's most livable state. We have a very rich social service environment. (Minnesota is the healthiest state in the country, a position we've enjoyed for 9 of the 15 years in which the national survey has been compiled.)

We also have a very rich cultural environment. The Twin Cities is second only to New York in per capita attendance at theater and arts events. Minneapolis has more than 100 theater companies and more than 30 venues and two internationally renowned orchestras.

As my dad started to get older he enjoyed more and more putting his name, or his name and my mom's name, or the Carlson name on things. I remember wondering at one point, why? It seemed to me that the most noble thing to do was to make anonymous contributions and not get credit for them. When I happened to mention that to my dad, though, I got quite a lecture. "The only way I can try to impact the family's long-term support for an organization is to have our name on the building, or our name on the program, because it will be harder for you, or for your children to let an organization fail that has our name on it," he said. "If it is anonymous, maybe that seems more to the glory of God, but the fact is, it doesn't create any tension within subsequent generations to support that organization."

What we've found since my father's passing is that he was right. To this day, my sister and I and our children all have a very strong connection with the Carlson School of Management, which is the business school at the University of Minnesota. In keeping our commitment to the Keystone Program, we still contribute 5 percent of our earnings to our foundation to improve the community, and about one-third of that goes to the University of Minnesota with a good part directed to the Carlson School. (Our objective is to make sure it is one of the top-10 public university business schools. We've seen the results of our efforts: every year it has increased in the rankings since it was first named the Carlson School.)

The other two-thirds of our foundation money is dedicated to child-related endeavors, including educational initiatives and programs for homeless and runaway teens. One of these specific efforts is the World Childhood Foundation, which sponsors projects that preserve the rights of abused and exploited children around the world. In addition to contributing to this with our corporate funds, we also have a policy at all of our hotels that offers guests the option of contributing $1 per night stay to World Childhood. Through this program we have been able to help raise $160,000—a number we believe we will be able to expand significantly as we continue to grow the program.

Funding for these types of programs certainly helps ensure the safety of children, but it's been necessary to make other types of commitments as well. We were the first North American corporation to sign the End Child Prostitution, Child Pornography and Trafficking (ECPAT) Code of Conduct for the protection of children from sexual exploitation in travel and tourism. (It's estimated that each year as many as two million children are exploited for this purpose.) The code is an international set of guidelines by which travel and tourism companies have pledged to operate in order to end the commercial sex trade of children. As part of the code we have informed our employees and our customers and our suppliers that we do not do business with people who profit from the trafficking and exploitation of young people.

We have promoted the code actively, and now the three major travel and hotel industry associations have endorsed it. We have spoken about the code everywhere, from our annual hotel and travel agency conferences, to an international tourism conference in Delhi, India. The Carlson Credo is a set of guidelines by which we run our company, and part of it states, "Wherever you go, go as a leader." We've been thrilled that our signing of and communicating about the code has actively inspired others to make this important commitment. The Japan Travel Bureau has signed on, and now their suppliers, customers, and employees are aware of their stance. Following our lead, Accor, our French partner with one of our travel companies, Carlson Wagonlit, also officially endorsed the code as did the American Hotel & Motel Association and the Travel Industry Association of America. Currently, we are working to encourage the World Travel Tourism Council to sign on.

While my dad always strove for an optimum return on our investment on the business side, he expected to leverage our philanthropic investments as well. In short, we had to be as good a steward of the philanthropic capital as we were of the corporate capital. Our ambition is to have this company last to the fifth or sixth generation and so the first thing we have to do in terms of corporate social responsibility is to make decisions that are not short-term decisions.

We believe that our reputation is as important to our bottom line as dollars.

We have to invest in long-term relationships that have a two-way win. For example, when we build a cruise ship we build one that is environmentally friendly; we would never take a short-term view and build a ship that was cheaper but polluted the environment. We are thoughtful about water usage with our hotels; we try to be environmentally friendly with the way we manage energy.

In the case of our company, our shareowners are family. While they of course need to get a fair return, they also need to see us participating in bettering their communities. They need us to care about education; they need us to hire people that have integrity; they need to create an environment that is diverse. We have seen the impact of having this sort of perspective. Instead of just asking, "What can I get," our shareowners also ask, "What can I give?" Together, it's a much more powerful way to positively impact our children's and grandchildren's futures.

In short, we aren't looking to get the highest possible return each quarter at the cost of making investments in our community and doing the right thing at our company. To us, this is smart business. We believe that our reputation is as important to our bottom line as are dollars.

There's a poem by the Swedish-American author Carl Sandburg, that begins, "It has cost to build this nation," which I believe captures where we started: the heritage and fight for the free market system and the shared responsibility of community that makes it work.

Where we came from as a nation is from people who sought freedom to succeed, freedom to fail, freedom to worship, or not, and a free trade society in a democratic context.

Corporations—just like citizens—earn the right to enjoy the freedoms if they fulfill their responsibilities to build community and to bridge the gap between those who have and those who have not, those who win and those who lose. This is what gives people opportunities—and reinforces opportunities. This is the very idea that informs our need to ensure that the education system moves people along and that we build human services programs and that we take care of our communities. We must remember the legacy of those before us who have built what we have—and we must continue to improve upon what we've been given.

CHAPTER 14

LEADING CORPORATE SOCIAL RESPONSIBILITY IN JAPAN: NEC

NEC has annually sponsored Make a Difference Day, which encourages employees to spend time working in their communities, since 1999.

For the past 100 years Tokyo-based NEC has been a leader in bringing technical innovation—from the dawn of telephony to the beginning of broadband internet technology—to people around the world. It has also emerged as a leader in bringing the practice of corporate social responsibility to Japan.

The global Fortune 100 company, which did more than $45 million in sales in 2005, was founded in 1899 as the Nippon Electric Company by Kunihiko Iwadare, a telegraph engineer, who had worked for Thomas Edison in the United States, and Takeshiro Maeda, with a dream to build the electrical industry in Japan. The company was established with the Western Electric Company of the United States, making it the first Japanese joint venture with foreign capital. From its earliest days, it focused in the production, sales, and maintenance of telephones and switching systems.

Many organizations relied on NEC's technologies, including the Japanese Ministry of Communications, which used the common battery switchboard supplied by NEC to eliminate the need for a permanent magnet generator in each of its subscriber's phones. Telephony proved to be an industry ripe for explosion. Between 1899 and 1907, the number of telephone subscribers in Japan rose from 35,000 to 95,000. NEC expanded internationally with entry into the China and Korean markets in 1908, and by 1912 sales grew to 2 million yen.

The fast-paced growth came to an abrupt halt, though, when the Ministry of Communications delayed its third expansion plan of the Japanese phone service in 1913. Although sales suffered due to the delay, NEC approached the situation as an opportunity for diversification. It began to import appliances such as washing machines, vacuum cleaners, and electric fans (something that had never been seen in Japan before). By 1916, the Japanese government resumed its telephone expansion plan, adding 75,000 subscribers and 32,600 kilometers of new toll lines, and NEC emerged from the period as a company poised for success.

In 1923 another problem would shake the company when Japan was struck by the Great Kanto earthquake, which killed 140,000 and left 3.4 million people homeless. Four of NEC's factories were decimated in the disaster, killing 105 of its workers. Thirteen of Tokyo's telephone offices were destroyed by fire. Telephone and telegraph service was interrupted by damage to telephone cables. In response, the Ministry of Communications accelerated major programs to install automatic telephone switching systems and enter radio broadcasting. NEC became involved in the installation of the automatic switching systems—and ultimately became the general sales agent for the British company Automatic Telephone Manufacturing. By the next year, NEC had developed its own automatic switching system, a first in Japan.

Over the next several years, the company had a hand in furthering the communications industry in Japan. Radio Tokyo, Japan's first radio broadcaster, went live in 1925 with Western

Electric Company broadcasting equipment that was imported by NEC. By 1930, NEC began manufacturing its first 500-watt radio transmitter. They provided the Chinese Xinjing station with a 100-kilowatt radio broadcasting system in 1934. It also developed fast and high-quality photo-telegraphic equipment that was used to transmit the most prized photos of the day, including those of the accession ceremony of Emperor Hirohito.

NEC began transistor research and development in 1950 and computer research and development in 1954. It unveiled its first transistorized computer, the NEAC-2201, at the UNESCO Automath show in Paris, where the product won positive reviews. By the 1960s, the company expanded into integrated circuit research and development. It soon supplied satellite communications ground facilities for Trans-Pacific TV broadcasting of the Olympics in Tokyo, and provided one of Japan's overseas telecommunications carriers with submarine cable systems to be laid in the Pacific Ocean. In 1963 Nippon Electric New York (now NEC America Inc.) was incorporated. Over the next two decades, NEC continued to expand globally and supplied its cable systems to countries all over the world.

By the late 1970s, NEC launched a new marketing concept, C&C—the integration of computers and communications. It acquired a California company, Electronic Arrays, Inc. to start semiconductor chip production in the United States. In 1980, NEC created the first digital signal processor (a specialized microprocessor) and a year later it introduced the 16-bit PC-9800 series personal computer.

In 1983, the company changed its English name to NEC Corporation. (It's still known as Nippon Electric Company in Japan.) A year later it started manufacturing computers and related products in the United States. Its supercomputer, SX-2, was used by the environmental organization Houston Advanced Research Center, and its NEAX61 digital switching system was put into service by the Bell Operating Company. By the late 1980s NEC Technologies was established in the United Kingdom to manufacture VCRs, printers, and color TVs for the European market.

In 1998, NEC opened the world's most advanced semiconductor research and development (R&D) facility. A few years later it built the Earth Simulator Computer, the fastest supercomputer in the world at the time. Today the company makes high-end computers (servers and supercomputers) and peripherals (monitors and projectors) and competes neck-in-neck with Fujitsu for the number-one spot among Japanese PC makers. It also manufactures everything from transistors to display modules, and it rivals Toshiba as the world's largest semiconductor maker. NEC is also successful at selling broadband and wireless networking equipment. The company, which has 147,000 employees, continues to build upon its legacy of innovation. Over the past five years it has ranked consistently in the top-10 companies for the number of U.S. patents issued—averaging 1,764 patents granted each year.

In the past number of years, Japan—the world's second largest economy—has been demonstrating a growing interest in corporate social responsibility (CSR). After a series of corporate scandals beginning in 2000 (a major food company lost consumers' loyalty after failing to take sanitary precautions in its factory; another food company was faced with a boycott for disguising foreign beef as domestic in order to receive a mad cow disease subsidy; and a large energy company was caught routinely falsifying the inspection record of nuclear energy plants), many organizations and companies began to place more emphasis on the importance of good corporate behavior.

Further spurring the trend, financial institutions began offering socially responsible investment funds—something that has encouraged companies to begin assessing and improving their efforts in acting responsibly. The growing CSR movement became well documented: in October 2002, the Japan Federation of Economic Organizations (Nippon Keidanren) amended "The Keidanren Charter for Good Corporate Behavior," which placed a new emphasis on strengthening compliance and building trust from consumers.

The Association of Corporate Executives (Keizai Doyukai) published its fifteenth Corporate White Paper, entitled "Market Evolution and CSR Management: Toward Building Integrity and Creating Stakeholder Value." By 2003, mentions of CSR in Japanese newspapers increased fourfold. The result? Recent studies have shown that about 80 percent of large Japanese companies (those with more than 1,000 employees) make some type of contributions to their communities.

NEC has long been committed to giving back to its consumer community all around the world ("Better Products, Better Service" was the first NEC corporate slogan). It has been recognized for its efforts, including a ranking on the *Nikkei Business Daily*'s survey of the best Japanese firms from the perspective of workers and has been included in the Dow Jones Sustainability World Index and several major socially responsible investment funds.

While Japan has long encouraged interaction between business and civil society, social contributions were historically marked by traditional philanthropy. NEC expanded the model by integrating giving back into its operational efforts. It organized a Social Contributions Office as a dedicated unit in 1991. It's since built upon this formalized effort by launching a CSR Promotion Unit and a CSR Promotion Committee, and by appointing a senior executive with responsibility for CSR in 2004. NEC also appointed "CSR Promoters" in each of its business units to foster a deeper awareness of CSR-driven management throughout all NEC group companies.

The company encourages employees to give back—an idea that fits naturally into modern Japanese culture. The Japanese Ministry of Labor established a "Workers Refresh" movement to encourage workers to use their paid time off in ways they would find satisfying. The goal was to make individual lives more balanced—something of concern during the era of Japan's so-called economic miracle, which was marked by excessive worka-holism—and volunteering exemplified a way to achieve that.

At NEC, contributions by employees take several forms, including participating in annual collection drives (these brought in nearly $100,000 from employees in Japan for major earthquake disasters in Turkey, Taiwan, India, and Iran; another drive to collect unused foreign coins helped UNICEF to raise money for underprivileged children in developing countries). NEC has annually sponsored Make a Difference Day, which encourages employees to spend time working in their communities, since 1999.

Education and developing programs that foster the creativity and skills of young people is a key focus of NEC's community activities. Since 1996, the NEC Galileo Club has offered children the opportunity to participate in scientific experiments to help them to develop a greater appreciation for the physical sciences. In 2004, 321 elementary school students in nine cities participated in the classes along with 26 volunteers from NEC who served as assistant instructors.

Looking ahead, NEC plans to make such classes available to children living in areas outside major Japanese cities and will continue to build the program overseas after successfully expanding the program to Malaysia. The program has already proven effective; the young people who came to the first workshops 10 years ago are now university students who have decided on careers in science. Equally telling, many have come back to teach Galileo Club classes.

Another one of NEC's programs, the "NEC Training Program for Social Venture Incubation," teaches students how to start and manage business-oriented nonprofit organizations. The impact from the 2005 program is already apparent: after seven months of training, one group completed procedures to form a nonprofit and began operations and another group started a company. The program, which was launched in 2002, has worked with 13 groups, 7 of which have formed their own enterprises designed to tackle social issues.

NEC's responsible leadership includes a focus on reducing its environmental impact. One of its achievements includes developing the world's first recyclable bioplastics that hold their shapes—an invention with excellent recycling properties. The newly developed bioplastics (based on polylactic acid made from corn) can be returned to its original shapes when heated, which allows it to be melted and molded into other shapes for recycling. Additionally, the company has structured a nationwide distribution network that maximizes efficiency by promoting scheduled and shared transportation shifts, which has resulted in a reduction in the numbers of deliveries and transport distances—and therefore carbon dioxide emissions.

One of NEC's most interesting environmental efforts—and one that has inspired a new profitable line of business—is a program it offers in Japan called NEC Refreshed PC. Refreshed PCs are used NEC PCs that are bought back by the company for thorough cleaning and regeneration. All data is deleted and the Refreshed PCs carry an NEC warranty. NEC has bought and sold a total of 20,000 Refreshed PCs, and the program has been operating at a profit since its first year. In 2005, the company expanded the initiative by committing to plant one tree in Australia's Kangaroo Island for every PC bought back.

In his essay here, Akinobu Kanasugi, a 30-year veteran of NEC who served as president from March 2004 through March 2006, and who is now vice chairman of the board, discusses NEC's commitment to giving back and what it has meant to the company and to him personally.

Empowered
by the Community

Akinobu Kanasugi, Vice Chairman of the Board, NEC

I have found . . . that by branching out beyond the basic fundamental principals of business, my career has become more rewarding.

I believe that it is the communities in which our employees live and work that enable them to perform well in every corner of the globe. Companies can never prosper without coexisting with the communities. As a basis of promoting social responsibility, NEC has issued the "NEC Group Charter of Corporate Behavior." One of the 10 principles of the charter is "maintaining good relations with the community." We believe that companies should get involved in their communities proactively and contribute their resources to solve the challenges that societies are facing. I believe that communities and companies can thrive together under such a relationship.

NEC views compliance as something we should always address as a company and something that would become a baseline of CSR. To be more specific, we have clarified six major risk areas (quality safety, environment, information security, fair trading, occupational health and safety, and human rights), and we provide education to our group executives and employees around the globe to make sure the idea takes root in them. This activity does not stay within our NEC family but has been expanded to the supply chain business partners to mitigate the CSR risks in the partnership.

The very fundamental of business management is to comply with regulations and to fulfill financial responsibilities through sound business activities. That alone, however, does not ensure that we are living up to our social responsibilities. To be successful, we must make contributions to improve the situations in our communities, and this must be an integral part of our business operation and management.

We aim to do this in an efficient manner. We promote programs with a priority on activities that address social challenges with the greatest needs, have deep relations with NEC business domains as an IT company, and allow us to leverage NEC-owned resources. Resources do not only include funding, but products, facilities, people, as well as know-how and expertise.

One of the areas where we believe we can make a real impact is in dissolving the digital divide. A program that exemplifies this objective is the "NEC IT Training for Mothers Raising Small Children." In 2004, in cooperation with child-raising support groups and local governments, we organized IT workshops in six regions across Japan for a total of 120 women. This program serves a dual purpose by targeting mothers raising small children who want to improve their IT skills and women trying to reenter the workforce after completing the most demanding phase of raising children.

Since August 2003, when the first workshop was held in Niiza City, Saitama Prefecture, 10 workshops have been held throughout Japan by request of each region. Former NEC employees, who work as volunteers, teach the classes. We believe sponsoring this program will help develop our next generation. Here in Japan, where the birthrate is declining rapidly, the challenge is how mothers can get assistance in keeping balance between work and motherhood.

Similarly, we sponsor a PC Training Program for senior citizens, the "NEC Senior IT Supporter Training Workshops," which promotes the community participation of senior business people and retired employees. It is a nationwide effort that aims to eliminate the digital divide by training senior citizens with PC skills to become "Senior IT Supporters" who can lead more fulfilling lives by teaching the elderly and people with disabilities. Social participation of senior citizens will become increasingly important in Japan with a full-fledged aging society right around the corner. There are many seniors—including NEC employees—who are hoping to be of service to society. NEC is providing a stage for senior citizens to use their PC skills and at the same time promote their contribution to the dissolution of digital divide.

At NEC we believe that technology has afforded society great advances, but we are also aware that it has introduced new challenges. Privacy protection is one such modern-day issue. The "NEC Kids Internet Safety Program," which was developed in 1999 in partnership with the nonprofit organization Japan Guardian Angels, was designed to teach children and their parents how to protect themselves from harmful information and crimes on the Internet. The program is held at NEC facilities and elementary schools in Japan. To date, more than 5,000 children and their guardians have participated in the program. With mobile phone crime rising rapidly, two classes on safe mobile phone use were also organized. NEC plans to extend these classes in the future to children of middle-school age.

Under the slogan "Nature, Education, Community: The Heart of NEC," NEC has been sponsoring "NEC Make a Difference Day" (the name changed to NEC Makes a Difference in 2005) in every corner of the world, since 1999. Each NEC entity around the globe chooses a date for their "Make a Difference Day," and each office acts on issues related to nature conservation, education, or community needs.

Each year NEC employees achieve significant results. In response to the Niigata Chuetsu earthquake and the Sumatra off-shore earthquake and the Indian Ocean tsunami, numerous NEC group employees worked together to conduct fund-raising drives and support programs. Our employees in Germany have contributed to their communities by donating PCs and monitors to facilities for the mentally disabled and by providing PC instruction to facility staff members. In New Zealand, NEC workers built a mountain bike course and conducted tree-planting activities.

Employees have communicated what participating in Make a Difference Day means to them. Some of their comments include:

> *I'm proud of myself working for NEC, a company that supports employees to take part in community contribution activities.*

> *Team work at the office has improved.*

> *I was able to expand a network with employees from other NEC entities, whom I usually have no exchange with, when I participated in the joint event with other NEC group companies in the region.*

> *I realized that I am a member of NEC family when I found out that NEC entities around the world are participating in the campaign.*

These comments indicate that the activities did not simply end with the contributions to the community, but that they have created a good impact on employees by providing a sense of unity and morale enhancement. Encouraging employees to give back has proven to be an idea that stays with them—even after they no longer work at NEC. When Hurricane Katrina brought devastating damage to southern states of the United States in August 2005, a team led by a former NEC employee went to the afflicted area on a truck immediately after the disaster to deliver clothes, food, and drinking water to the victims. I am impressed and proud of the fact that former NEC employees are involved in such activities.

Being involved in improving our communities has had an enormous impact on our company. I've found that is has been of the utmost importance to me personally as well. In my late forties, I lost my first wife who suffered from cancer. To ease the shock even a little, I took a vacation for 10 days, visited a friend from the time when I was studying at UCLA, and we engaged in many conversations. It was during that visit that I realized that neither title nor rank in society is important to me in my life. Until then, the company was my first priority, and I was working in a self-centered way. However, when I returned to Japan after the reunion with my old friend, I tried hard to figure out a way to inspire others rather than myself. As part of my effort in setting up stages for others, I started to consider the power of embracing diversity. Effective involvement of diverse human resources and their contribution to our business leads to a better society for people with wide range of backgrounds.

NEC Corporation established a subsidiary (NEC Friendly Staff, Ltd.) that is specially equipped to employ people with mental disabilities in Japan. We aim to find opportunities for people with physical disabilities too, including employing visually challenged employees to develop our Universal Design products. We are also committed to supporting the success of women in the Japanese workplace. The ratio of women in managerial roles at NEC Corporation has been increasing every year. Fiscal year 2005 saw the first woman at NEC Corporation become certified as a chief systems architect—the most senior level in the NEC Certified Professional system in Japan.

NEC is very proud of the fact that we were selected as one of the "Preferred Establishments Employing People with Disabilities" for year 2005 by the Japan's Ministry of Health, Labor and Welfare. As a corporate manager, I take this as encouragement—it's shown me that we have made real contributions and it has inspired me personally to consider how we can continue to engage our talented and diverse workforce and enable them to thrive.

My work is still of the same importance to me. I have found, however, that by branching out beyond the basic fundamental principles of business, my career has become more rewarding. Fostering and supporting programs that have a positive impact on society have made my life richer—in every way imaginable.

CHAPTER 15

CREATING FORUMS FOR CHANGE: WORLD ECONOMIC FORUM

Each year, 2,250 of the most well-known and powerful people from 96 countries convene in the small alpine town of Davos, Switzerland, to focus on the world's problems and find solutions.

K laus Schwab is a serious-minded European business professor with university degrees in mechanical engineering and economics, a Master of Public Administration from Harvard, two doctorates, one in science technologies and the other in political economy, as well as honorary doctorates from prestigious institutions including the London School of Economics and Ben-Gurion University. He's also known for his unique ability to gather a world-famous crowd that includes Tony Blair, Bill Clinton, Quincy Jones, Bill Gates, Michael Dell, and Oprah Winfrey as well as a bevy of European and Middle Eastern royalty.

Globally recognized as the visionary founder and executive chairman of the World Economic Forum—the global partnership organization that attracts business, political, and intellectual leaders and celebrities from around the globe—Klaus is renowned for getting unlikely groups to connect. Each year, 2,250 of the most well-known and powerful people from 96 countries convene in the small alpine town of Davos, Switzerland, to focus on the world's problems and find solutions. It's said that global trends are first identified at Davos, and Klaus, the entrepreneur behind it all, has been instrumental in shaping that global agenda for the past 35 years. His work behind the scenes has been responsible for bringing together even the most bitter antagonists, such as the Israelis and the Palestinians, to search for ways to generate positive social change.

In 1971, Klaus founded the World Economic Forum as a nonprofit foundation with the mission to "improve the state of the world." It was his belief that the challenges of the globalized world couldn't be met by governments, business, or nongovernmental organizations (NGOs) alone but through the collaborative efforts of all of the stakeholders of global society. The Forum, which was originally designed to serve as a platform for a European-wide dialogue of business and political leaders, has long created global communities and task forces and published groundbreaking research. Work catalyzed by the World Economic Forum has played a role in important global developments.

In 1979, for example, the Forum became the first nongovernmental institution to initiate a partnership with China's economic development commissions, later spurring economic reform policies in China. In 1988, Greece and Turkey turned back from the brink of war by signing the "Davos Declaration" at the Forum's annual meeting. North and South Korea held their first ministerial-level meetings in Davos in 1989, and at the same meeting, East German Prime Minister Hans Modrow and German Chancellor Helmut Kohl met to discuss German reunification.

While the Forum provides a platform for decision makers to meet, discuss, and debate, it's run as an impartial organization, not tied to any political, partisan, or national interests. The Forum is supported by its members—among the 1,000 foremost global companies, including Microsoft, Citigroup, Coca-Cola, and Dell, and is formally under the supervision of the Swiss Federal Government. In 1995, the Forum was awarded NGO consultative status with the Economic and Social Council of the United Nations.

Today, the World Economic Forum, headquartered in Geneva, is composed of 180 professionals from over 30 countries. It is recognized as the leading organization of its kind. Recently, with the financial contribution he received as part of the Dan David Prize from Tel Aviv University—a one million dollar award honoring outstanding scientific, technological, cultural, or social impact programs—Klaus launched a new foundation in partnership with the World Economic Forum: The Forum of Young Global Leaders.

The new foundation aims to bring together 1,000 diverse people under 40 years of age who have demonstrated their commitment to improving the state of the world. The organization encourages them to work together to create social change over a five-year span. In the inaugural 2005 meeting, one group of Young Global Leaders committed themselves to setting up a free University for Africa, which is properly accredited and offers recognized qualifications. One of the Young Global Leaders has already created a successful venture of this kind in South Africa.

As the World Economic Forum expands its reach through harnessing the power and passion of young people, it is expanding its geographical scope as well. It is currently in the process of opening an additional office in New York (to "be close to the pulse of business and of industrial strategies," Klaus explains). Additionally, it is in the midst of launching another office in Beijing, which will focus on the emerging multinationals in the world.

"The Forum is a membership organization of the top Fortune 500 companies, but there are many companies in developing countries that are very dynamic, family owned, and have around $1 billion revenue, which are considered too small to be accepted as members of the World Economic Forum," explains Klaus. "We created a special membership category for those companies, and we will service them from Beijing. A number of these companies are in China and in Asia, and all companies of this size will be particularly interested in China itself," he adds.

Klaus's sphere of influence goes beyond big corporations, governments, and NGOs. In 1998, Klaus and his wife, Hilde, created a family foundation, the Schwab Foundation for Social Entrepreneurship, which seeks to identify, recognize, and disseminate initiatives in social entrepreneurship that have improved people's lives—and that have the potential to be replicated on a global level.

The foundation, which is a separate entity from the World Economic Forum, also differs in its approach in that it doesn't depend on only the high-level cooperation of global decision makers, but it looks to broader-based community-driven social entrepreneurship. "My belief always has been that in the end, economic and social progress can only be achieved through entrepreneurship of all kinds," Klaus explains. "The foundation enables us to encourage and foster entrepreneurs working for the public interest—to support them and provide them with access and funding to an international platform for experience exchange that they might otherwise lack."

The Schwab Foundation does not give grants. Rather, acceptance into the network connects its selected entrepreneurs to corporations, high-net-worth individuals, and other foundations that are looking to support socially responsible initiatives. (It is almost as if the foundation acts as a broker between social entrepreneurs and social investors.) The foundation also introduces social entrepreneurs to one other and each year holds the Social Entrepreneurs' Summit, an event where they can exchange best practices and strengthen their community of fellowship. Schwab entrepreneurs are also invited to attend the meetings of the World Economic Forum, where it connects its community of accomplished social entrepreneurs with corporate and government leaders. Davos corporate participants also benefit from social entrepreneurs' know-how.

Many world leaders have said they were inspired by the efforts of the social entrepreneurs who were present at the meetings. At the Forum's regional meetings, social entrepreneurs have the opportunity to meet leaders in their own countries to whom they would not otherwise have access, and are invited to participate in discussions and task forces on pertinent topics including health, education, and the digital divide.

As a direct result of the foundation's efforts, social entrepreneurs report that they have mobilized a total of $76 million last year alone. (This means that each social entrepreneur has been able to raise, on average, about one million dollars, not including in-kind resources.) As a result of nominations made by the Schwab Foundation, its social entrepreneurs received a total of 41 other awards that have brought additional financial support and international recognition to their efforts. Because of the foundation, their stories have been featured in 366 articles and television programs.

Perhaps most importantly, since inclusion into the network, the efforts of Schwab social entrepreneurs have increased 3.5 times. Today, they work directly with a total of 600 million people—that's an average of about eight million persons per social entrepreneur.

The Schwab Foundation recently unveiled its most recent effort, a collaboration with the media to select a "Social Entrepreneur of the Year" from various countries. The award winners will join the global Schwab Foundation's network and have access to the benefits provided by the foundation.

In addition to his work with the World Economic Forum and the Schwab Foundation, Klaus has been a business policy professor at the University of Geneva since 1972 and has lectured around the world. He has also written several books. He maintains close affiliations with Harvard University, MIT, and the United Nations, where he's served as a member of the high-level Advisory Board on Sustainable Development and as the Vice-Chairman of the Development Planning Committee.

He is the recipient of many prestigious honors, including the Candlelight Award, presented by UN Secretary-General Kofi Annan, the Guggenheim Humanitarian Award, and the Annual Award of the International Institute of Education. He's also been recognized for his peace and reconciliation efforts in several regions, with national honors including the Knight of the Légion d'Honneur of France, Grand Cross of the National Order of Merit of Germany, and Highest-level Order of Friendship of the Republic of Kazakhstan.

When we spoke with Klaus from the Geneva headquarters of the World Economic Forum, he was gearing up to climb Mount Rosa, a 4,000-meter peak in the Alps that he climbs every summer. We talked about the organizations he's founded, leadership, and the importance of collaborations between businesses, government organizations, and NGOs. As he reflects on the past 35 years, he admits he had no idea that his brainchild would blossom into what it has become today. He relates his lifelong work to his current challenge, climbing Switzerland's highest mountain: "You always have big aspirations, but you concentrate on what you have just in front of you."

SUSTAINABLE CAPITALISM

Klaus Schwab, Founder, World Economic Forum, and
Schwab Foundation for Social Entrepreneurship

*The key to sustainable capitalism is reasonable profits as opposed to
maximizing profits.*

I t has been clear to me for some time that the pressing problems
we face are too complex to be left only to the public, the corporate, or the charitable sector. My life's work has been about advancing innovative concepts and practices to facilitate the coming
together of different stakeholders. The World Economic Forum,
the Schwab Foundation, and the newly formed organization of
Young Global Leaders are all expressions that reinforce that
approach.

We all know that proponents of capitalism believe that individuals pursuing their own interests will also maximize the ful-
fillment of the interests of society as a whole. This so-called
trickle down theory posits that the capital created by the wealthy
will eventually reach the poor as a result of investments, increases
in productivity, and employment opportunities. While the theory has many critics, we do know that the last decades have demonstrated that countries and economies that provided citizens
with high degrees of economic freedom have had much faster
economic development, benefiting hundreds of millions of poor,

in comparison to other countries that relied mainly on collectivism and state control.

There is little doubt that business as we know it today has empowered individual genius and bestowed great social benefits. Yet it has also done social harm. Many of the ills of modern life—nonsustainable levels of personal and institutional debt, toxic air and water, workplace injury, loss of livelihoods for communities, political bribery—can be traced to corporate lack of responsibility to one or more constituencies. This is not intentional. No one wants to cause poverty, pollution, disease, unemployment and corruption. Rather, they want to make profits. But in that pursuit, they may find antisocial behavior pays. To achieve profits in the short term, corporations exact a "social and environmental price," and that price is high and rising.

The key to sustainable capitalism is reasonable profits as opposed to maximizing profits. In the current system, a segment of society is trying to maximize profits without concern for the impact on the well-being of the society as a whole, while another segment of social organizations have to deal with the fallout. The system is not working. The reality is that capitalism has to be seen in the broader social context, and not just defined by economic capital but also human and social capital.

I founded the World Economic Forum as a membership organization that brings the world's leaders from business, government, and the media together with thought leaders and social change agents, such as social entrepreneurs. The Forum is unique in providing a multistakeholder platform to raise awareness for decisions to be made and to make sure that the opinion and best know-how of every stakeholder is heard and considered when shaping the global agenda. We are not a decision-making body—decisions in our world are made by those who have the necessary mandate to do so, such as international organizations on a global level, governments on a national level, or corporations on a business level. We are, however, a decision-facilitating mechanism. In fact, there is no other organization that is so involved in the pre-decision-making and post-decision-making phases.

There are many examples that illustrate the hand we have had in decision making. At the 2005 Annual Meeting at Davos, for example, we were able to put the fight against poverty at the top of the global agenda and provide a platform to come up with ideas and initiatives of what should be done. It now appears that the international community, and particularly the G-8 [The Group of Eight (G-8) consists of Canada, France, Germany, Italy, Japan, Russia, the United Kingdom, and the United States. The hallmark of the G-8 is an annual political summit meeting of the heads of government with international officials.], will create the necessary action. Another initiative that stemmed from the meeting is our work with the office of United Kingdom Prime Minister Tony Blair to look beyond the Kyoto Protocol to address the challenge of climate change. Together, we are making sure that the best ideas for action will be integrated by the United Kingdom presidency into the proposals for the G-8.

The Forum has had a unique role in creating public-private partnerships long before such partnerships were part of international lexicon. Those partnerships have always been based on pragmatism and action. We have many examples of this including, our Global Health Initiative, our Jordan Educational Initiative, and our Disaster Relief Network (DRN).

The formation of the Disaster Relief Network, for example, was initiated as a result of the 2001 earthquake that devastated Gujarat, India. Using the platform of the World Economic Forum, our members in the engineering, construction, and logistics fields created the DRN when they concluded that there was no established mechanism for putting their resources to work for relief workers on the ground. The DRN has become a point of contact and coordination for companies that want to provide support to disaster management efforts in developing countries.

Today, the DRN is a Swiss nonprofit private foundation that coordinates the donations of goods and pro bono services contributed by members of the World Economic Forum. The donation of time and administrative expertise from these corporate executives keeps overhead costs to a minimum. In just three years, through its global alliance of business partners, the DRN has contributed resources to humanitarian relief efforts on four continents. It's had real impact: after the Asian tsunami in 2004, for example, we were able to tap into the network's logistics capabilities and have the airport at Colombo running within 48 hours. The DRN's work demonstrates how much can be accomplished when, in the face of disaster, business is organized to effectively dispatch assistance to the site.

Companies that become members of the World Economic Forum are responsible global corporations. But over the last 10 years, they have become much more aware of the importance of being more proactive stakeholders in global society.

There is a saying, "Top down doesn't work but bottom up is not enough."

There are many reasons for this, but let me highlight two that are historic. First, there is a shifting locus of control from those who sell to those who buy. The uninformed, subservient, passive, loyal customer and employee are rapidly becoming history. They are being replaced by women and men—and even children—who are powered by information technology that gives them instant access to relevant information about anything. They use that information not only to find the best deals for every product and service on the global market, but also to collectively organize and demand transparency and accountability from their "leaders," including those in the corporate sectors. The power has been transferred from those who sell to those who buy, from those who exercise public or corporate power to those who have the capacity to mobilize others and blow the collective whistle when power is abused. Information technology fosters the ultimate in mass participation.

A second factor in the power shift is the explosion of choices. The world in which we now live abounds in goods and services and information about them. Many of these goods and services are similar. Whether one is looking for sports gear, household appliances, or a charitable cause, for a household handyman, a strategic consultant, or a project that addresses HIV/AIDS in Africa, there is an abundance of choice.

Suppliers have to work hard to get noticed. Economics and business have traditionally been the science of scarce resources. But in an age of surplus supply, something else has to attract the customer besides the product or the service. Successful companies today are those that have been able to appeal not only to the rational side of people but also to their emotions. If nothing else, adherence to principles set out in the Global Compact[1] would support a company's "emotional" value proposition.

So while there are other factors at work, these two highlight why it is in a company's enlightened self-interest to incorporate global corporate citizenship into its core business—and more and more are beginning to do so.

There is a saying, "Top down doesn't work but bottom up is not enough." While we think the World Economic Forum has successfully demonstrated the power of bringing the world's leaders from many sectors together to work on changes at the macro level, we found that we also needed to find a way to identify people who have discovered practical solutions to social, economic, and environmental problems at the local level.

We knew that innovative solutions that have been shown to transform people's lives could be adapted to solve similar problems all around the world. We wanted to create a way to disseminate their accomplishments so others can support them or emulate their approaches. Together with the facilitating structural supports at the macrolevel, those microlevel innovations can improve the state of the world and the state of the people in it.

With that philosophy, we established the Schwab Foundation to invest its resources in creating unprecedented opportunities where social entrepreneurs, who have successfully implemented and begun to scale their transformational initiatives, can further the legitimacy of their work, have access to usually inaccessible networks, and in consequence, mobilize financial and in-kind resources that enable them to continue to strengthen and expand.

It's interesting to recall that when we started this foundation, the concept of social entrepreneurship was virtually unknown. In fact, we had a difficult time registering the name of the foundation with the Swiss authorities! In the past few years, though, "social entrepreneurship" has had a meteoric rise. Click on Google and you will find 1.5 million entries for "social entrepreneurship" and 2.3 million for "social entrepreneur."

While we are excited about this rapid acceleration of the notion of social entrepreneurship, we also regard it with cautious optimism. It seems everyone these days who does any social activity is calling himself a "social entrepreneur." Most are well-meaning people running nonprofits doing good things for the unfortunate—and that is a wonderful thing. And while all of us may have some entrepreneurial traits to a greater or lesser degree, in our experience, a true social entrepreneur is a rare breed. They possess the exhausting and exhilarating energy to imagine, innovate, implement, measure, improve on innovation, scale up, diversify, defy the usual, break the patterns, move in a new direction, and create new organizational arrangements.

The Schwab Foundation does not give grants; we leverage our expertise as well as our close, but separate, relationship with the World Economic Forum. The social entrepreneurs we select to our community report that our networking capabilities have represented a much greater value to them than any single grant that we could have provided. For example, thanks to the facilitating role of the Schwab Foundation working together with the Forum, the John Deere Company has invested $3 million in Kick Start, a nonprofit organization that develops and markets new technologies in Africa, which was founded and run by two of our social entrepreneurs, Martin Fisher and Nick Moon. Specifically, the funds will go to enable 80,000 African families—approximately 400,000 people—to raise their standard of living by introducing small, inexpensive irrigation pumps and other agricultural-based money-making equipment. Kick Start would have been much less likely to have access to John Deere had it not been for our work to bring them together.

We have seen the accomplishments of the entrepreneurs supported by the foundation. Take, for example, Javier Hurtado, an entrepreneur from Bolivia whose focus has been getting indigenous peoples' organic agricultural products to global markets. He started his organization, Irupana, in 1987.

Today, Irupana works with 1,700 subsistence farmers who would otherwise have few markets for their goods. Irupana teaches them how to farm organically and buys their produce, which it then processes organically into 80 different products and distributes these nationally to 18 Irupana stores and 300 outlets, including large supermarkets and overseas markets in the United States and Europe.

Irupana typically raises indigenous families' incomes from around US $700 up to the national average of about $1,000 a

year. Growing organic crops that sell for higher prices to mid-
dle- and upper-income families allows farmers to receive 20 to
50 percent for those crops more than for nonorganic crops. Seeing
the indigenous farmers as business partners with considerable
entrepreneurial potential—not as aid recipients—has been a key
to Irupana's success. Because of access to the Schwab Foundation's
network, Irupana has been able to establish partnerships with
major grocery stores in Switzerland and Germany. It sells $2.2
million of certified organic products a year, and its market is
rapidly expanding.

There is no doubt that large parts of the population feel that
business interests are no longer aligned with social interests. The
recent corporate scandals, the greedy and fraudulent behavior of
some CEOs, and the drive by some corporations to maximize
profits at all costs—despite social and environmental destruc-
tion—have been real and have been appalling. But it is not capitalism and globalization that are the problem. At the heart of it
is the deterioration of a sense of public purpose and global citizenship within the corporate community.

The only way to stop this wave of antibusiness sentiment is for
business to take the lead and to reposition itself clearly and con-
vincingly as part of society. While we have built the Forum on
the basis of the stakeholder concept, given today's challenges we
have to add a new dimension of global corporate citizenship. The
stakeholder concept defines the economic, social, and environmental responsibilities of the management of an enterprise vis-à-
vis its own stakeholders, individuals and groups, which usually
have a direct stake in the company.

Global corporate citizenship goes far beyond the stakeholder
concept. It means that the company in itself is a stakeholder in
global society, a global citizen with rights and duties. It means
that the company has to engage with other stakeholders of global
society, such as governments, civil society, science, education, and

cultural organizations to address the challenges we collectively face and shape the global agenda.

I have always been a strong believer in the capacity of leaders to change our world, and I have been privileged to get to know many world leaders on a personal basis. These men and women come from all age groups and cultures and display different leadership styles. But the greatest leaders who exercise transformational leadership are those who combine brains, heart, and soul.

To be a true leader, you must be among the best professionals in your field. A leader's professionalism breeds respect in others, and so brains are essential. But there must be a harmonic relationship between brains and heart. These leaders' belief in what they are doing unlocks the drive and creativity needed to succeed. Unlike most people who focus on what they feel they *should* do to advance their professional careers, these leaders make a point of focusing on what they really *want* to do: contribute their faculties to the creation of a more dignified and caring society. Doing what makes them feel passionate in service of society breeds love and loyalty and empowers others to do the same, forming the foundation of true community.

The world needs many more of these types of leaders in government, business, and civil society. We are currently very enthused about our newest project, a global advisory group, which is a group of about 100 people that includes leaders in very top positions such as ministers, heads of state, top CEOs, and Nobel Prize winners. These people will be available on request to advise governments and international organizations on specific policy issues. Our passion for putting together this new group and our continuing work through the World Economic Forum, the Schwab Foundation, and now the Young Global Leaders, is rooted all in the same idea: a continuing quest to identify true leaders, who by working together, have the capability to improve the state of the world.

CHAPTER 16

THE EVERYDAY PHILANTHROPIST: WORKING ASSETS

In addition to allowing its customers to give at no extra cost, the company aims to turn customers into active citizens.

The comedian Paula Poundstone once joked that her "Master-Card spending alone could rescue a third world country." Unfortunately, we can't assume that she was talking about a Working Assets MasterCard, but if she had been, some of her purchasing would actually have gone to making a difference in lesser-developed countries, as well as in her own backyard.

Working Assets, a San Francisco–based for-profit company, offers a credit card that donates 10 cents per transaction to non-profit groups working for peace, human rights, equality, educa-tion, and the environment. The company first launched the credit card in 1985, before affinity cards such as airline miles cards and nonprofit credit cards were in existence. The idea was to create a more progressive philanthropic model and help people make a difference through everyday acts like using a credit card. "The big question was, could you use consumerism to help improve the world and effect social change," says Laura Scher, the cofounder, chairperson, and CEO of Working Assets.

Now, 20 years later, Laura and Working Assets have proven that you can indeed use consumerism to make a positive difference. In addition to the credit card, which has attracted more than 100,000 customers, Working Assets has launched long-distance and wireless telephone service and most recently an online flower delivery service that donates a portion of its revenue—regardless of the company's profits—to progressive causes. To date, the company has donated more than $50 million to hundreds of nonprofit groups, including Amnesty International, Doctors without Borders, Greenpeace, Oxfam, and WITNESS.

Each year, customers nominate the organizations they want to give to (each nonprofit must be national or international in focus and has to have been in existence for more than one year). An independent foundation evaluates the hundreds of nominees, and Working Assets employees select 50 groups in five categories (civil rights, education and freedom of expression, the environment, peace and international freedom, and economic and social justice) to be listed on an annual donations ballot. Customers then vote on how to distribute the funds. (They can suggest 5 percent for one organization, 45 percent for another, and 50 percent for a third, for example.) Working Assets counts every vote—they had 150,000 votes in 2004 and disbursed nearly $7 million to the selected nonprofits.

In addition to allowing its customers to give at no extra cost, the company aims to turn customers into active citizens. It gives its customers information about public issues and offers them the opportunity to speak out—an initiative that has created one of the country's most powerful citizen-action groups.

Each month, Working Assets customers generate approximately 80,000 calls and letters on issues of public concern. Some recent political victories include saving the Arctic National Wildlife Refuge from oil drilling, defeating conservative judicial appointments, and thwarting a controversial energy policy. In 2004 Working Assets customers generated more than four million calls, letters, and e-mails to Congress, the White House, and corporate leaders.

The company lives by its progressive ideals as well. It prints its bills on 100 percent postconsumer recycled paper with soy-based ink and commits to plant 100 trees for each ton of paper used. And, Laura, the only female CEO of a U.S. telephone company, drives to work in a hybrid car, a Toyota Prius, which gets 42 miles to the gallon.

It makes sense that Laura, whose father made environmentally friendly chemicals and whose mother was an economics professor and the president of the League of Women Voters, says that upon graduating Harvard Business School, she wanted to have a job doing something that she "could believe in." Growing up in New Jersey, her family worked on presidential campaigns, cleaned up a local river, and carried their recycling around in the trunk of their car before curbside pickup came to their neighborhood. But when Laura graduated Harvard Business School in 1985— right in the hullabaloo of the decade of greed—the idea of socially responsible business was still somewhat of an oxymoron.

Today, with the current boom of social entrepreneurship, it's apparent that Laura, who's been called a "modern-day Robin Hood," was onto something early. Her ideas to merge caring and commerce—once perceived as unusual by her peers at Harvard— are now embraced by a new generation of students. (The business school now offers an entire Social Enterprise Initiative.) And, Working Assets has emerged as both a progressive organization (it's the only telephone company endorsed by Nell Newman and Gloria Steinem) and as a viable business that does $140 million in revenue and made it to the *Inc.* 500 list of "fastest growing privately held companies in America" for five years in a row.

For her innovative approach that melds business and philanthropy, Laura has been the recipient of many accolades. She was honored as Entrepreneur of the Year in Northern California in 1997, and the San Francisco League of Women Voters has named her "one of four women who could be President." She has also been recognized by *Working Mother* magazine as one of the "25 most influential working moms." In her essay here, Laura talks about the founding of Working Assets and what the company has achieved in its 20-year history.

CONSUMERISM WITH A CONSCIENCE

Laura Scher, Cofounder, Chairperson, CEO,
Working Assets

*By using both the Web site and the bill, customers generate about a
hundred thousand phone calls and letters every month.*

Working Assets was founded 20 years ago with a mission to
create products that allowed people to spend in a socially
responsible way. Of course, that concept needed to be defined
because there weren't really any models of socially responsible
business back in 1985. Our first product was modeled on a program launched by American Express in which Amex donated a
penny to restore the Statue of Liberty each time someone used
their American Express card. We asked ourselves "What would
happen if Working Assets donated more than one penny? What
else could we fund this way?"

The Working Assets credit card was launched in December
1985 with Visa and MasterCard. At that time we donated a nickel
per transaction (now it's 10 cents), and we funded four different
issue areas: peace and international freedom; human rights; economic justice (then called hunger and homelessness); and a cleaner
environment. We thought this was an obvious idea for everyone
who already used a credit card since this card would give money to
a nonprofit group with every transaction, at no extra cost to the
customer. We wanted to build a business model where consumers

didn't have to pay more to be socially responsible. In fact, we found that switching to Working Assets actually saved customers money because we had lower interest rates.

While we thought we had come up with the best idea ever, it's important to mention that I was fresh out of business school, and at that stage in my career it was easier to take a risk. Although we expected to be successful, the idea was underestimated by the bank issuing the credit cards, which believed we would acquire 10,000 customers in our first three years. In fact, we had that number of applications after only eight months.

From the outset we called the venture Working Assets Funding Service rather than Working Assets credit card, because we knew that we wanted to add other products. In the fall of 1987 we began to consider what exactly we might offer. Like the credit card, we were looking for a product in everyday use. There were two services we considered: long-distance telephone service and electricity.

Despite presenting a real chance for customers to use their buying power to determine how electricity was generated in the United States, it became clear that there wouldn't be an opportunity for outsiders to enter that industry. On the other hand, long-distance telephone service proved to be a viable market for Working Assets.

In 1988, after a year of searching for a phone company that would allow us to market long-distance phone service, we launched Working Assets Long Distance through Sprint. At first, we didn't handle the billing or customer service, we just signed up customers. Sprint paid Working Assets a very small percentage and we made a 1 percent donation to a pool for nonprofits, which in the beginning were mainly environmental groups.

The bill itself is an activism newsletter.

Telecom was a very different world when we started. Customers had to be convinced to switch from AT&T, and there was some skepticism because it wasn't thought Working Assets would offer quality phone service. Despite this landscape, over 50,000 customers signed up during the first year. We soon realized, however, that we weren't doing everything we could. Many of our customers didn't even know they were with Working Assets because all their billing came from the carrier Sprint. The only item customers received from Working Assets was a ballot sheet for the selection of donor recipients, followed by a report after the money had been donated. In 1990 Working Assets changed the way it operated and became a reseller, buying telephone time in bulk, which was sold on to customers at competitive rates. This change enabled us to bill the customer directly.

I believe Working Assets is the only company that decided to become a reseller in order to manage billing—after all, that's the most onerous task! However, we thought it would be a great opportunity to communicate with customers. As long as we had to send them a bill, why not do something more? Customers already had to get out their checkbook, stick on a stamp, and mail back the payment. We wondered what else we could do while we had the customer's attention. That's how we become much more innovative and created what is in some ways our product—the bill.

The bill itself is an activism newsletter. Every month it includes two or three issues directed at decision makers. Customers can check a box and for a small fee we'll send a letter under their name, or they can make a free phone call to the decision maker, be it a representative, senator, or corporate leader. We also include an option to round up the monthly phone bill payment to the nearest $1, $5, or $10, and we donate the difference. The contribution is 100 percent tax deductible for our customers, and although it's really like the penny jar at the cash register, collecting funds this way really adds up. We raise $100,000 a month for our nonprofits in this way.

In the late 1990s and early 2000, Working Assets started using the Web to disseminate information. In addition to information on our company and products, we have WorkingforChange, our news and information site, and ActforChange, focusing on activism. On ActforChange we can publish "Actions," particularly those with a very short time frame. For instance, if Congress is going to vote on a bill in three days, we can advise people on how to immediately take action, as opposed to the 60-day window needed for actions presented on the bill.

By using both the Web site and the bill, customers generate about a hundred thousand phone calls and letters every month supporting such issues as voting rights, energy efficiency, and the prevention of drilling in the Arctic. Working Assets is also involved in grassroots organizing, whereby meetings are set up between our customers and their elected officials to discuss issues of concern. We give them advice on how to speak at these meetings and how to become active citizens. For instance, in February 2005 we had 24 meetings with senators around the country where citizens had the opportunity to express their concerns about President Bush's continuous resubmission of contentious judicial nominees. We also planned meetings for customers to voice their opinions on the proposed privatization of Social Security.

Our customers' activism has resulted in many victories. Several years ago Mitsubishi wanted to build the world's largest salt plant on the coast of Baja California, Mexico, an area where the California gray whales breed and the home to many endangered animal and plant species. After concerned citizens wrote more than a million letters, including tens of thousands written by Working Assets customers, Mitsubishi agreed not to build a plant. Mitsubishi admitted that the decision to cancel the project was due to pressure from individuals. On another occasion, Working Assets customers became involved when Pacific Bell (now SBC) was going to cut down trees in the Tongass National Forest, which would be used in the production of the Yellow Pages. We joined with Rainforest Action Network and were able to persuade them not to go ahead. In another example, when Mercedes Benz was going to buy Chrysler, we called on them to compensate slave laborers who worked for them during World War II. Because of American consumer pressure—and before other companies were doing this—Mercedes contributed to a compensation fund.

As a company, Working Assets is proud of its achievements. At the outset one of our goals was to reach a point where we were donating $1 million to nonprofit groups annually, which seemed quite impossible in 1985. We reached our goal in 1993. Around that time AT&T, which had been giving $50,000 a year to Planned Parenthood, bowed to a vocal minority and ceased funding the organization. That year we wrote a check to Planned Parenthood for $55,382. There we were, the little phone company start-up, writing a check to a group we cared about, for an amount larger than AT&T's contribution. As an aside, this all seemed much more important when AT&T had 85 percent dominance of the market. Now, it seems that Working Assets has prospered, while AT&T has not—an interesting irony and perhaps validation of the idea that companies do well by doing good.

It was Working Assets' top-line commitment to social change and bottom-line commitment to running a good business that has allowed us to survive and thrive. I don't think we would be here, no matter how big our hearts were, if the only goal was raising money for nonprofit groups. We had to figure out how to run a successful business and to do that we employed the same analytic tools for both commercially and socially responsible business decisions.

Working Assets is a success because we offer great quality products and exceptional service, but we choose to spend our marketing dollars on making donations rather than running expensive television commercials. The weekly, or even hourly, advertising budget for Cingular Wireless is probably greater than our entire marketing budget. For Working Assets, making a socially responsible business decision has also been a sustainable business decision. Apart from being the right way to go, I would argue that being socially responsible—sometimes in the short term, and definitely in the long term—is financially beneficial for all companies. Think how happy Toyota must be with their investment in hybrid technology. It became an excellent business decision. Think of Ford's chagrin at not making that investment. It now licenses the technology from Toyota.

We are sometimes asked if we miss out on customers because of our stance on issues that are deemed controversial. These include protecting a woman's right to choose, supporting gay and lesbian rights, and saving the rainforest. It's our belief that the causes we select are actually the opinion of the majority, although the vocal minority might make you think otherwise.

However, that's not the reason Working Assets promotes progressive causes. We give these issues our support in response to our customers' votes. I'm sure there are some who don't join Working Assets because we fund certain issues, but there are clearly many more who become members because they are confident that we represent their beliefs through our funding and activism. Working Assets was created with this mission: to build a company that is more just, humane, and environmentally sustainable. We're sure that for our one million customers, and for the hundreds of nonprofits which have shared over $50 million in donations, this is the right company.

CHAPTER 17

REVOLUTIONIZING HOW WE GIVE BACK: REVOLUTION

There's more to Revolution than making money. The company is working to give consumers more choice, more control, and more convenience—in a number of sectors.

Steve Case—the serial entrepreneur who started his first business when he was six (selling juice from the limes in his backyard); launched a mail-order enterprise that offered greeting cards, seeds, and watches as a teenager; and made the Internet accessible to millions of consumers by founding AOL—has admitted that his addiction to building companies could one day land him in "Entrepreneurs Anonymous." It's not likely that day will be anytime soon, though. At the moment, Steve is too hooked on building his newest venture, called Revolution, which he officially launched in April 2005.

Steve is pouring $500 million of his money into Revolution, a private holding company that will invest in health care, wellness, and resorts. The company looks to buy early-stage, consumer-oriented businesses that Steve plans to develop into highly profitable companies.

Revolution has already had success with Exclusive Resorts, a luxury vacation club that Steve acquired a percentage of in 2003.

Since the investment, Exclusive Resorts has grown from 50 members who vacationed at a dozen of the company's homes to more than 1,700 members and more than 300 residences. Revolution also acquired a 70 percent stake in Miraval, a top-rated "life in balance" destination in southern Arizona, which will be expanding in the years to come.

There's more to Revolution than making money, though. The company is working to give consumers more choice, more control, and more convenience—in a number of sectors. In health care, for example, Revolution Health is investing in health clinics inside major retail centers, where consumers can be seen quickly and affordably—something that will be especially helpful when the doctor's office is closed and the only other option would be an expensive and time-consuming visit to the emergency room. It's also developing a Web site where consumers can get reliable information about health-care providers in the same simple fashion they can access restaurant or movie reviews.

Steve's latest entrepreneurial act represents the culmination of years of thought on how to create a bridge between the nonprofit and for-profit worlds. "What I'm most interested in is building organizations in this 'sector blending' space—running a business that also serves a valuable social objective, or running a nonprofit that earns part of its income through viable commercial activity," he explains. "This new kind of business paradigm will generate social benefits as well as financial returns. It will not only make a profit, but make a difference."

The genius of Steve Case has always had less to do with computers and whiz-bang technology than with brilliant marketing and creative vision. His warm-up to AOL began not with a tech-head pulling apart PCs, but with a Pizza Hut executive spending too much time on the road. After Steve graduated from Williams College (with a degree in political science—"the closest thing to marketing," he explains), he joined Procter & Gamble and later managed development for Pizza Hut, then owned by PepsiCo. The job required endless travel in search of new ideas for pizza toppings, and Steve would spend many nights in his hotel room with his computer. Steve subscribed to The Source, one of the first online services, and became absorbed with the possibilities of a community that existed online.

In 1983 Steve attended the Consumer Electronics Association's convention in Las Vegas, where he was introduced to a company called Control Video, which distributed games for Atari using a phone line and modem. Although Control Video was struggling financially, Steve eyed an opportunity to enter the world of computer-based communication, and he signed on with the company.

Although Control Video was unable to get traction with its Atari service, Steve was able to establish a strategic alliance with Commodore and launch a new company, called Quantum Computer Services, in 1985. Quantum's initial service was Q-Link for Commodore computers, and in the years that followed, Quantum scored deals to provide custom-built online services for hardware companies including Apple and Tandy. (Steve, known for his persistence, practically camped out at Apple's headquarters for four months before he struck a deal.) In 1989, the small company found itself in a predicament when Apple decided to manage its own online service and Quantum lost a needed customer.

Sometimes, as the Dalai Lama has said, not getting what you want can be a wonderful stroke of luck: needing to reduce its dependence on the big hardware manufacturers, Quantum created its own branded online service. The new product—named America Online—rolled out nationally for use on any type of computer in 1989. (Quantum changed its name to America Online a few years later.)

As a subscription-based online community, AOL was in direct competition with the better-known services including Compu-Serve, Prodigy, and Genie—all of which were owned by giant corporations. Steve, who became CEO of AOL in 1993, always had a unique vision for the service, though. His mission was to make the power of the online medium available to the average person—not just the computer-savvy techies who were already on the larger text-based versions. To that end, AOL was designed with colors and icons that made it "friendly" and easy to use. While its competitors focused on games, shopping, and business, AOL aimed its attention on building "community" via chat rooms and message boards. The idea worked, and AOL gained subscribers.

Although AOL was criticized by some technology folks for its "novice interface," it eventually proved that ease of use was what reigned supreme with the consumer. In 1995, *PC Magazine*, *Family PC Magazine*, and *Online Access Magazine* all rated AOL the "Best Consumer Online Service." In 1996, AOL, which first went public in 1992 as "AMER" on the Nasdaq, moved to the New York Stock Exchange and got the new ticker "AOL." (The Wall Street sign was changed to "WAOL Street" for the day.)

In just over a decade, after its modest start as beat-up computer gaming company, AOL swelled into a company with 10 million subscribers—a circulation higher than any U.S. newspaper—and delivered more daily mail in form of e-mail and instant messages than the U.S. Postal Service. The company reaped the financial rewards as well: revenue reached $1 billion.

When it looked like the tides could turn for the worse for AOL as more home-computer users gained access to the Internet through their phone companies, AOL swiftly navigated the changing marketplace. Steve wanted AOL to be the most popular portal for the average consumer to enter the Internet, and to achieve this he repositioned AOL as "the Internet and a whole lot more" and launched an aggressive marketing push, mailing "try AOL for free" disks to computer owners. In addition, AOL snapped up companies including its former rival CompuServe, and later Netscape Communications, which made a popular Internet browser, and MovieFone, Inc., the number-one movie and ticketing service.

Over and over, AOL bounced back from the trying circumstances it faced (something that earned it the nickname "the cockroach of cyberspace"[1]). Eventually, it became the first blue-chip company of the Internet (the stock would double again and again), introduced millions and millions of people to the Web, and ushered in a new kind of electronic community—and *zeitgeist*. (AOL became so embedded in our culture that a popular movie starring Tom Hanks and Meg Ryan was titled *You've Got Mail*, one of AOL's friendly electronic greetings.)

By 2000 AOL had established itself as a new media giant, and Steve orchestrated what the business press then called "the deal of the century." For $106 billion, AOL acquired Time Warner, the entertainment and media colossus that owned Warner Brothers film studio, Time Inc. publishing, and CNN. Steve served as chairman of the combined enterprise, AOL Time Warner—the largest media company in the world.

The merger, as many do, struggled with clashing corporate cultures. Problems were compounded by the end of the dot-com bubble and the crash in Internet stocks. The deal eventually caused the stock to lose $135 billion in market value. In 2003, Steve stepped down as chairman. He resigned from the board of directors in 2005 to focus on building his new company, Revolution.

Although Steve is no longer an AOL executive, the legacy he's left on the company—and the industry—is indelible. AOL provided the first instant messaging service, the first parental controls, and the first service designed specifically for broadband consumers. It remains the world's largest Internet service provider, with about 26 million subscribers across the globe. And, after he helped to make the personal computer—connected through the Internet—as much a part of the American home as television or the telephone, Steve stepped up as an industry leader on issues that arose from the new technology—protecting consumer privacy, integrating technology into schools, and ensuring the safety of children on the Internet.

While AOL has always had a very comprehensive program to give back to the community (among other things, it focuses on improving the skills of underserved youth, increasing technology literacy in disadvantaged communities, and encouraging its employees and members to participate in volunteer activities), Steve has personally dedicated himself to making a difference in the community as well. In 1997, Steve and his wife, Jean, founded the Case Foundation, which seeks to achieve sustainable solutions to complex social problems by investing in collaboration, leadership, and entrepreneurship.

The foundation currently invests in several areas including education, health care, youth development, community development, and international projects. Over the years, the Case Foundation has done direct giving, including granting start-up funds to help launch City Year in Washington, DC, providing the seed money for PowerUP (a program designed to close the digital divide by building computer centers for underserved youth), and granting $10 million to Habitat for Humanity to build affordable homes.

But now the work of the Case Foundation goes well beyond traditional financial giving. The Cases employ an approach that taps their entrepreneurial talents to help organizations achieve growth and sustainability. This is illustrated in the foundation's work with Accelerate Brain Cancer Cure (ABC^2), an organization Steve founded with his brother, Dan, shortly after Dan was diagnosed with brain cancer. (Dan, who was recognized as one of the world's leading investment bankers, passed away in 2002.)

The nonprofit is based on the idea that the same entrepreneurial model that has made so many technological innovations
possible can also help develop promising therapies for brain cancer—and, one day, Steve says, help to find a cure.

Steve saw the possibilities of the online world before the rest
of the world had ever heard of the Internet. Once again, he is
aiming to create a new community—one where nonprofits and
businesses overlap to achieve social good. Here, Steve discusses
how in balancing the goals of purpose and profit, we can maximize both—and "pay dividends to the community as a whole."

A Hybrid Approach to Business and Philanthropy

Steve Case, cofounder, AOL; chairman and CEO,
Revolution; chairman, The Case Foundation

Too many people act as if the private sector and the social sector should operate on different axes, with one all about maximizing profits and the other all about maximizing social impact. A better approach is to integrate these missions.

There are few more rewarding experiences than making a donation of time or money that literally changes a life. I am grateful that I have had the opportunity—through both my business and philanthropic interests—to invest in making the world a better place.

However, over the last few years I've become increasingly aware—and uncomfortable—with the fact that I appear to wear two distinct and very different hats. There's *Steve Case the Business Executive*, and *Steve Case the Foundation Executive*, and it often feels that if I put on one hat, I have to take off the other.

This became most apparent recently with the launch of my new company, Revolution. A lot of people came out of the woodwork and asked if they could be investors in the new company. "Steve Case was lucky once with AOL, maybe he'll strike gold again," they think. "I want to be part of that." It's interesting (and quite frankly, bizarre) to juxtapose that frenzy with what happens when I'm wearing my philanthropy hat, where typically there is more reluctance to invest.

In both cases, there's the same person at the helm of the organization, but on one hand there's an eagerness from people to invest, and on the other hand there's a reluctance to invest. It makes some sense considering the way that many people typically view not-for-profit donations. They pledge money with the expectation that it will be well spent by others, but with little expectation that they will earn a measurable return on their investment. Every dollar they contribute is seen as a dollar they are never going to see again. If they make a business investment decision, though, not only do they expect to get their dollar back, they expect to get a return—and in some cases, a significant return.

I believe we need a new paradigm for giving back to the community. Too many people act as if the private sector and the social sector should operate on different axes, with one all about maximizing profits and the other all about maximizing social impact. A better approach is to integrate these missions. Businesses can be "not-only-for-profit." They can have a sense of social responsibility that isn't in a silo part of the organization. At the same time, social service groups can integrate business models that earn income and help achieve sustainability. By building a bridge between these two worlds, each of these groups can create positive, durable, and significant social change.

Although many people don't recognize it, the fact is the U.S. nonprofit sector's commercial activities generate billions in revenue annually. In today's climate where competition for philanthropic dollars is rising faster than the dollars themselves, nonprofits are finding that earning income (ideally through well-planned programs that develop products that people actually want) is imperative for survival. Without sustainable revenue, many nonprofits—despite good intentions and excellent programs—can barely scrape by. And, relying on the a priori model, where talented nonprofit leaders are forced to spend the majority of their time chasing money, there's less energy available for improving the world.

The idea of revenue-generating nonprofits isn't new. A good example is the National Geographic Society, an organization that was founded by geographers, explorers, teachers, lawyers, cartographers, military officers, and financiers more than a century ago with the purpose of educating people about the world. To sustain the organization, the Society built a membership model; one aspect of that was the magazine, which the organization launched nine months after it was founded.

The magazine, which also advances the group's social mission, has always been a significant source of revenue. Most recently that revenue stream has been supplemented with the National Geographic cable network and other businesses such as films, videos, and DVDs. National Geographic is now the largest nonprofit scientific and educational institution in the world, as well as a billion-dollar business. National Geographic is accomplishing the social goals it set out to achieve a century ago—and doing so in a far more significant way than its founders could have imagined.

Another example is the Girl Scouts. Since 1917 the organization has held an annual cookie sale, which uses the organization's resources—an army of Girl Scouts—to sell cookies (they used to bake them too!) and bring in revenue to sustain the organization.

These days we are seeing more and more innovative approaches, including nonprofit groups working with private-sector companies.

For example, Share Our Strength, a national hunger-fighting organization, has created a partnership with kitchenware maker Calphalon. We are also seeing a rise in social entrepreneurship— where individuals launch a business whose revenues can underwrite a social service—as evidenced with the Yonkers, New York–based

Greyston Bakery, which sells brownies to help finance the Greyston Foundation's community development programs.

Technically, the business of business is business, but thinking about it in a more blended way is smart business.

I try to use a hybrid approach in both business and philanthropy. For example, I am trying to bring this type of blended thinking to Maui Land & Pineapple, a Hawaiian business where I am the principal shareholder. Maui Land & Pineapple is involved in rebuilding the Kapalua Resort, which it owns and operates. Simultaneously, it is building Pulelehua, a new 300-acre residential community near the resort. Pulelehua, which means "butterfly" in Hawaiian, will be a for-profit venture. But it will also be a community that respects the ecosystem and provides a healthy life experience for those who live, work, and visit there. It meets a real need as well. There's an acute shortage of quality affordable housing in Maui. Half the residences in the community will be affordably priced. With schools, hospitals, wellness facilities, and trails and paths, this community will offer a more convenient place for people to live and will shorten the drive time to Kapalua for employees.

Building Pulelehua is a synergistic and positive development for the business of Kapalua. Ultimately, a resort is only as good as its people. If a resort's employees live close by and are living in a community that they are really proud of, it will be a source of satisfaction. It will also ultimately make it easier for the resort to attract, retain, and motivate employees. So this project benefits not only the community, but the company as well.

Technically, the business of business is business, but thinking about it in a more blended way is smart business. That is the idea behind Revolution. The company focuses on revolutionizing industries, but we are only interested in industries that have a direct impact on consumers. Revolution is doing some things in the resorts area, some things in the wellness area, but our particular focus is in the health-care area. We are trying to change the health-care system to be more consumer-centric.

We are focused on health care because it is a huge industry—one of every six dollars in the U.S. economy is spent on health care, and the costs are going up. Additionally, our current system is not effective. Most patients don't feel like empowered customers; they feel as if they are on the fringe of the system with virtually everybody but them making the decisions that most impact their lives and the lives of their loved ones. In the current system, important choices are made for people by third parties like HMOs, employers, and government agencies.

We are trying to build health-care businesses that give consumers more choice and control and convenience, which includes new tools to help them pick doctors. Everybody knows how to pick a restaurant, or how to pick a movie, but nobody knows how to pick a doctor. That's kind of crazy, if you think about it. Why isn't there a simple way to keep track of what is happening with something like a health savings account where it's possible to see where the money is going and how much is left? In our current system, parents have few choices if their child wakes up on a Saturday morning with a sore throat that seems to be strep. Either they go to the emergency room to get antibiotics (and wait a long time) or wait until Monday morning when the doctor is seeing patients again (mostly likely among a swarm of other patients who waited throughout the weekend for care). Why can't there be a simple, quick, and affordable way to serve this family, such as having nurse practitioners in convenient locations like retail outlets and mass merchandisers? These are the things that, to us, make a lot of sense.

Yes, Revolution is a for-profit venture. Yes, we are trying to build it into a significant valuable business. But if we are successful at building the business, we will have some impact in shifting the health-care system to be more consumer-oriented and serve the public good as well.

ABC^2 is a nonprofit organization that we run with a for-profit mindset. The focus at ABC^2 is brain cancer, which is a disease that historically has not gotten a lot of investment or attention. Each year more than 17,000 people in the United States find out they have a primary brain tumor, of which more than half are extremely aggressive. Because brain cancer often strikes individuals at a relatively young age, brain cancer now ranks seventh for adults and first for children in terms of years of life lost. One half of the primary brain tumor patients affected die within 12 months and few survive five years. We need new and effective treatments.

The relatively small number of people who have focused on brain cancer, particularly on the research side, have thus far worked in their own silos. Researchers in California, North Carolina, Texas, and elsewhere were all doing their own thing. Our goal was to build bridges and encourage collaboration among researchers, educators, medical professionals, industry, government, patients, and family members.

This approach has had a remarkable impact in terms of accelerating what was being done in that space. Each year ABC^2 convenes a group of leaders from various fields who otherwise would not meet to share ideas and discuss creative approaches to addressing this most challenging of diseases. The results of these meetings have been substantial. Several collaborations among academic groups and between academic and corporate groups have been forged, and new therapeutic approaches have been created and are being tested in laboratories and then on patients. Ultimately, success will be measured by prolonging lives of patients with this disease.

ABC^2 carefully selects the most promising of applicants to receive our annual investigator awards. To increase the number of scientists who focus on brain cancer, awards are given to encourage young physicians or scientists to pursue a career and research in the field of neuro-oncology. ABC^2 also gives funding preference to scientists who are focused on programs that will benefit patients with advanced brain cancer in the near term, and we have a fast-track award process to get money to them sooner. The award application is only five pages and, being true to our commitment to accelerate a cure, they are reviewed within a matter of weeks after the submission deadline.

ABC^2 has also created and funded a partnership with the Brain Tumor Center at Duke University to test molecules submitted by developers at no charge to the drug sponsor. This enables rapid testing of molecules with potential utility that may not otherwise be tested against brain cancer. To date, ABC^2 has entered more than 100 therapies for evaluation at Duke and for other members of our preclinical screening network.

Another part of our public-private partnership strategy is to create beneficial relationships between businesses and nonprofits. For example, the leading biotechnology company, Genentech, has agreed to focus more of its resources on brain cancer therapies, and ABC^2 has committed to sharing development expenses and providing access to its resources, including relationships with leading researchers and clinicians. It's a model that works because it reduces some of the business risk for Genentech (this is especially important since it doesn't make much economic sense for Genentech to focus too many of its research dollars on a disease that affects a smaller patient population than other cancers). It also offered opportunity for ABC^2: if the therapies become commercialized, Genentech will pay a small royalty on product sales back to ABC^2. This will help ABC^2 recoup investments and hopefully create additional dollars with which the organization can invest in other things. A more important indicator that the public-private partnership strategy is working: Genentech has already released encouraging early results on a drug called Tarceva.

Last year, the founders of ABC² determined that more capital needs to be available to start-up companies that focus on developing new therapies to treat brain diseases, and that ABC² is unable to raise such capital on a philanthropic basis. The Brain Trust Accelerator Fund has been organized as a for-profit venture capital fund, which will make investments in promising companies/technologies in the development of brain disease therapies (not limited to brain cancer). In assisting with the organization of the fund, ABC² seeks to promote its core purpose of furthering the development of brain cancer therapies. Although the decision has been made that the fund will operate separately from ABC², ABC² and other brain disease charities each will be given a portion of the management fee and the carried interest in the fund that would ordinarily have gone to the general partner.

Pulelehua, Revolution, and ABC² all demonstrate the potential benefits of combining philanthropic and business approaches to address important community needs. And each of these investments is an extension of what I learned at the time we were building my first business. At AOL, there was a dual passion behind what we were doing. We were building something that was a business, and we wanted it to have market share and be profitable and valuable, but we also were building something that had tremendous impact in terms of society and people's lives. AOL became a tool to empower consumers and give them more access to more information and more people. Trying to figure out how to do that in areas like health care, which are obviously crying for more innovation, is where I think I can make the greatest contribution. By applying a more entrepreneurial and collaborative approach to nonprofits and by building businesses with a purpose beyond profit, I believe we can create organizations with the ability to change the world.

The Case Foundation invests in a number of diverse organizations, but there are three areas that unite everything the foundation does. "It really comes down to trying to encourage more collaboration, fostering more entrepreneurship, and developing more leaders," says Steve. Here's an explanation of the three-pronged approach:

Collaboration: It's essential to find ways to knit together disparate organizations. "They can have more of an impact together than they might separately," Steve says. ABC², for example, has gone beyond its focus on brain cancer research to create a "Brain Trust" that focuses on all brain diseases, including amyotrophic lateral sclerosis (ALS, commonly known as "Lou Gehrig's disease"), Parkinson's, and Alzheimer's. "A lot of our focus is to try to get separate organizations working together toward a common goal."

Entrepreneurship: Steve believes that not-for-profit organizations can benefit from more of a for-profit orientation; entrepreneurs are often the force behind many of the ideas that can be sustained and scaled. "We believe that entrepreneurship is the source of great innovation and passion, and we want to build on that and try to take entrepreneurial start-ups and help build them," Steve says. "We are trying to develop this whole social enterprise sector and link social entrepreneurs to others—whether it is other nonprofits or other corporations."

Leadership: Ultimately improving the world is about leaders. "We've always been struck with how one person could have such a huge difference on an organization," Steve says. The foundation helps to develop leaders and brings leaders together around common goals. It has also helped several nonprofits strengthen their management and build their capacity to better achieve their objectives.

CHAPTER 18

WITNESS TO THE WORLD: PETER GABRIEL

Meeting many human rights victims around the world inspired Peter to create WITNESS.

Everyone knows Peter Gabriel is a well-known musician. He started the band Genesis, debuted his solo career with the song "Solsbury Hill," and created Rolling Stone's number-one video of all time—*Sledgehammer.* (Not to mention the man invented "stage diving.") Some people, like "Gabrielites," as fans are called, know that he also broadened the pool of music available to western audiences by founding both the international festival World of Music, Arts and Dance (WOMAD) and the record label Real World Records.

Few people are aware, though, that he has also used his interest in technology and his penchant for video making to create WITNESS, a nonprofit organization that empowers human rights defenders to use video to transform personal stories of abuse into powerful tools of justice. Throughout a 35-year career—and a wide range of media—Peter has strived to use his voice, creativity, and influence to make a difference. "On my passport it says 'musician,'" says Peter. "I would have preferred 'humanist.'"[1]

While Peter is revered as far more than a musician, it is music that first offered him the vehicle to effect positive change. He was born into a musical family (his mother and her four sisters each played piano and sang) and he studied piano when he was five years old. He began writing songs by the time he was 12, and his unique personality as a lyricist was evident early on (his first song was called "Sammy the Slug").

By the time he was 16, he had founded a songwriter's collective with some of his school friends. The group, which called itself Genesis, authored songs ranging from those that explored classical themes like love, or good versus evil, to those about more personal and prosaic ideas ("Get 'Em Out by Friday" is a protest song about an exploitative landlord). Peter's natural ability as a showman—which included dressing up in bat wings, animal heads, and Egyptian collars, and flying on high wires across the stage (something that had never before been done at a rock concert) was also met with outrageous enthusiasm.

By 1975, Genesis had released seven albums and established a cult following and a strong foothold in the progressive rock movement. It was somewhat surprising then, that at the zenith of the band's commercial success, Peter decided to quit. He felt that the near loss of his first baby was not treated sympathetically by the band and he wanted to spend time with his new family. He also had very mixed feelings about the fame game and retreated to the English countryside to pass the time gardening and to focus on his own music. In 1977, he released his first solo album, *Peter Gabriel*, which featured "Solsbury Hill," an autobiographical song that explored his thoughts on leaving Genesis. (His first solo success, it's now called a "classic," an "evergreen," and an "anthem.")

He soon released two other self-titled albums, followed by a third, known as *Melt* because of its melting face cover image, which was regarded as his most ambitious and innovative album to date and revealed an interest in the music of other cultures and technology. Peter's affinity for ethnic sounds began with an African band he had heard on a Dutch radio station.

He often made tapes of the music he liked and put them in a rhythm machine in order to write themes around them—a process later done by a booming generation of recording engineers who popularized dance music. His third album also debuted "Family Snapshot," inspired by the gunman who had shot Alabama's Governor George Wallace and "Biko," about the murdered South African civil rights leader Stephen Bantu Biko. Although the album was turned down by Peter's record label, Atlantic (one record executive called it "commercial suicide"[2]), it went on to sell twice the amount of his previous record, and "Biko"—the first pop song to talk about the effects of apartheid—became one of the biggest protest anthems of the decade. That song also led to the banning of all Peter Gabriel recordings in South Africa. (The ban has since been lifted.)

Peter's next album, *Security*, was his first to "go gold," and Peter continued to use his music as a medium to advance political awareness, as seen in the song "Wallflower," a response to reports of torture in Argentina. In 1986, Peter released his fifth solo album, *So*, which had hits including "Sledgehammer," "In Your Eyes," and "Big Time." The album reached the number-one spot in the United Kingdom and in the United States, where it received a Grammy nomination—and hurled Peter into international superstardom.

It also established him as an innovative video maker (an interest he'd later cultivate for WITNESS). The *Sledgehammer* video, which relied on special effects and animation to show fruit, fish, and a model train flying around his head, won nine MTV awards—more than any video in history—and was named the best video of all time by *Rolling Stone*.

Peter Gabriel—called "one of the world's major talents" by music mogul David Geffen[3] —has had an enormous influence on the music business through his music as well as his use of his celebrity status. While there have been some aspects of fame that Peter has disliked, he has always seen his role as a rock star as an opportunity to provoke change. "Celebrities can help with political causes," he says. "While they can't always express all the complexities of an issue, they can be a part of the process in raising awareness and in getting stories into the news." From early on in his career, Peter has used his celebrity to catapult fringe issues into the mainstream.

While weaving ethnic sounds into his own music, through WOMAD Peter also created a way for musicians from around the globe to gain attention in the West. Although the first WOMAD event in 1982 lost money (Peter even got a death threat from a creditor), the festival eventually gained a loyal following; it is now recognized as the first festival to bring world music to a popular audience. It takes place in several countries each year and is a great success.

WOMAD, which often brought together as many has 300 artists from 21 countries, also spawned the idea for Real World Records. "I never really wanted to have a record company," says Peter. "But we were getting all these artists in the UK for WOMAD who couldn't get recorded and promoted properly." Peter decided to allow the musicians to make recordings in his studio so the world could hear music by artists outside Western Europe and North America (until then difficult to do without traveling) and the musicians could gain recognition—and royalties (a new and life-altering concept for many of them).

Peter didn't just work from his studio. He also went on the road to promote social justice. In 1986 he coheadlined with Sting and U2 in the first benefit tour for Amnesty International, "The Conspiracy of Hope," and in 1988 he worked with Amnesty

International to set up the Human Rights Now! tour. His participation in this tour begot other cause-related events (he worked on the Nelson Mandela Tribute concerts, which raised awareness about Nelson Mandela and other South African and Namibian political prisoners and donated one of his songs, "Red Rain," to the Greenpeace album).

Meeting many human rights victims around the world inspired Peter to create WITNESS. Since it was launched in 1992, the organization, which is rooted in the principle that "a picture is worth a thousand words," has partnered with groups in more than 60 countries and been involved in creating thousands of hours of videotape and dozens of productions that have been viewed by a variety of decision makers including international tribunals and UN committees, as well as television viewers worldwide. The documentaries have helped to combat injustices on a variety of issues—from the abuse of women and girls in Sierra Leone to sweatshops in the United States. WITNESS has been widely recognized for its work as a change agent: among other honors, WITNESS was recognized with The Fast Company/Monitor Social Capitalist Award, the only award program that quantitatively measures a nonprofit group's innovation and social impact, as well as the viability and sustainability of its business model.

From the Real World offices in Wiltshire, England, Peter reveals his entrepreneurial epiphany for WITNESS, as well as a new project that is designed to help effect change through the wisdom of elders.

GLOBAL VOICES

Peter Gabriel, Musician, Entrepreneur,
Human Rights Activist

*It was unfathomable to learn that these people had not only suffered
greatly, but their whole experience had been denied, ignored, and
buried.*

I f we look at music throughout history—such as the antiwar
movement in the United States, or civil rights campaigning in
South Africa—we can see a long tradition of music that is linked
to social causes. While there is always room for straightforward
entertainment—and lots of it—one can argue that music that is
blind to the world isn't as relevant or potent. People respond to
music that has meaning and makes it possible for them to plug in
on an emotional level (and, hopefully, gets them interested
enough to read up on the issue, follow the news, and get
involved).

The first solidly political (in the sense that it was about a specific person and a specific situation) song that I wrote was "Biko."
I had been following the story of the antiapartheid activist
Stephen Biko's detainment. At the time, it seemed as if there was
enough publicity to protect him from murder. It was pretty
shocking when we eventually heard that he had been killed.

That got me more interested in the cause of human rights, and
it is what put me on that road with Amnesty International in

1986, and again in 1988. We always performed "Biko." At the end of the song there is a sort of anthemlike chant and the whole crowd would join in and sing. It was always a very moving moment; you felt as if they were singing not just for Stephen Biko and his struggle, but also for the many others fighting for human rights around the world.

We went around the world on that tour, and I met people from all over—Africa, Southeast Asia, South America, and China—who were victims of human rights abuses. These people had suffered all kinds of torture—some had even watched their families murdered in front of them—and they would gravitate to our shows because they felt as if it was their time, that their story finally had a chance to get heard. Meeting these people and hearing their experiences was emotional and eye opening. It was unfathomable to learn that these people had not only suffered greatly, but their whole experience had been denied, ignored, and buried. It was just as shocking to discover that the perpetrators often avoided prosecution. Although written reports had been published, it didn't seem to make a difference. Justice was rarely served.

I had a video camera with me on the trip, and I thought about the idea of arming these people with cameras so they could document these abuses. I felt if there were video evidence, or good photos, we could open the eyes of the world to human rights abuses and make it far more difficult for those in power to bury the atrocities.

At that time I was asked to be a board member of the Reebok Human Rights Foundation. I proposed the idea for WITNESS to the foundation right after I got back from the tour in 1988. There was little enthusiasm at first, but in 1991 the Rodney King incident happened. The amateur video footage of Rodney King being beaten by Los Angeles police officers was played all over the world, the images giving the incident an impact and immediacy that words could not. The lasting impression of the beating and the riots that followed demonstrated just how emotionally powerful video could be in galvanizing a global conversation. When I proposed the idea for WITNESS a third time, right after the King incident, everyone by then understood that if you have a video camera in the right place at the right time, you can have an impact on truth and justice.

We got the seed money for WITNESS from the Reebok Human Rights Foundation, and the Lawyers Committee for Human Rights made a home for the organization in 1992. It had a bit of a rocky start, but in 1995 WITNESS gave a camera to Gillian Caldwell, a human rights activist who was in Russia investigating an organized-crime ring selling women and girls for sexual slavery.

The documentary she made, *Bought & Sold*, was featured worldwide on BBC, CNN, and ABC News, and in many national broadcasts. Influenced by the ABC special and a *New York Times* front-page story, President Bill Clinton issued an executive order allocating $10 million to fight violence against women, with a special emphasis on trafficking. In 2000, the United Nations passed a new protocol to prevent trafficking, and the U.S. Congress passed the Trafficking Victims Protections Act, which gives victims who are willing to testify against their trafficker the ability to remain in the United States legally. In the wake of her successful campaign using video as a WITNESS human rights partner to create change around the issue of trafficking, WITNESS hired Gillian as director in 1998.

WITNESS has evolved more rapidly over the past few years, and today is an independent organization that partners with local human rights groups around the globe. Over time, we've realized that WITNESS's initial mission—to arm people with cameras—wasn't enough. We needed to provide technical training to teach people how to use the technology. Now, in addition to providing cameras, we provide training and assistance in editing footage,

and even disseminate editing equipment to more advanced partners. We've found that giving them the ability to edit footage in
the field allows them to produce more timely videos and reduces
the danger of transporting sensitive images.

We recently developed a new two-pronged approach that consists of a Core Partner portfolio of about 15 key advocacy campaigns designed to achieve high impact and visibility along with
a Seeding Video Advocacy initiative that provides short-term
training to hundreds more groups around the world each year.
(Since launching the Seeding initiative in 2004 we've trained
more than 600 new human rights defenders in over 110 countries
around the world.)

To date, WITNESS has partnered with groups in more than
60 countries to bring unseen images, untold stories, and seldom-
heard voices to the attention of key decision makers, the media,
and the masses. The organization has worked with women in
Afghanistan, for example, who used hidden cameras to capture
the abuses under Taliban rule. (They used the cameras again to
depict the aftermath of the U.S. military campaign.) Garment
workers in sewing factories in Saipan used video to show women
working 14-hour shifts—often without pay—to make clothes for
American retailers. Women in Sierra Leone have used video to
speak out for the first time about the widespread use of rape during the country's decade-long civil war.

There are millions of situations that need the help of video.

We also help to create distribution plans to ensure that the
videos are seen. WITNESS documentaries have been broadcast
on television, shown at film festivals, streamed on the Web, and
presented as evidence in federal courts and international tribunals. They've had real impact. In the Philippines, President
Gloria Arroyo ordered the setting up of a national crime office

after seeing a film documenting land right disputes where indigenous people were attacked and murdered. In Mexico, the government reformed its mental health system after the footage revealing the inhumane abuse and neglect of children with mental disabilities aired on national television in Mexico and the United States. (The images were horrific; kids were kept in filthy subhuman cages. Although page after page of written documentation had been previously put forth on the issue, no changes were implemented until the film was seen.)

In the United States, WITNESS and Books Not Bars, a project of the Ella Baker Center for Human Rights, teamed up to create a powerful 30-minute documentary called *System Failure: Violence, Abuse and Neglect in the California Youth Authority*, which depicted abject human rights violations including sexual abuse, beatings, forced medication, and medical and educational neglect in the California Youth Authority (CYA), one of the largest youth correctional agencies in the United States.

The video was shown to the California legislature and staff at the State Capitol; five days after viewing it, Senate Majority Leader Gloria Romero announced sweeping legislation to reform the system. Since then, the CYA has committed in writing to transforming the state's juvenile justice system to a rehabilitative model based on a therapeutic environment.

Those are just a few examples of the impact that WITNESS has had—there are many powerful ones. And this is just the beginning of what WITNESS could be doing. There are millions of situations that need the help of video. We are now focused on teaching other human rights groups and some of the bigger umbrella groups how to create their own video advocacy campaigns. We have also compiled a book, *Video for Change*, which serves as a how-to guide on using video in advocacy and activism.

A few years ago, we embarked on a major initiative to catalog and preserve the footage—much of it on fragile tape stock—that has been compiled by our human rights partners since 1992. The WITNESS Media Archive, which is housed on the Web, contains over 2,000 hours of video covering a broad range of issues including people displaced by the Burmese dictatorship, landmine victims in Senegal, and the aftermath of the ethnic cleansing in Kosovo.

Our mission with the archive is to preserve this living record of human rights violations as well as to provide affordable access to the media, lawyers, historians, educators, and policymakers. While the raw footage—most of which has been shot on digital handicams—may lack the polish of professional news footage, it offers unparalleled access and insight into untold issues. Our archived video has already been used as a tool for justice. Among many other examples, it was used in investigations by the International War Crimes Tribunal for the former Yugoslavia.

While we have made many advances in today's society, there's still a lot of racism and prejudice, governments paying only lip service to human rights issues, and corporations that could be more responsible. All of us can be more conscious and do more. I'm also working on another project called the Council of Elders. It's based on the idea that has long existed in many traditional cultures in which the elders fulfill a very important role in bringing wisdom and long-term thinking to any policy debate.

If we are to truly be a global village, we need our global elders. The UN tends to represent the views of the governments of the world rather than the views of the people of the world. We know it's ambitious, but we believe a group of 12 elected representatives, who are geographically, racially, and religiously diverse—and are men and women outside of active politics—may best represent the hopes and fears of the people worldwide. We've discussed this project with Nelson Mandela, who has endorsed the idea and offered an example of his work in Burundi where the young leaders of the Tutsi-Hutu conflict had told him they found it easier to negotiate with him because he seemed more of a father figure and he had no agenda other than peace. Others, they felt, still engaged in politics, were more influenced by their own countries' political and economic goals. It's our goal for the Council of Elders to function both privately and publicly in areas of conflict resolution, strategic planning, human rights, and disaster response. Moral authority is an underused natural resource, and if millions of people participate in the election of the elders, they could have a real influence in a world that has responded more to military, economic, and political authority.

I have seen the benefits of unlikely groups banding together. I have participated in the World Economic Forum for the past several years—something Bono and I have gotten a lot of flak for—but it is something that interests me intellectually and something that has helped us raise money and awareness for WITNESS. Additionally, I have been a member of the Reebok Human Rights Foundation for more than 10 years. While I have seen complications relating to public and private partnerships (some corporations may have a back garden that is not as perfect or as clean as you would like), it's fair to say that corporations are made up of people and families, and everyone wants to feel good about what they do. Despite growing up seeing Big Business as a big part of the problem, we have learned that you can often achieve more under the umbrella of, and with the support of, a corporation with a conscience.

It has been through my work with Reebok and their annual Human Rights Awards that I have met some of the most extraordinary people receiving awards. I've also been rewarded with an education about what's going on in different countries from a political and musical point of view. I have always tried to get my kids to attend the Human Rights Awards that Reebok gives because I felt it was a better education about the realities of the world in those few hours than they would get the rest of the year in the classroom. The young people who receive these awards are lit up from the inside. Inspiration is certainly high on the list of how I've been affected personally. The more inspired I am, the more engaged I want to become, and I spend less time making music, but that's the only downside. The upside is that together we can be one of the many catalysts for change.

NOTES

Chapter 5

1. Rajiv Lal and Arar Han, "Citizens Banks," Harvard Business School Case Study N9-505-034. October 29, 2004.
2. From Citizens Bank company documents.

Chapter 8

1. Ken Howe, Alan T. Saracevic, Sam Zuckerman, et al., "On the Record: Steve Burd," *The San Francisco Chronicle*, August 29, 2004.
2. Christina Veiders, "Identity Crisis: Retailers Are Rethinking Who They Are, and Seeking Ways Their Brand Can Resonate with Today's Shoppers,' *Supermarket News*, October 10, 2005.

Chapter 9

1. Carla Power, "Paying for AIDS," *Newsweek*, March 19, 2001.

Chapter 10

1. Joshua Cooper Ramo, "A Survivor's Tale," *Time*, December 29, 1997.

2. David Lidsky, "Intel: Gordon Moore," *FSB:Fortune Small Business*, September 2003.
3. Lidsky, "Intel: Gordon Moore."
4. Walter Isaacson, "Man of the Year: The Microchip Is the Dynamo of a New Economy," *Time*, December 29, 1997.

Chapter 11

1. Patricia Sellers. "The Next Generation," *Fortune*, April 4, 2005.
2. Kristen Millares Bolt, "Jim Donald Brings New Energy to Starbucks CEO Post," *Seattle Post-Intelligencer*, March 31, 2005.
3. Christine Edwards, "Neighbor Howard Schultz, Chairman of Starbucks," *Dan's Papers*, July 8, 2005.
4. Edwards, "Neighbor Howard Schultz."

Chapter 12

1. Peter Burrows, "Cisco: Giving Back Is 'Good business,'" BusinessWeek Online, August 11, 2005, www.businessweek.com.
2. Joseph Nocera, "Cooking with Cisco," *Fortune*, December 25, 1995.

Chapter 13

1. From Carlson Companies documents.
2. David Saltman, "Global Heavyweight," *The Chief Executive*, August–September 2003.
3. Saltman, "Global Heavyweight."
4. Saltman, "Global Heavyweight."

Chapter 15

1. The Global Compact is a UN initiative announced at the World Economic Forum's Annual Meeting at Davos in 1999

by Kofi Annan, who called upon business leaders worldwide to join in a "Global Compact" and "contribute to more sustainable and inclusive global markets by embedding them in shared values." As of March 2003, 717 companies around the world have become signatories to this voluntary initiative that promotes global corporate citizenship.

Chapter 17

1. Kara Swisher, *AOL.com: How Steve Case Beat Bill Gates, Nailed the Netheads, and Made Millions in the War for the Web*, New York: Crown Business, 1998.

Chapter 18

1. Chris Welch, *The Secret Life of Peter Gabriel*, London: Omnibus Press, 1998, p. 122.
2. Welch, *The Secret Life of Peter Gabriel*, p. 114.
3. Welch, *The Secret Life of Peter Gabriel*, p. 122.

INDEX

ABOUT THE AUTHORS

Marc Benioff is chairman and CEO of salesforce.com. He founded the company in March 1999 with a vision to create an on-demand customer relationship management (CRM) solution that would replace traditional enterprise software technology. Benioff is regarded as the leader of what he originally termed "The End of Software," the now accepted idea that on-demand applications can democratize CRM by delivering immediate benefits to companies of all sizes at reduced risks and costs. Under Benioff's direction, salesforce.com has grown from a groundbreaking idea into a publicly traded company that is the market and technology leader in on-demand business services.

Benioff, a 25-year software industry veteran, is internationally recognized as one of the preeminent thinkers in information technology. Most recently he was named on *Computer Business Review* magazine's "Top 10 Most Influential Movers & Shakers" list and he was ranked on the "50 People Who Matter" list published by *Business 2.0* magazine. Additional recent acknowledgments include: "Silicon Valley Visionary," from the Software Development Forum, the leading source of information and education to the technology community; "Alumni Entrepreneur of the Year," from the University of Southern California's (USC) Marshall School of Business; "Northern California Entrepreneur of the Year," from Ernst & Young; and "Entrepreneur of the Year," from SunBridge, the leading incubator in Japan, which recognized Benioff for his work in catalyzing technology change. He has been widely recognized in many leading magazines. Among others, *Selling Power* named him "International CEO of the Year;" *Fortune* magazine called Benioff one of its "Top 10 Entrepreneurs to Watch;" and *BusinessWeek* named him one of the 25 people responsible for turning e-business around.

Throughout his career, Benioff has been determined to use information technology to produce positive social change. In July 2000, Benioff launched the Salesforce Foundation, a multimillion-dollar global philanthropic organization. Pioneering the "1 percent model"—where the company contributes 1 percent of profits, 1 percent of equity, and 1 percent of employee hours back to the communities it serves—the Salesforce Foundation has demonstrated the power and impact of integrated philanthropy. Benioff is the coauthor of *Compassionate Capitalism*, the first-ever best-practices guide for corporate philanthropy that illustrates the success of the integrated model. He has been widely lauded for his work to effect change: members of the World Economic Forum selected him as a "Global Leader of Tomorrow," one of 100 leaders in business, politics, and the arts committed to addressing social issues; he received the Promise of Peace award from the Prime Minister of Israel, Benjamin Netanyahu, for his work using technology as a means to further Middle East peace; and he was honored with the Bridge award from the nonprofit organization HEAVEN (Helping Educate, Activate, Volunteer, and Empower via the Net) for providing Internet access to the underserved in America's inner cities.

Prior to creating salesforce.com, Benioff spent 13 years at Oracle Corporation, where he held a number of executive positions in sales, marketing, and product development. Before joining Oracle, Benioff worked at Apple Computer and founded Liberty Software. Benioff received a Bachelor of Science in Business Administration from the University of Southern California in 1986.

Carlye Adler is a freelance journalist who has been widely published in magazines such as *Fortune, FSB: Fortune Small Business, BusinessWeek*, and *Travel+Leisure*.

While based in Hong Kong, she wrote articles for *Time*-Asian Edition, and covered the film and television business as the Hong Kong correspondent for *Daily Variety*.

Formerly a senior writer at *FSB*, Adler wrote dozens of feature investigations and received several awards.

Her story on the hefty price of investing in a Krispy Kreme franchise was selected for inclusion in the compendium The Best Business Stories of the Year. She was twice named one of the most influential business journalists under the age of 30.

Adler lives in New York with her husband, Anthony Fieldman, and their daughter, Mia.